EMPATH

THIS BOOK INCLUDES

A survival guide,Empath healing and Highly sensitive people. How to manage emotions and avoid narcissistic abuse. Develop your gift and master your intuition.

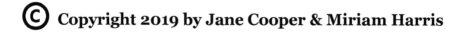

TABLE OF CONTENTS

Highly Sensitive Empaths:

Empath Healing Made Easy. The Practical Survival Guide for Beginners to Psychic Development. How to Stop Absorbing Negative Energies, Setting Boundaries, and Manage Your Emotions.

Chapter One: What Does It Mean to Be an Empath?

The range of human emotion and the breadth of human experience is vast. While what drives us to survive and what enables us to create thriving communities can be in conflict with one another, one thing has helped the human race survive for so long: empathy.

Empathy is often confused with sympathy. While both characteristics have similarities, the term is not interchangeable.

Sympathy is the ability to feel sorrow for someone else's misfortune. Sympathy is most easily differentiated from empathy because sympathy is triggered by someone else suffering an obviously painful event. These events are things like a well-loved family member passing away or someone experiencing an unfortunate vehicle accident. Sympathy is a fundamental human emotion: even young children often show sympathy for their friends' injuries or disappointments.

Empathy, on the other hand, is the ability to feel what another person is feeling. Any time you are happy for another person's success, you're experiencing empathy. If you're the kind of person who can cry for the characters in a fictional story, you're experiencing empathy. Does your heart pump faster during a suspenseful scene? Do you feel connected to a musical artist through a song? If so, you're experiencing a degree of empathy.

While there's a connection between sympathy and empathy, being an empath is something far more complex than being sympathetic and empathetic. Empaths are keenly tuned in to at least one part of their world. Usually, we understand the empathic ability as directing our gift toward other people. That is, empaths can often walk into a room and sense the energy and emotions of the people there. Often, the empath's own energy level is altered immediately, without their consent.

Most empaths learn early in life how to "turn down the volume," if you will, on this sixth sense. They do this in order to function. Otherwise, strong emotions – even without actions or words – are like an assault. Empaths are easily over-stimulated and easily drained of energy.

For empaths who don't learn to cope with their gift, the most basic activities in life can be completely overwhelming. They don't know why simple things like going to the post office or making a phone call can cause their heart rates to skyrocket. They may be almost physically bound to their beds with anxiety they don't understand. Sometimes, they'll be fine and behaving normally for weeks, and then suddenly find themselves in an anxiety-depression loop that threatens their work and personal relationships.

Likewise, an empath who "turns down the volume" on his gift will also suffer. These souls tend to be logical and pragmatic in many ways. The numbed empath is focused and has professional and personal drive, so they systematically conquer tasks, but this takes its toll in interesting ways. They may chalk frequent illnesses up to having a weak immune system. They may suffer migraines or have extreme muscle pain that comes and goes without any known cause.

Worse yet, empaths who don't understand their power often find themselves in toxic relationships. Predators such as clinical narcissists instinctively seek out empaths because they offer so much of the positive energy the narcissist needs. While healthy people absolutely will seek out positive energy and good relationships, too, the narcissist differs in that they don't return the goodness for long. The relationship may be mutually gratifying at the beginning, but it soon turns into a cycle of negativity, verbal and emotional mistreatment, and possibly even physical abuse. Then, as the empath victim begins to step away from the relationship, their narcissistic partner will show the attractive, loving side again. It's wrong for the victim to think that perhaps the narcissist has come around, that the relationship can be recovered, and that there is a bright future ahead. This is because as an empath, the deepest desire is for peace and harmony.

An empath can have more than just a connection to other people, but to places, animals, health, and even the earth. A geomantic empath finds an emotional connection to places. She can walk into an empty room and absorb the energy there. It can be an exhilarating feeling, even spiritual, or it can be chilling to the point where she must leave. It may be difficult to separate the energy of a location from any people who may be in it or near it, so it can take geomantic empaths a multitude of experience to realize that they have this particular gift.

Animal-oriented empathy has been explored in reality television with shows such as The Pet Psychic. These gifted individuals are able to go beyond the standard animal lover's expertise in caring for pets and have an extraordinary ability to understand an animal's needs, both psychological and physical.

Empaths can be highly aware of the energy-based physical needs of people, too. Practitioners of alternative medicines, like Reiki and chakra healing, are able to determine where negative energies are clustering in a person and creating toxicity in the body. This is not limited to alternative medicine: many traditional, licensed practitioners have an almost supernatural awareness about what's really going on with their patients. Medical empaths are a treasure to their community, but, like other empaths, can suffer if they don't know how to protect their own energy properly.

We say people with the talent to keep plants alive have a green thumb, and horticulture and agriculture is absolutely a skill that can be learned. Some people have more than a textbook mastery of those fields, though. Earth empaths have an uncanny knack for knowing what different kinds of vegetation needs in order to thrive.

One other aspect of this is that of the intuitive. An intuitive person has the capacity to comprehend something with no substantial rationale or evidence. We tend to call these people psychics and clairvoyants when their knowledge is predictive of short- or long-term events. This may be a disservice to people with true intuition, as their gifts can be dismissed by mainstream culture as being worthless or ludicrous. Intuitive are more numerous than we realize, but because of the stigma attached to their abilities, they learn to stifle them instead of mastering them.

Conversely, when intuition is of a more material nature, mainstream society tends to call the intuitive a prodigy, a savant, or genius. This material intuition can be mechanical or artistic, and people with these gifts have a beautiful impact on the world around them.

The idea of mechanical intuition may first seem strange, but history is full of instances of mechanically minded people working on a physical problem, and then the solution comes to them subconsciously, even while they're sleeping. These intuitive represent the array of what we call STEM: science, technology, engineering, and mathematics. They can have a preternatural aptitude for any of these areas. There is a unique beauty in these people in how they connect with the tangible world. Athletes can be intuitive as well: they understand the mechanics and physics required to make their bodies perform extraordinarily.

Some people are intuitive in leadership or teaching roles. An intuitive leader can quickly determine the needs of those in his charge and how to delegate parts of the solution to the appropriate people. An intuitive teacher doesn't struggle to communicate knowledge to the student to ensure the student's success.

Artistic intuitives have a strong presence in the performance, design, and visual arts, but some are inclined in all things culinary, communication, or hospitality. Chances are, you've met some of these people: maybe they pick up a pen and everything that comes from it is beautiful, or perhaps they tried crocheting for the first time and seemed to understand the concepts and were able to visualize the patterns without referring to them repeatedly.

When an intuitive is given freedom to cultivate their abilities, wonderful things happen for them and the people around them. But when an intuitive suppress them in order to conform to traditional roles, they can become physically and emotionally unhealthy even to the point of substance abuse or needing prescription medication. They were created for something other than what they are living. Countless stories in cinema and television illustrate this conflict between the gifted calling and the societal requirements.

An empath can also be intuitive. When these two characteristics reside together, you get what is known as a highly sensitive person. This doesn't mean that she will always cry at Hallmark commercials, and it doesn't mean that she is easily insulted or wounded. It does mean that the highly sensitive person is naturally more in touch with the energy of his surroundings than most people. She tends to use these readings on that energy in order to make decisions and react to stimuli.

If any of these descriptions remind you of yourself or someone you love, this book was written for you.

Before you embark on this journey, take the time to find a good journal. There are many revelations and events you'll need to record, and many things you'll need to work out on paper. It's best to have a single, dedicated place for all you're about to discover!

A Note about Journaling

It is strongly recommended that you skip using tech for any sort of intuition-based writing. Aside from the scientifically proven benefits to writing by hand, it keeps you anchored to the present, even as you write about the past. By joining the present sensory experience to the past memory, you are better able to access things you might not have remembered. Besides, there is something sacred about a handwritten journal.

Highly sensitive people often are very picky about the things they buy and use. If you're already accustomed to writing in journals, you probably have favorite notebooks and pens. If you're new to the practice, play around with different notebooks, types of paper, and writing utensils. Some people prefer the sound of a nice fountain pen's nib against toothy paper while others might prefer a fine point Sharpie pen on the smooth pages of a Moleskine notebook. You might find it more pleasurable to write on blank or grid paper than on traditional lined paper, and you might be inclined to add illustrations or ephemera to your pages. All of these things are welcome!

Chapter Two: Signs of a Highly Sensitive Empath or Intuitive

There are limitless ways for an empath to connect to more profound things in this world. Do any of the following traits sound familiar to you?

- Do you feel the emotions of others as your own or close to it?
- Do you ever feel claustrophobic in open places that are crowded?
- Is it difficult to watch bad news on television?
- Do you ever feel like you should hold back on believing certain people, even though you try to be an open-minded and easy-going person?
- Do people—even strangers—open up to you far too quickly?
- Are you extra-sensitive to sounds or visual stimuli at times, but fine with them at other times?
- As much as you love people and doing things, you need a lot of time on your own.
- Are you prone to depression or anxiety?
- Do you use food or other substances in order to numb?
- Have you ever gone to the doctor with a physical symptom, only to have them not be able to diagnose you?

- If you see someone in need, are you compelled to stop what you're doing to help them, even if it's not a particularly good time to do so?
- Have you ever found yourself in a relationship you thought was good, but it seemed to turn sour, then extremely toxic?
- Do you easily lose yourself in another person's life, even visualizing yourself in their private lives as an observer or speaking to them?
- Does nature soothe you?
- Are you inexplicably fatigued one day but perfectly fine most others?
- Do you feel like you're responsible for being a peacemaker on a regular basis?
- Is it difficult for you to separate yourself from others' expectations of you?

These are just a few of the fairly universal indicators of empathy. Below, you'll find more statements that might resonate with you. Some may be framed in different ways because sometimes, we need to hear things said in a different way in order to connect with them.

- When you start feeling drained or overwhelmed, you need a lot of time doing things at your own pace, be it work or leisure.

- You often feel as though you should be doing something else or be somewhere else entirely. If you don't follow those needs, you may become somewhat paralyzed where you are.

- Frequently you will have some sort of impression that you need to contact someone you know, and if you follow through, they will tell you that they really needed that interaction.
- When you have money to spend, you may be selfish because you tend to spend it on things that give you physical comfort.
- When you're feeling good, you can be generous with your money and time. When you're not, you may hoard both things for the sake of security.
- If you're an extrovert, you sometimes get mistaken as an introvert because of your ability to stay quiet when everyone else is loud or hectic.
- You tend to see the people who others pay no attention to.
- You can feel the energy in a room shift when certain people walk into the room.
- You've checked into a hotel room, and even though there wasn't anything visibly wrong with the room, you wanted to change rooms or hotels.

- You have experienced anxiety around someone without even speaking with them.
- You occasionally feel unromantically drawn to people you don't know.
- You have found yourself saying something encouraging to a stranger in passing without particularly meaning to.
- People end up telling you deeply personal things upon your first meeting.
- You've been told that you turned someone's day around for the better just by making contact with them.
- You sometimes seem to be the only person in the room who listens to quietest people when they speak up.
- You feel physical pain after a verbal conflict with someone.
- You prefer social situations where you can connect to at least one other person on a deep level.
- You can be in a large group of people if you're not expected to interact with most of them.
- When it comes to acquaintances having successes, you tend to feel happy for them more often than you feel jealous.
- You can see things around people, such as lights or colors, that no one else can.
- Upon meeting a person, you've felt a negative presence that you thought about multiple times later, only to find out much later that they were involved in criminal activities.
- Parents notice that babies seem to be "extra-good" when you're caring for them.

- You are known for giving good advice.
- You can see what other people can't about their own situations.
- Specific locations feel particularly warm or cold, regardless of the actual temperature.
- You have walked into a non-religious building and felt that it was sacred.
- You can feel when you are not welcome in a place, or when you're welcome there suddenly seems to shift.

- You can read in dreams. This is supposed to be almost impossible since the parts of the human brain required for reading are significantly more inactive during sleep than others.
- You get the "heebie-jeebies" more often than you care to admit.
- Conversely, some places seem safer than others.
- You have been looking forward to a trip or an event, then suddenly you strongly feel as though you should back out, even if not showing up costs you money in cancellation fees.
- You are highly scent-sensitive. Even good, synthetic-free scents can overwhelm you.
- When your personal space gets cluttered, you feel anxious or claustrophobic.
- Animals, even only selective kinds, seem drawn to you.

- You can look into an animal's eyes and understand its needs.
- You can differentiate between an animal's different sounds upon just meeting them. Example: You understand a dog's certain bark is his way of asking for play, as opposed to its defensive one.
- If you're in a room with multiple animals, they all seem to gravitate to you.
- A specific species of animal seems to favor you on repeated occasions.
- There seems to be more animals in your neighborhood or yard than there "should" be, or than there are in other parts of the area.
- Sometimes, it seems as if you have no immune system at all, regardless of how healthy of a lifestyle you lead, and doctors can't tell you what's wrong.
- You occasionally have inexplicable pains in certain areas of your body after having just interacted with someone.
- You have felt the temperature drop or rise when a certain person has been nearby.
- You feel the need to research conditions and diseases and their remedies even though you have none of the symptoms, only to find out someone you know has been diagnosed with that condition or disease.
- You experience migraines out of the blue, and there is no medical explanation for them.

- You have brought the outdoors indoor by bringing live plants into your living space.
- You feel changes in weather or barometric before those changes are reported by a tech application or the news.
- When walking through the forest or a garden, you somehow are able to hear your own inner voice better when you really tune in.
- You're more likely to decorate spaces with botanicals than other forms of artwork.
- You are drawn to useful items made from natural sources.
- You have a deep internal conviction for environmental issues and sustainability.
- Déjà vu isn't uncommon to you.

- You have avoided what proved to be a certain injury by a narrow margin without trying to.
- You can look at an abandoned, run-down space and vividly see its potential, and have a good grasp on all the steps it will take to get it there
- You could swear you've heard someone's voice minutes before they were present.
- You've reached for your phone to call or text someone and you've got a call or text from them instead.
- You can begin a new project in a fairly unfamiliar medium and complete it without construction.

- You sometimes find yourself staring at an object long enough that you lose a sense of time.
- When looking at a photograph, you can sense what's missing or not shown in the scene.
- You're very good at shell games.
- You can sense when someone in your household is coming home before you hear their car or speak with them.
- You gain energy by seeing another person master a new skill.
- You get as excited as – or more than – someone when they have a Eureka! moment.
- If someone makes a statement that seems off to you, you're able to quickly determine what pieces of information they lack to make their statement more solid.
- You have fantastic organizational skills: if given some space and ample time, you can create a functional system out of a mess.
- You can read poor handwriting quite easily.
- You can remember multiple times where people you've only just met have opened up to you and told you far more than normal about themselves.
- You understand that sometimes, people are too upset to be able to communicate clearly at the moment, and you're completely at ease with waiting even months or years for them to be able to tell you what you need to know.

- You anticipate other people's needs and have items ready for them before they ask.
- You are not easily offended if a person doesn't like life's comforts the way you like them if they're not rude about changing things to their liking.
- You ensure that supplies around the home or work are well-stocked for the ease of your own life, but that of others'.
- Conflict drains your energy to the point that you need to retreat from even people you like.
- If, when asked a question, you immediately know the answer, but pause before giving it because you're trying to figure out why you know it.

These are, but a handful of the ways one's empathic abilities can be seen. You may have read some of them and thought, "Yes! All the time!" On the other hand, you may only agree greatly with a handful of them, and some none at all. If even a few of these are representative of you, however? You're probably an empath, intuitive, or highly sensitive person.

Chapter Three: Empath and Intuitive Stories

You may ask, how do these things look in the real world? Let's look at one particular family of empaths. Roberto and Ana (names changed at their request) were a young couple who had hit it off immediately. Ana saw wisdom and kindness in Roberto, and Roberto was quickly sure that Ana was to be his wife. They were married at a fairly young age, and though things were tight sometimes, they soon built a business together.

A Connection to Animals

When Roberto and Ana first moved into their home in the Midwestern United States, they had the usual amount of wildlife coming in and out of the yard. Squirrels, birds, and the occasional bunny came on and off their property, but upon the birth of their daughter, Paloma, animals seemed to congregate near their home. Chipmunks became a usual occurrence, and in the summer, a family of large groundhogs moved into a space near their split woodpile. Toads and gentle possums, little brown bats, and even the occasional deer wandered across their historic district driveway. Every time the weather warmed up, a new box turtle would make its way into the young family's life and take up residence in their indoor aquarium, to be released at the end of the summer. They began calling their daughter Snow White because of the way butterflies and birds—pardon the pun—flocked to little Paloma.

When visiting the zoo one day with their daughter, now five years old, they paused by what they thought was an empty enclosure to pass around water bottles and snacks. Soon enough, a small crowd had gathered nearby, because three turtles had made their way over to the fence where the family stood. Paloma leaned over the partition a little and began speaking sweetly to the tortoises, and in return, the reptiles began to push against the fence. One even seemed to try to climb up the posts.

When Paloma finally began to walk away, all three turtles followed on their side of the fence. Even though there were plenty of other people around, some trying to get their attention by dropping contraband food into the enclosure. Still, the turtles followed Paloma until she was out of sight.

Four years later, the family was on a trip to the southeastern coast. One afternoon, they visited a historical site that was bordered by a beach. When the sun began to set, the family turned around to head home. That's when Paloma noticed a sea turtle moving quickly away from the water. The family had visited a sea turtle sanctuary the day before and learned that sea turtles could die if they got lost on land and were unable to find their ways back to the ocean. Paloma cried out, "Mom! I don't think it can tell which direction the water is!" She carefully approached the turtle, and the turtle changed direction and walked toward Paloma's shadow. Paloma began walking slowly back to the soft sand of the beach, and the turtle was sure to stay in her shadow.

Paloma then looked up at her parents, "I think it wants to lay eggs, so I'm going to stop for a minute." There was no way the young girl could have known the turtle was female, and the parents quietly noted that, but agreed to wait a minute to see what might happen.

Sure enough, the turtle began to dig with her flippers. Minutes later, she positioned herself over the carefully made hole. Once again, a small crowd had gathered, and together, they watched the turtle lay egg after egg into the hole. When the turtle was done, Paloma walked her back to the water, and the crowd cheered as the turtle disappeared into the waning tide.

Paloma clearly had a special connection with animals, and clearly with a particular species.

A Connection Via Dreams

Paloma wasn't the only empath in the family. At multiple times during his adulthood, Roberto would dream about people he hadn't seen in years in such a way he felt the need to get in touch with them. Usually, he'd call the day immediately after the dream.

One night, Roberto dreamed about a coworker from almost a decade before called Charles. They had lost touch at that time, but when Roberto phoned him the next day to check-in, the phone number took him to his friend's voicemail. He left a message and didn't think much of it until two months later when he had another dream about Charles and his family.

Once again, Roberto felt the urge to phone Charles to check-in. This time, Charles answered. After the initial greetings, Charles apologized for not returning Roberto's previous call. "That day you called, my wife was in the hospital. She miscarried the night before, and we've all had a rough time with the loss since then."

The two reconnected then and made plans to have lunch together. But again, over the course of the years, life seemed to get in the way of their friendship. Still, Roberto didn't think much of it, as that's the way the world seemed to work. But then, Roberto had another dream about Charles and his family. Upon waking, he told his wife that he was hesitant to call Charles, because the last time it was in the middle of a tragedy, and he didn't like being connected to the tragedies.

His wife encouraged him to phone Charles anyway, so Roberto did. Charles answered quickly this time, too. "I was just thinking about you!" Charles exclaimed. "The last time we talked, I told you about my wife's miscarriage. I'd meant to call you earlier to tell you the good news—my wife got pregnant again. I'm sorry I didn't, but you won't believe this! Last night, she delivered the baby! She's doing well, and the baby is healthy, too!"

Other people Roberto knew popped up in his dreams from time to time. One other memorable instance was when the father of a friend from high school in Colorado made an appearance. Roberto woke in the middle of the night with an anxious heart, and he dreaded calling his friend the next day. So, he began to pray for his friend's father. The following day, his wife encouraged him to call his friend. "It could be important."

He did, and when Adrian answered, Roberto, explained that he'd had a dream about Adrian's father the night before, and felt the need to check-in.

"You won't believe this," Adrian said, his voice quiet and serious. "Last night, my father was driving down the mountain in his truck and trailer from a long trip. The rest of us were at home, but my mother got very nervous and couldn't sleep, so she called me over to pray with her. Dad was supposed to be home, but she couldn't get hold of him at all. We prayed all night until there came a knock at the door. I opened it, and the police were there."

At this, Roberto began to feel sick. Adrian continued, "They found his truck and trailer off the side of the mountain. They didn't find his body, though. We were devastated but kept praying. He walked in at seven this morning, having had to climb back up the side of the mountain and hitch a ride home. He lost his phone in the dark and couldn't call to let us know what happened."

In these instances, Roberto couldn't have helped at the moment, but he was clearly meant to check in with those friends, even though they weren't people he engaged with much anymore.

Mental Health Intuition

Roberto's wife, Ana, exercised a wholly different sort of empathic ability, and it manifested itself notably when Ana was visiting her sister Maria for a few weeks. Things were initially good. They had a few good talks and good meals together, but Maria's work schedule kept her busy during the day. Toward the end of Ana's trip, Maria's mood seemed to shift. She began talking about various illnesses she'd suffered, most of which was new information for Ana.

A recent divorcée, Maria made a few comments that should have been alarming to Ana regarding her own health and longevity. She mentioned having had an operation for cancer, which was brand new news to Ana. Their parents hadn't mentioned such a thing, and they were in contact often. Ana had even spent time with their mother on the trip, and nothing had come up at all. Her family was close-knit: how had this passed under Ana's radar?

When Ana asked Maria for more details, Maria remained vague, even about the specific diagnosis and procedure. Maria shifted the conversation and asked if, before Ana left, if Ana would go with her to get Power of Attorney paperwork taken care of. Maria didn't want any of the responsibility falling on her two daughters, who were young adults. As Ana sat, curled up on the couch across from Maria, she realized that she should be feeling concern, fear and that specific sort of compassion that comes with someone dealing with such issues. Ana was a fairly sensitive and compassionate person, but she felt none of those things. As a religious person, she prayed for discernment in the situation: Lord, if I'm supposed to be concerned for her health, please put that feeling in me because I feel none of it.

Instead, she became concerned about her sister's mental health.

Even though Ana agreed to go with Maria to take care of the Power of Attorney paperwork, Maria seemed disinterested whenever Ana mentioned it. As her visit drew to a close, Ana filed away the strange conversation.

Over the next few years, Maria's actions grew more erratic, and their relationship became strained. At first, Ana worried that Maria was suffering from bipolar disorder, because of the extreme emotions she'd showcase: being Ana's very best friend one day, then screaming irrational accusations the next. Other members of the family were being victimized, too, and eventually, it came out that Maria had a narcissistic personality disorder.

Ana agonized over this. Why hadn't she known? Could it have been stopped? Could Maria have been helped? But the more Ana began to understand the disorder, the more she realized it was nothing she could have fixed. As Maria descended into abusive behavior, alcoholism, and was suspected of a number of petty crimes, Ana continued to study the disorder and learned that one of the root causes was a lack of empathy.

Ana also learned that Maria was showing markedly different faces of her social circle. To strangers, she lied and said that a family member who had been diagnosed with a terminal illness was her own daughter to gain further sympathy, when, in fact, the child was not. When anyone tried to correct her or call her out privately, Maria embarked on a no-holds-barred smear campaign against them. She was soon accusing her family members of horrible things Ana knew none of them had done. Maria had no boundaries.

It took years of this behavior for Ana to learn what the term covert narcissism meant. While narcissists are named as such because they are in love with grandiose ideas of themselves and manipulate others to their wills, covert narcissists manipulate people into thinking they are victims and not at all responsible for any negative thing around them. Both types fed off the attention of others, and, Ana discovered, empaths were their favorite source of narcissistic supply.

Ana thought back to that day on her sister's couch. She'd since learned that her sister had been mistreating other people for years before that day when Ana saw Maria shift. She'd learned that each of her victims had thought the abuse was only toward them; that they somehow deserved it. In retrospect, armed with knowledge, Ana was able to understand what she was feeling—or rather, she hadn't felt—during that strange conversation.

Ana realized she initially hadn't been worried about her sister's health because Maria never had surgery for cancer. She probably hadn't ever had a diagnosis close to that, either. Ana still didn't know what triggered the change in her sister's attitude, but she realized she hadn't felt sympathy or concern because, as an empath, there was nothing to worry about in that regard.

Cultural Connection

Ana had a friend from her school days with whom she'd lost contact for several years. As adults, they regained contact with one another. Meredith was a Caucasian who had been adopted as a newborn into another Caucasian family. When the women reunited, Ana was surprised to hear Meredith's tale.

After university, Marjorie and her adoptive parents traveled to Japan. Meredith said it was phenomenal: she had an almost immediate understanding of the language and cultural intricacies. She'd gone back several times and was intending to move. Even though Meredith had been adopted, she was now able to verify that neither of her parents came from Japanese lineage. While there was a possibility they had traveled or lived in Japan, Meredith had never had much personal contact with the culture outside of anime cartoons.

In houses of worship which permit the speaking in tongues, many instances have been reported one member speaking in a language unknown to them. Theological structure traditionally dictates that if one member of the congregation speaks in tongues that someone else will be given the gift of translating and has the responsibility to translate for the congregation.

In one church service, a member stood up to address the congregation in a language unknown to any of the other members. They waited for someone to translate but did not prompt it from the pulpit. After the service, a visitor from a small African tribe approached the minister. Brightly, he exclaimed that he was so touched that someone would speak in his native language.

Practical Premonitions

Paul began having the strangest dreams when he was in middle school. He couldn't remember the context of the story when he woke, but he was left with the image of an object firmly imprinted on his mind. One morning, he had the impression of a tennis ball in his mind. Near the end of the school day, he found out that the administration had agreed to add tennis to their sports roster. In another instance, he had the image of rain boots and a raincoat in his mind upon waking. He couldn't shake it, even though it made no sense. His area was well into week two of drought. He checked the forecast, but there was no rain in sight. After lunch, the sky turned dark. He watched as clouds formed and then split open with rain. The rain turned into flash floods on the parched earth that day. A few more instances like these, and he began taking note, preparing himself for the day according to what his dream suggested.

Advance Meetings

One day while sitting in her cubicle at work, Valerie drifted off. It was more than a daydream, and yet she wasn't quite asleep, either. In it, she had a dream about an introduction to new associates to the business.

The details of the meeting were vague, but Valerie remembered very specific things about the new associate. The letters ZM were emblazoned in her mind, as was the other woman's vocal tones and ability to make Valerie laugh.

Three weeks later, Valerie arrived at work and was introduced to Zoe Morena, the head of the company's new marketing firm. As soon as she heard Zoe's laugh, Valerie was taken back to those dream remnants. The women had the same sense of humor and common goals and quickly became close friends. A year later, Zoe extended an invitation for Valerie to join her marketing company. Together, the women were able to triple the firm's net worth within eight months and began taking more clients whose purposes mattered to the women. Their friendship grew along with their business, and that was the most valuable thing, as far as they were concerned.

Not only had Valerie been prepared to meet Zoe in her dream, but she'd also been prepared to feel comfortable and like her.

The Wrong Place

Nick was touring with a popular band, standing in as a rhythm guitarist. It was their third UK stop out of eight. They made it to an old but updated inn one afternoon and would have a few days there as the band had some promotional things to do in the city.

After he unloaded his things from the bus, Nick was given his room assignment and headed up. First, he walked past the door to his room, even though he was paying attention to the numbers. When he backtracked, he found the room, but when he moved to unlock the door, his hand opened, and he dropped the key. After he picked up the key, he felt a cold that made his skin clammy, and his bones ache.

Nick stepped back from the door, trying to understand what was going on. Was he getting sick? He couldn't afford the flu! If the air conditioning was on too high, he'd just turn it down and explore the neighborhood until it leveled out. He went to insert the key into the lock again, but the same thing happened as before: he dropped it.

Annoyed at himself, he grabbed the key from the floor and finally opened the door. The room was bright and well-appointed with high-quality furniture and amenities. Still, he felt something wasn't right. Nick always avoided being a pest at a hotel, since rock bands always got a bad rap, but he knew he couldn't stay in the room.

Nick took his things back downstairs with him. The older man at the desk seemed alarmed to see him again so soon. Nick explained that he'd prefer another room. The clerk's mouth pressed into a thin line. "Did someone tell you about what happened there?"

Nick told him no and asked what happened. The clerk hesitated, then told him a story about a young man who had been killed in that area of the hotel. The young man's fiancée had found him. He was laid to rest, the case unsolved. Devastated by the whole ordeal, the young woman pleaded with the hotel not to use that room again.

For years, the hotel complied. When it was bought out and renovated, the rooms were re-partitioned, and some of the room in question was integrated into the space Nick had initially been given. Since then, some of the maids and maintenance workers had "bad luck" when working in that room.

The clerk changed Nick's room with no argument. Later that night, Nick called his cousin back home to check-in. He told her what happened. As they talked, Emma looked into the story on the internet.

"Nick," she said abruptly. "I'm sending you an article."

The link she'd sent was almost a decade old. It was about the unsolved murder. Halfway down was a photo of the victim. "He could be your brother. Your twin, even," Emma said quietly.

She was right: they had quite a bit in common, at least from what he could gather from the photograph: similar golden complexions, similar light-colored eyes, strong jaws, slightly cleft chins. A chill ran down his spine. What hadn't wanted him in that room? Was it the victim? Or was it the fiancé, still projecting her will on the room from wherever she was now? Perhaps it was all Nick's doing. Or maybe his intuition surged when he first got near the place. Whatever the case, it seems that someone didn't want him in that particular space.

Understanding your power and accepting it for what it is can be the most exciting and freeing experience you'll ever have. Learning that there's not something innately wrong with you, but instead innately right and in contact with the world around you should encourage you.

Chapter Four: The Newly Awakened

On former federal prosecutor and former FBI agent Jim Clemente and former state and federal prosecutor Francey Hakes's podcast Best Case Worst Case, guest Maureen O'Connell tells the story of her first case after becoming a mother.

Based in Los Angeles, FBI agent O'Connell was on maternity leave and due to return to work in a few days. She was on a walk, her infant son in the stroller when she came across a flier posted on a light pole. She paused and read about the young man, a curly-haired blonde like her son, who was missing. Suddenly, she was hit with a horrible question: How am I going to tell his mother he's dead?

She recovered a moment later and rationalized the thought. She'd been in that line of work long enough that she just assumed the worst. Perhaps it was further triggered that her son resembled the man in the photo, and her newly found mothering instincts made her sensitive to other mothers. She shook off the feeling and got on with her day.

Her first day back at work, she was called to respond to a body found on federal property near where she'd seen the poster. As she approached the scene, she felt mounting unease. The face had been disfigured—by nature or human hand they still had to determine—and there was no form of identification on the body.

She didn't need it: she knew who it was. Agent O'Connell returned to where she'd seen the flier and pulled it off the post so that they could begin the process of legally identifying the victim.

She and her partner went to the apartment the victim shared with his roommate. The victim's family was from out of state, his mother in Ohio. But it was his mother who opened the door.

Agent O'Connell understood that she, not her partner, was going to have to break the news that a body presumed to be the woman's son had been found.

Clearly, Agent O'Connell had a high degree of empathy and intuition before having a child. Her profession demanded both, but something seems to have intensified her intuitive gifts after having a child. This frequently happens with parenthood. There's the old adage about a mom having eyes in the back of her head, but what if a sixth sense does develop during maternity?

A 2012 study of women found traces of fetal DNA in various regions of the mother's brain. Nearly two-thirds of cases showed male Y chromosomes marking the DNA. These chromosomes could not have come from the women's fathers and had to belong to the sons they were had carried. The study focused on women who carried males because the chromosomes would be more easily identifiable. Children have a life-long impact on women, it seemed, as the oldest woman carrying her son's DNA was 94 years old.

Perhaps that explains the phenomenon called mother's intuition. And with all the physiological and psychological changes that happen during parenting for both men and women, perhaps the act of parenting activates a part of some peoples' minds to allow them to be more sensitive to energies and invisible truths.

It's not only parents whose enhanced empathy and intuition can blossom over time or appear overnight.

Some signs your level of intuition may be increasing include:

- You may see colors or light attaching to certain people.
- People with a similar interest or profession, different than yours, come into your life seemingly all at once.
- You may have a sudden aversion to certain foods, such as dairy or wheat, without negative symptoms associated with intolerance.
- Your success rate of discerning lies is improving or is almost 100%.
- You may begin craving more whole, fresh food than you ever have before.
- When shopping for household items, you may feel particularly drawn to something you didn't intend to buy.
- Conversely, you may also feel uneasy with other items.
- You recently are noticing and remembering things from dreams that never appeared to you before.
- You feel less of the need to apologize for being honest about your meaning, need, or feelings.
- You can visualize how events, people, and ideas are connected—it's like a giant web in your mind.
- You "pick up" on things about people's private lives and they strike you as fact, but you have to remind yourself that they have not actually shared those things with you.

- If you walk into an empty space, you can easily see where things belong.
- When you walk into a place, you can easily envision what it looked like in previous eras.
- You know things about your infancy you "shouldn't" be able to remember.
- You are increasingly comfortable trusting your gut instinct.
- It's almost painful not to ask *Why?*
- You feel less of the need to explain your decisions if confronted about them.
- You experience sudden, clear changes of mood: you may be brought to tears, you may laugh for no apparent reason, you may worry about an undefined issue or unknown person.
- Lights seem to go out more often when you're around.

But really, when it comes down to it, you will probably just *know*. That's the tricky thing about intuition.

Chapter Five: The Unhealthy Empath

The internet is full of stories of people who realize that they're not just sensitive, but empathic. Most of these people often find themselves distressed by it, even in pain from it.

Some people are so accustomed to reading between the lines when it comes to others that they forget that is not the norm in society. They expect friends to understand and anticipate their needs in the same way the empath does for them. The empath may not even realize they haven't expressed their needs to their loved ones. They find themselves feeling neglected. If this goes on, and they fail to communicate in return to others, the empath may isolate themselves further and further, not wanting to experience that perceived betrayal again. When left unchecked, this self-protection can turn into a full depletion of empathy in the once-sensitive person.

Sometimes, a lack of empathy sounds like a relief. Don't be fooled: the lack of empathy is directly tied to dangerous personality disorders such as psychopathy, sociopathy, and narcissism.

Instead of wishing your gift away, learn to harness it. When you can direct your empathy away from toxic sources and toward positive, clean ones, you can find peace and fulfillment anywhere.

Emotional health can be directly related to physical health. Those of us who are highly sensitive often experience a myriad of physical symptoms. These can include:

- Elevated blood pressure when triggered
- Irritable Bowel Syndrome (IBS)
- Skin inflammation, such as a rash or hives
- Abdominal cramping
- Vertigo
- Flushing of the face
- Weakness in the limbs
- Difficulty breathing / feeling like you're hyperventilating
- Weight loss to the point of cachexia
- Weight gain to the point of obesity
- Insomnia
- Muscle pain
- Joint pain

It's as if highly sensitive people are allergic to negative energy, somewhat in the way those with celiac disease have painful, disruptive reactions to gluten or the way dander can trigger hives and respiratory distress for those allergic to cats.

The human body's sympathetic nervous system, its fight or flight or freeze system, activates when we are threatened. It creates slower digestion, increased heart and breathing rates, and triggers adrenaline and other hormones and neurotransmitters, which, in turn, increases muscle tension.

If you have ever had a near-miss with an auto collision, you probably experienced the following: you held your breath, your muscles seized up, bracing for impact, and your brain started looking for an escape route, even if it didn't have time to act on it. Minutes after, when everything is fine, and you're continuing on your way, your heart may still be pounding in your chest. You may still hear the thump of your blood moving through the vessels near your ears. You may experience pain in your shoulders and back from where you tensed.

But it doesn't take a life-or-death situation to launch the sympathetic nervous system into responding this way. Many people involved in high-stress relationships have similar reactions when they have to interact with certain people. Highly sensitive people often have a difficult time separating themselves from others' demands and ignorance of boundaries, and their bodies react in much the same way.

The parasympathetic nervous system works to counteract those things. When activated, it decreases the heart and breathing rates, it assists in digestion and relaxes muscles. Highly sensitive empaths need to create a lifestyle that will nourish the parasympathetic nervous system. We also need to indulge in rituals that can help us expel our negative emotions—more on this in later chapters.

Roots in Trauma

Post-traumatic stress disorder, or PTSD, first appeared in American Psychiatric Publishing, Incorporated's Diagnostic and Statistical Manual of Mental Disorders, Edition 3 in 1980. Since its inclusion in the manual, it has become part of the American vernacular. Many people claim they have PTSD from watching a poorly made comedic film or being inconvenienced at the Department of Motor Vehicles. But for millions of people worldwide, PTSD is not something to joke about. It is disruptive and agonizing. When it triggers a severe anxiety attack, the sufferer worries she might lose her job, or not be able to take care of her kids. It can severely limit every aspect of her life.

PTSD can present itself in a multitude of ways, from obsessive-compulsive disorder, hyper-vigilance, attention deficit disorder, or depression. Most of us can sympathize with a soldier returning home from war. We don't understand his need to scan rooftops or be wary of suspicious packages. We don't know what it's like to leave the present moment and have to relive a battle when we're enjoying fireworks. We don't know, but we can imagine. We can accept that their PTSD is real and agonizing.

In cases of extreme childhood abuse, we can stretch our imaginations and conceptualize why survivors are afraid and why they are easily triggered. We can sympathize with them, and often, we can hurt for them even if we're blessed enough not to have endured anything like what they have gone through. Unfortunately, many peoples' grace doesn't extend to adulthood for the victims. Once they pass adolescence, childhood PTSD survivors seem to be expected to "be over it by now" or otherwise pretend that the abuse didn't occur.

The same could be said for adult victims of violence or psychological torture. It's been three years, Laura. Why do you still freeze when you hear that sound?

But some people are different. Some are ready and willing to be patient, to listen, and to accept a survivor in whatever state they come. A large number of empaths were once victims of trauma themselves. Instead of becoming cold to the world and using their injuries as an excuse to hurt other people, they chose to use their understanding to better the world around them. Many stepped into a deeper role and became empaths, whether intentionally or not.

Why Do Empaths Get So Tired?

Empath fatigue is cited as the most frustrating thing about being sensitive to energy. No one jogs for twelve hours a day, every day, with only a few short interruptions for rest. That would destroy a human body. Not many people can do any singular voluntary movement consistently for 12 hours a day without major repercussions coming to the body. Empaths, however, are expected to (and expect themselves to) be emotionally available during every waking hour.

For an undeveloped empath or intuitive who doesn't know how to protect and regenerate their own energy, any interruption in their flow can punch a hole in their dam, causing energy to leak out at an alarming rate.

Professions such as teachers, doctors, first responders, veterinarians, and counselors are often filled by empaths. When an empath is in a role that requires them to deal regularly with people who are hurting, they may experience secondary trauma. Some people go a step further and call this phenomenon empath compassion fatigue.

When emotionally sensitive people are past their limit of empathy, they tend to shut down. They not only need extra sleep, but they also need a space to be awake but alone as they process everything that has come in. Sometimes this looks like an escape to an off-grid cabin in the woods. Sometimes this looks like going on a solo vacation and being pampered. Sometimes it looks like holing up for an extended weekend and enjoying your favorite foods while binge-watching multiple seasons of a new show.

In 2012, Scientific American reported on research regarding the positive effect that intense special-visual processing video games can have on post-traumatic stress disorder sufferers. The subjects were instructed on how to play the game Tetris, then played it for around 20 uninterrupted minutes per day for a week. A control group was given no game to play. After the week was over, the group playing Tetris logged 8.7 "intrusive memories" such as flashbacks or panic attacks. The group that didn't play suffered nearly four times as many during the week.

While Tetris won't cure PTSD, it has been shown to alleviate flashbacks and panic attacks. Doctors have made correlations of this form of alternative therapy to the highly successful eye movement desensitization and reprocessing (EMDR) therapy that is gaining traction in the traditional psychology world.

This tells us that the human mind—empathic or not—requires time to process difficult things in the background while occupying itself in the foreground.

Processing Activities

- Reading a book
- Watching engaging television or film
- Listening to an audiobook
- Listening to podcasts
- Playing a video game
- Knitting or crocheting
- Boxing
- Play music
- Practicing yoga
- Writing fiction
- Driving
- Listening to music

- Cooking
- Walking a dog
- Running
- Painting
- Learning a new hobby
- Play with a pet

When engaging in media as your processing tool, you may feel even more tired or frustrated. Binging *Game of Thrones* or reading a forum may be fine for some, but it may compound stress in ways you don't immediately notice. Check in with yourself during your processing period to make sure you're improving and not spinning your wheels.

If you have taken time for yourself and feel like it's not refreshing you, or if you're just as anxious as you were before, please talk to a professional who's able to walk you through your energy depletion and see you to the other side of it. Your wellness is more important to the world than you know.

Adrenal Fatigue

In *The Empath's Survival Guide* by psychiatrist Dr. Judith Orloff discusses why and how empaths are so frequently misdiagnosed by doctors. Adrenal fatigue is likely to blame for the empath's sometimes sudden lethargy, and not laziness or physical diseases such as anemia or hypothyroidism.

Adrenal fatigue is said to be caused by stress. Our adrenal glands are part of the endocrine system and located over each kidney. They are small sacs responsible for the production of vital hormones, most notably here for adrenaline and cortisol. If you think back to the first chapter, you'll remember that the sympathetic nervous system is linked to the fight-flight-freeze responses to stress, and to adrenaline manufacture.

Cortisol affects many different systems in the body, as there are cortisol receptors in nearly every kind cell. Cortisol is responsible for the regulation of metabolism, the reduction of inflammation, blood sugar levels, sodium balance, blood pressure, and even the formulation of memories.

When under stress, the adrenal glands snap into overdrive, producing the proper substances to keep you running at the required pace. The theory is that when they are in overdrive too long, they, too, run out of steam and are no longer able to produce the helpful hormones until given time and resources (in the form of lifestyle changes and dietary supplementation) with which to heal.

Often, adrenal fatigue is overlooked by medical professionals. In fact, regardless of growing research on the topic, the Endocrinology Society does not recognize adrenal fatigue as a condition. Mayo Clinic addresses these problems as adrenal deficiency, which suggests a different causality than the idea of overused glands. Holistic and homeopathic doctors, however, rarely overlook the symptoms and are willing to help treat the disorder. Still, the best practice is to first have a physician rule out problems like anemia.

Do You Have Other Signs of Adrenal Fatigue?

- Migraines
- Irregular menstruation
- Insomnia
- Salt cravings
- Muscle weakness
- Irritability
- Feeling constantly dehydrated
- Low blood sugar
- Low blood pressure
- Loss of appetite or weight
- Gaining and holding weight in disproportionate places

- Abdominal and digestive problems
- Sensitivity to temperature changes
- Depression

- Brain fog
- A dependency on caffeine or other stimulants

If these symptoms ring true and other causes have been ruled out by a doctor, keep reading. You can live a full life and protect the energy you have while gaining more instead of simply losing it to other people.

Is This Really a Gift?

Be assured, being a highly sensitive empath is a gift and not a curse whatsoever. When a person is untrained in integrating and using their abilities, they can very much feel like a curse. Once he begins to accept these powerful parts of himself, he will feel stronger and healthier on a regular basis.

When healthy, the empath can have an undeniably positive impact on the world around them. A healthy empath is able to lift the energy of those whom they cross paths. The following is a story of two friends who experience another friend's sadness differently.

Jennifer, Cassandra, and Leah are meeting at a cafe to support Leah, whose father was just diagnosed with a terminal illness. Each of the ladies is empathetic and sharing in Leah's concern and fears. The mood at their table is tense: Jennifer and Cassandra are genuinely concerned and don't want to give false hope or cheer when the facts are solid. Cassandra has been through something similar when her mother passed away two years ago from cancer. She has literally brought her own fears and trauma to the table, as she watched her mother suffer and languish for months.

On the other hand, Jennifer hasn't had to deal with any personal tragedy firsthand so far in life.

Jennifer isn't sure how to go about helping her friend. But before their meetup, she already did some research and tried to find out what the next months will look like for Leah and her family.

As the women meet and Leah begins to talk about her father's last appointment, the mood is supportive but subdued. After a while, Cassandra shares what her own experience was like and gives Leah some practical pointers on navigating the future. Jennifer listens quietly and attentively, and at one point, squeezes Leah's hand to show her support. Having done the research, she understands most of the terminology her friends are using and doesn't have to interrupt to ask questions.

Both of Leah's friends are showing empathy in useful ways. When the women part ways, Leah feels as though some of the emotional burdens have lifted. She's able to face the next week in a better frame of mind than she'd had when she first walked into the cafe that day.

When Cassandra gets home that night, she steps back into her roles as wife and mother and says a prayer for Leah and her family. She cares, and she'll be there to help in the various ways Leah needs, but she hasn't lost sleep over this. Even though she has lived through a similar tragedy, she also took time to heal from it and is able to focus on her own family's needs.

Jennifer, however, goes home and finds it difficult to tackle any of the chores she needs to complete before dinner. By the time Jennifer makes it to bed, she's sore and doesn't know why, as she hadn't done anything physical out of the norm during the day. After a few hours' sleep, she wakes with her heart pounding and can't get back to sleep easily. The next few days are similar, but eventually, she gets back to her normal energy level. Then, she has another day with the pain and anxiety and realizes that it began after she received an upsetting update text from Leah.

Vicarious Trauma and the Psychic Connection

It is common for emotional empaths to take on the form of another person's trauma. As discussed in the previous chapter, people in certain professions are subject to secondary trauma. Empaths seem like they'd succeed in these roles, and it's true. They have a unique ability to understand difficult situations and create steps to correct them, but it takes a special type of empath for their abilities to send them spiraling down into anxiety and depression.

Neither Cassandra nor Jennifer have jobs that require them to exercise their empathy for trauma victims on a daily basis, but Jennifer has the propensity to absorb things and store them in her body as if it were her own trauma. It's as if she actually lived through a degree of that trauma herself.

While Cassandra is clearly both sympathetic and empathetic, Jennifer shows signs of being both an empath and an intuitive, albeit an underdeveloped, unaware one. There's a good chance Jennifer has a psychic connection to Leah.

If we look at the term psychic in a clinical way, we are quick to learn that it means relating to the soul and mind. It's important to let go of the idea of psychics being a colorful caricature of 19th-century fortunetellers. Instead, you probably know multiple people with psychic inclinations, even though they may be at different levels of awareness. You may even possess psychic abilities yourself.

In a positive way, you have the uncommon ability to shift your energy to provide for another person, in much the same way a mother's body changes to nourish her child. In order to have plenty for yourself so that you can give, you must spend time alone with yourself and without the distractions of technology, listening to your own needs over the demands of the world. This is how you will begin to let go of any negative things holding you back and open yourself up to refill yourself with goodness.

Chapter Six: The Healthy Empath

So, what does a healthy empath look like? With all this talk of the negative aspects of true empathy, it may seem like it truly is a curse. The good news is, an empath or intuitive who has learned how to create and maintain boundaries, and how to nourish themselves while filtering out the things that do them harm can live the fullest, richest lives of all.

Even those things might sound exhausting, like a full-time job. Rest assured, all it takes is some practice. Once you experience how good life can be as an empath, you'll begin naturally taking steps to thrive!

Meet Kara, a 36-year-old freelance writer from Brooklyn. She has been living in New York City for almost a decade. Kara has built up a client list that keeps her busy and comfortable in the apartment she shares with Rachel, a graphic designer she met through a mutual friend.

A typical day for Kara begins with making her bed, then ten minutes of yoga in her small bedroom, so that she can connect to her body and have some idea of what she's feeling physically and emotionally today. She then goes to their tiny kitchen and makes breakfast: oatmeal with chia seeds, because she has learned that that combination gives her energy but also fills her up. She doesn't have a gluten intolerance, but most glutinous foods tend to go straight to her brain and make her tired. She can't afford to nap all day long, so she has found out what foods sustain her and what foods should be reserved for special occasions when she doesn't have to work.

She'll make sure to drink a full 16 ounces of water with that, for the sole sake of hydrating well first thing. If she's not hydrated, she feels all sorts of aches and pains she usually wouldn't. She also takes a few supplements to help reduce inflammation and to regulate her physical energy levels throughout the day.

Kara makes sure that she takes breakfast either outside on their small balcony, when the weather permits, or at least beside the window because natural light soothes her. If it's raining in a good direction, she'll eat inside with the window partially open so that she can breathe in the petrichor—she's learned that the scent of rain fuels her creativity.

Then comes the coffee. A few months earlier, Kara began to have an energy crash mid-morning, sometimes so badly that she'd fall asleep while at the computer. She did some research and had to admit to herself that it was probably because her metabolism and adrenals were changing. She made the decision to switch to decaf, and within the first week noticed her energy stabilizing. While she still has the occasional caffeinated drink, she only brings home decaf coffees and teas.

While the coffee is brewing, Kara washes her dishes. A year ago, they realized that they had developed a bad habit of using too many dishes, then letting them pile up in the sink. It was taking too much time and energy to wash that many dishes, and it was also taking up a lot of precious real estate in their kitchen to have six plates, eight mugs (albeit cute mugs!), ten glasses, six bowls, seven small plates, et cetera. They downsized to one of each piece of table service a person and stored away the extra items for when they had company visiting. To make sure they could differentiate between what they were responsible for, they each selected recognizably different pieces. Kara's plates, bowl, and mug set were a faux copper, as were her utensils. Rachel's plates, bowl, and mug were Tiffany blue, her favorite color, and her utensils were pieces of real silver she'd picked up at Brooklyn Flea. Downsizing the kitchen in this very simple way had proven to be a fantastic way to save time and ease the frustrations that often came between them.

When the coffee is ready, Kara takes a few minutes to journal the things rattling around in her head. She may be a professional writer, but when you read her journal, you might not know that she is. It's not a beautiful prose to be cherished for generations, published posthumously. It's sentence fragments, and random thoughts untethered to one another by logic. It's all those things floating around, threatening to slow her down later in the day if she neglects them.

The temperature is beginning to drop. Need to save for new snow boots.
Dan and Leslie's puppy cried half the night. Woke me up at 2, couldn't get back to sleep for an hour.

Feels like it will rain again soon.

Rachel's father has another treatment today. I need to check in with him this afternoon.

I received confirmation that my airline voucher was properly processed. I wasn't feeling very anxious about it, but whatever anxiety I had is gone. Excited for the Greece trip!

I need to schedule a massage. I'm feeling heaviness in my solar plexus again.
Realized why I've been feeling tension in some places. It's because of the upcoming election. Couldn't stay at the coffee shop yesterday because of it. Cab driver and I had a good talk about immigration. It didn't drain me; he felt strong and positive, even though he was concerned. His is a voice I need to integrate into my worldview.

She takes another minute to enjoy her coffee, trying to see if anything else going on that she needs to pay attention to, but can't think of anything else that requires ink. As she finishes her coffee, she adds anything she needs to her daily to-do list and checks her calendar to be sure she remembers her appointment times for the day.

Then it's time to get ready. She'd showered the night before – something about going to bed clean always helps her get better rest – so this doesn't take long. Before leaving the house to meet her first subject of the day in Queens, Kara dabs a blend of essential oils onto her pulse points – partially for fragrance, partially for emotional grounding. She's going to be talking to victims of an arson today. She knows this has the potential to affect her, so she wants to be able to absorb the story but not carry the emotions with her all day.

Rachel has begun her morning routine, too. She tends to be more frenetic in the mornings, sleeping in longer and then rushing to get out of the apartment on time. At first, this was very jarring to Kara. She tried to be social, but the hurried manner and loud sounds that came from the whirlwind that was Rachel's routine irritated Kara. It took Kara a long time to attach the word irritating to her friend. She loved Rachel like a sister. Rachel worked hard and did her part in the chores. They had a fantastic time together when they were entertaining or out with friends, so calling a part of Rachel's persona irritating felt like a betrayal of some sort. But when Kara finally realized that it wasn't a slam on Rachel's character, and more about the way they gained and held and spent their energy, she was able to admit that yes, any rushed, loud action in the morning irritated her.

Understanding that busy mornings were a simple fact about Rachel, Kara decided it would be easier to change some of her own habits than to confront her friend. So, she began waking an hour and earlier in the mornings to be sure that she was back in her own bedroom, getting ready for work when Rachel became active. The occasions when Rachel has to be up early are the hardest for Kara, but she can manage those disruptions to her routine, as long as they're not the norm.

Life outside her apartment can't be as structured as her mornings. It's New York City, after all! Having to depend on others for transportation can be frustrating for anyone, and public transportation can fully drain a highly sensitive person. She's learned some coping skills over the years that are fairly standard for New Yorkers, like listening to music or audiobook, or reading when on the subway or bus, so she keeps a paperback and earbuds in her bag. She also knows that even in winter, she can overheat while waiting for a train in a subway tunnel, so she makes sure she has a bottle of water with her at all times.

Kara makes it to the café in Forest Hills with twenty minutes to spare. This gives her time to get settled and not have to rustle around in her bag or otherwise distract from the attention her contact deserves. When her contact arrives, Kara is able to focus on making her feel comfortable and asking questions without leading or presuppositions attached to them. She takes notes and, with her voice recorder running, she's able to get a story worth telling. By the time Kara pays the bill for them both, she ensures that the interviewee is pleased with how things went, and lets her know that if she thinks of anything else she wants to say, to contact her.

Checking the time, Kara sees that she should be able to get to her next appointment with almost an hour to spare, so packs up and heads to the subway station. Things are going well until she has to switch trains and finds out that one has a 7-minute delay. It's not a very big deal, but she feels anxiety creeping in. When the correct train comes, she boards. One stop into her ride, the train slows to a halt again. Over the loudspeaker, the conductor says something about the tracks.

Minutes pass.

She checks the time again—if they stay at this standstill much longer, she'll be late. She types a text to the client she's supposed to meet, but she doesn't get a signal. Twenty minutes later, the train begins to crawl. Some of her old habits of anxiety have begun to flare up, so she focuses on her breathing. This is a new potential client; she's concerned he'll think she's unreliable. Kara pulls out the rollerball of oils she uses to help soothe anxiety and applies them, and then pulls out her journal and jots down some of her fears. Finally, the train picks up speed, and eventually, she makes it to her stop. Topside, the text sends, and she receives two from her client, Darnell.

I left your name with security. They know where to direct you. Just come in through the Astor Place entrance.

Then, a few minutes before her text had sent:

We'd said 11:30, correct? I have to leave for a lunch meeting at 12:15. Please respond ASAP.

This is the sort of thing that used to send her into a small panic. She wanted to work with this company on the project, a narrative script for a promotional social media video. The pay was going to be better than she usually received, and she already had been working on several different angles. Most importantly, she felt as though tardiness said something about her character, which was something she protected. Kara moves out of the flow of traffic and takes a break to assess herself.

She realizes her shoulders are hunching forward and her neck is retreating into her clavicle —one of her telltale defensive positions. She works herself through a few breaths while still on the sidewalk and stretches her arms above her head and then clasps her hands behind her. This takes but a minute, but she feels more in control again. This is New York: public transportation delays happen. She'd left with ample time to get here, too, so it wasn't an issue of neglectful planning.

"He'll be reasonable," she said out loud. And if he wasn't, then it was possible that this job wasn't meant for her.

She checks the time once more before texting Darnell again: 11:48. Her phone buzzes before she can check in with him, and it's a response to the message she'd sent explaining her lateness.

No problem! Let me know when you're here—I'll stick around as long as I can.

She responds quickly, saying she's just across the street, and she'll be up soon.

Soon enough, she's past security and meeting Darnell, who proves to be understanding of the situation. Though their meeting is short, she's able to ask helpful questions and pitch a few of her ideas, all of which are well-received. They schedule another meeting at the end of the week so that she can meet more members of his team before going through the contract process.

She makes a mental note to get to Astor Place two hours before the planned time, or to set back enough money for a cab ride directly over!

She leaves the building feeling hopeful but fairly tired. It's lunchtime, so she considers her options in the neighborhood. There are plenty of great places, but she knows finding seating will be difficult at this time of day. It's a nice day, so she opts to get takeout she can order through her cell phone. Once her food is ready, she scores a bench at Cooper Place. This way, she's not quite so overstimulated as she would've been in a busy restaurant, and she can think over her meetings from earlier that day and plan the remainder of it.

Afternoons are usually reserved for the actual writing part of her job, so Kara treks back home and takes a few minutes there to shift gears. By about 3:30, she's starting to have difficulty focusing and realizes she's tired, so she takes a break and rests on the couch, listening to some binaural music through her headphones. By 4, she's up again and is sure to drink another bottle of water, then works until 5:30, when Rachel gets home.

Together, the women make a light dinner and talk about the events of their day, and at 7:00, they meet up with some friends for trivia night at a local bar. While she'll indulge in alcohol, Kara makes a point to drink as much water, too.

They're out for a few hours, but it's a work night, so the women make it back to their apartment before it's too late. Kara showers and then once again checks her schedule for tomorrow to be sure she's not on a schedule like she was today.

She'd like to get a few thousand more words drafted on a project, so she settles in to pull some later hours, but sets the alarm on her phone for 10:30. When it sounds, she's still not as far along as she wants to be but knows she'll get even further behind if she doesn't rest, so she closes up for the night.

As she winds down, she has a decaf tea and reads a chapter in the book she's been enjoying. Before bed, she applies a blend of Roman chamomile and lavender oils to the bottoms of her feet, then frankincense oil diluted with almond oil to her sinus passages and chest, to open them up and aid in oxygenating her brain cells. Before she goes to sleep, she takes the time to say aloud what she's grateful for and to put positive energy toward the things she's prone to get anxious about. She doesn't leave out the new puppy next door, either. He and his parents need a good night of sleep, too!

Being self-employed, her one day's schedule rarely looks like the previous one. It's become important for her to keep routines in the times she's at home, and to be able to take some coping mechanisms—like intentional breathing and stretching, journaling, hydration, and the ability to find less-stimulating places to eat—along with as she's out in the world.

Does all of this sound complex and time-consuming? Rest assured, it's not! Later in this book, you will have a chance to build a system that supports your energy. Remember, it's not about making big changes all at once! It's something that needs to happen over the course of time. Master one habit before trying to take on another. Each one will lighten your load and increase your energy. If you're looking to heighten your intuition, know that you have to learn what your body needs in order to function at its highest capacity first.

Chapter Seven: Releasing Negative Energy

In Peter Levine's book, Waking the Tiger, he likens a human's stress response to be like that of a deer hearing a branch break in the forest. They become hyper-vigilant and freeze. The difference is, once the threat has passed, the deer go through a physical release of stress by shuddering in a specific manner. Humans, however, are quick to snap back to our rational brains. We try to process our scares and traumas verbally, on a superficial level, even if it is just in our own minds. Sometimes this works; often, it does not reach deep enough to soothe the damage.

Before you can become a healthy, strong empath, there are some very basic, yet possibly difficult things for you to confront. In order to confront our fear, we have to recognize it. How can you identify fear? It may be more difficult than you think if you've buried your emotions.

- Have you settled into your environment so well that you would immediately pass on an offer of a significant promotion if it meant you would have to move?

- Do you stay in relationships that you know are unhealthy and give excuses to people when they ask why you don't break it off with the toxic person?
- Do you avoid taking on new responsibilities at work?
- Do you keep your partner or children on a tight leash?
- Are you quick to jump into a heated political debate?
- Do you defend every unnecessary purchase you make, even if only to yourself?
- Do you keep most people, even your favorite family members, at a distance?
- Have you quit a hobby or sport you loved for "sensible" reasons?
- Do you lie to keep the peace?
- Do you keep your kitchen stocked with only your favorite convenience foods?
- Do you equate your worth with your weight?
- Do you drink more than one alcoholic beverage a day?
- Do you avoid housework or lawn work because of pain?
- Do you have a stockpile of something?
- Do you buy books but are unable to remember the last time you finished reading a book?
- Have you tracked someone's movements using GPS?
- Do you look for escape routes whenever you're in public or a new private residence?
- Do you bristle and close up when a stranger speaks to you in passing?

- Does anything that reasonably happens in daily life make your heart race in an unpleasant way?
- Does talking about anything make it hard to breathe?
- Do you dread phone calls or other forms of interaction?
- Does making decisions take a long time?
- Do you see your children talking negatively about themselves and do their words sound familiar?
- Does the idea of giving up any particular kind of food or drink make you laugh sarcastically?
- Do you have rituals that you perform wherever you travel, like a specific order of things you do before bed?
- Do you have goals you can't begin working on?
- Do you spend all of your money as soon as you make it?
- Do you make a list of things you need to do, but routinely get distracted?
- Do you do things a certain way just because your parents did it that way?
- Do you do things a certain way just because your parents wouldn't do it that way?
- Do you self-deprecate?
- Do you apologize for things even when you're alone?

Now, not all of these things are wrong in and of themselves. As you go through that list, ask yourself follow-up questions.

- Why?
- Is what I do different from what I say I want to do?

79

- Do I want something because I want it, or because it's logical?
- Do I want something because it's logical?
- What keeps me from acting on what I want to be?
- If I succeed, what will happen to me?
- What will my life look like?
- How will people treat me?
- What will I feel?
- What will people say about be?
- Who will still be close to me?
- How would I function with that success?
- Where exactly would my money go, if I achieve financial freedom?
- What would my new goal be?
- Will people use me?
- Will people want to be around me?
- Will I travel more?
- If I had financial freedom, would I make any legal actions, such as a divorce or put down roots and buy a home?

Some of these things require another "Why?" Perhaps that answer begs even another "Why?" Follow those trails until you have an "Aha!" moment. Know that you may be afraid to see or experience things, so time to meditate and affirm yourself that it is okay to see. It is okay to feel.

Stop Dissociating

Empaths have a difficult time staying connected to their own bodies in the present time. Here are some exercises to aid in re-establishing the mind-body connection.

Sense Yourself

Stand or sit in a comfortable position. Listen to the sounds your body makes even as you remain mostly still: the way your back pops a little when you correct your posture by supporting yourself with your spine instead of slouching into your ribcage. Listen to yourself swallow, listen to yourself as you begin to breathe deeply through your nose. Close your eyes, and feel your body. Where do you feel pain? What do you usually ignore because it feels just fine? Pay attention to the good things happening in your body for a few minutes. Speak your gratitude for those things aloud.

> *"I am grateful that my calves feel strong and are capable of propelling me through life."*
> *"I am grateful for the breeze that cools my skin and makes my hair dance."*
> *"I am grateful that I can breathe through my nose without congestion."*

Stretch Yourself

If you still feel pain in certain muscles, slowly begin to stretch in a way that engages that muscle. Don't press yourself so far that your breath hitches, and instead, stop before that moment. Beginning with your diaphragm, inhale deeply, thinking about the area holding the tension. Exhale slowly, imagining some of the pain leaving that area with your breath.

Repeat this action three times, returning to your original position between each time. You will likely be able to move a little further with each stretch! Move on to another area that is holding tension and do the same. After going through these movements, take a leisurely walk for about five minutes, and drink at least sixteen ounces of water to help deter the buildup of lactic acid in your muscles.

Journaling

It's helpful to record the good things as well as the bad. It's a way to find patterns in your life and to allow you to dig deep while using your rational brain, which is a more comfortable way to learn about yourself, your needs, and your world for some than going through psychological treatment.

Chapter Eight: The Intuitive

When Keysha's niece, Sierra, had a child, Keysha was thrilled. Finally, she got to be a great auntie! Keysha lived in a hefty seven hours away, but when she visited her family in Galveston, she was always ready to babysit. She adored her grand-niece, Faith, but was in full disbelief when, one day, she found out that Faith, now five, had just been diagnosed with a rare form of leukemia.

Because of her job, Keysha wasn't able to get back to Texas in the early days of Faith's treatments. She kept in contact with her girls, which helped, but her heart was always with both Faith and Sierra. Often, Keysha would find herself staring into space or at a blank wall, and even at the back of a work partner's head. She lost time this way. Once, when asked if she was all right, it took her a few moments to be able to answer.

In her mind, Keysha had been in the hospital room with Faith and Sierra. She could have told you details about the place: the way the room's trim didn't quite get along with the wall color, the layout of the furniture and the machines—the way the window sill was cluttered with flowers and stuffed animals, the view from the window. She even had a feeling of where different things were located in relation to the room: the common waiting area on the floor, the women's bathroom, the vending machines, and even the nurse's station.

Keysha realized she'd been doing this for weeks. She could even envision the nurses. A part of her had been there with the girls the whole time, and it was exhausting.

What Keysha was experiencing was called a soul tie. Soul ties can cause you to have unconscious reactions. In Keysha's case, it had become physical, too. She had begun clenching her teeth so hard in the night that a tooth abscessed and eventually had to be pulled out.

As soon as she was able, she visited her family in Galveston. She was surprised to find the details of the hospital were very close, if not dead on, to what she'd envisioned in those bouts of lost time. Even more, Keysha found out that her other niece, with whom she'd been close, too, had to have a tooth pulled because— yes—she'd been grinding her teeth so much that it had abscessed at the root.

Most of the time, people don't intend to create soul ties with intuitives. It's not an intentional, malicious thing, even though it can have negative effects on their partner. It's up to the intuitive to recognize the signs and take steps to free themselves from the aspects of the relationship that are unhealthy. Letting go of a soul tie to a person doesn't mean you must disappear from her life; it means that when you are present, you are your whole, thriving self.

Signs You Might Be Intuitive

- As an adult, you catch yourself losing time. You may not immediately know what you were thinking about, as you weren't actually daydreaming. When you try to access what you'd been thinking about, it's real people and situations, feelings and places, not fiction or fantasy.
- You are often struck by the beauty of things that go unseen by most people and can easily access stories about their origins.
- Patterns of abstract things, like emotions and events, emerge easily for you.
- When talking a friend through a problem, you know the right questions to help them untangle their emotions and thoughts.
- You are unintentionally aware of others' schedules.
- You sometimes to forget to look at a person's appearance when you're interacting with them. It's usually a secondary thought, as your primary attention was on something else about them. Sometimes, you have no idea what they were wearing or carrying after they were gone, even though you

had a face-to-face conversation with them that lasted ten minutes.

- Words can be hard to come by. If someone asks you a simple question like, "Where did you put the tape?" out of the blue and you weren't expecting it, you sometimes have great difficult remembering words like "mud room" and "drawer."

- You experience setbacks, like traffic detours, long lines, or a store being closed, and you're able to let it go when other people might get mad. You figure you're not supposed to be where you thought you should be quite yet, and that it will all work out.

- You suddenly develop a new habit, like nail biting or tapping your foot, and then see someone else doing it shortly after.

- You can find your way around a new town or building without much effort.

Intuition can be a pleasant and useful gift but keep aware of what belongs to you and what does not. Don't allow people to connect to you on a spiritual level without your consent, and don't feel obligated to share your insights or your energy with just anyone.

Chapter Nine: How to Stop Absorbing Negative Energy

Empaths and intuitives are like sponges in water. A sponge can't help but absorb what it's put into. If it's dropped into clear, clean water, it can be used to make the environment around it clean as well. If it's dipped into water that has bacteria like salmonella, however, it is no longer useful, but dangerous until it's been fully sterilized.

Even though it's impossible to guard against being in any negative situation ever, there are steps we can take to filter out negative energies trying to drain us.

Gabriel is nearly 30 years old. He escaped a highly toxic situation at home when he was 18. He proved himself more capable than his parents ever gave him credit for by not only graduating college but also obtaining a master's degree in a difficult field and a demanding, high-level job in Washington, DC.

Gabriel moved away from his small hometown early on, but he has several very good friends who still live there. When he's called home to attend his best friend's wedding and act as a groomsman, he immediately makes plans to stay with another friend in an attempt to minimize contact with his parents.

He knows it won't be that easy, of course. His mother is a queen bee and always knows what's going on in town. She's the type of person who seems to be everyone's closest friend, and very few people have caught on to her manipulative ways. His father is also well-known in town, and serves in a powerful job, too, as the sheriff. He's well-liked, few people knowing how hard he came down on his son, often crossing the line from corrective parenting to abuse.

The groom, Gabriel's best friend, is a police officer under Gabriel's father. The bride's mother is close friends with Gabriel's mother— as much as anyone can be. Gabriel knows his parents will very likely be in attendance. Regardless of how pleasant his parents will appear when they reunite with him, he's certain that he'll be affected by their negativity. As he heads back to town, he mentally prepares himself for whatever they may sling at him.

As an adult, he knows they can't harm him anymore. At the same time, they can pass off barbs that will annoy or bite at him. He can't control that, nor can he control anything they say to others about him behind his back. He knows he can't fake anything more than civility to them. Onlookers, who don't understand the complex and hidden history he has with them, will probably think poorly of him.

So, he thinks about what he can control. He is able to surround himself with his few trusted friends. He can honor his own personal workout regimen, which helps him manage stress, and he can tap into the things he knows about himself that they still refuse to recognize.

He gives himself permission to turn down any meal invitation they may offer up.

He makes plans to spend one-on-one time with the trusted friends he has in town.

He takes a bit of work along so that he can honestly decline anything that feels like it might be a setup of one his parents' "agents"—those people who do his parents' bidding without realizing they're being manipulated.

He reminds himself that when he can't politely avoid contact with them, he still doesn't have to give him anything of himself.

He makes a plan to take a hike up to his favorite waterfall during some of his downtimes and might invite a friend to go along.

And to those trusted friends of his, he explains where he is in his relationship with his family. He explains how he'd prefer for anything personal he shares with them doesn't get back to his family, as they tend to use it as ammunition against him. They agree and are supportive.

Gabriel also takes some time to examine the root of his fear. He no longer fears their physical power over him. His father can't do anything to him legally because Gabriel keeps his nose clean. His mother—

That's when he realizes that he's more concerned about his mother. He felt his blood pressure rise, and his heart rate goes up. What is it about his mother that's bothering him still?

With more thought, he realizes it's partially the way she'll tell amusing stories to her audience about his childhood, but in ways, he's sure didn't happen. He was a little boy, of course, he pushed limits and got into trouble, but he doesn't remember saying clever things or her reacting cleverly in return. He only remembers her anger and punishment. She tells the stories as if they were warm memories, leaving out anything that makes her look responsible for his reactions. These memories were not warm to him.

He's been dragged by his parents to social events in the past where he was expected to laugh along with those versions of the stories. He's been expected to smile when either parent made a thinly veiled negative comment about him.

Gabriel knows that calling either of them out at a wedding-related event would be disruptive, and he wants there to be peace for his friends. Before he gets into town, he takes some time and writes out a letter to each of his parents, detailing his issues with them. As he prepares for his trip, he mulls things over in his head a bit more, occasionally even taking them out to himself.

Forgiveness, he realizes, is a funny act. It has less to do with the other person's asking or admitting what they did, after all. He knows neither of his parents will likely ever do either. He's beginning to find forgiveness for himself, however. As a child, he was not responsible for their actions or reactions or failures as parents. He has taken responsibility for the ways he rebelled as a teenager, understanding that he'd had a misguided need to embarrass them as a way to punish them in return. He's learning to give himself the grace he'd give any child he came in contact with while at work with the Administration for Children and Families.

He chooses to focus on his friends and the good things that are happening for them. And by the time he gets into his hometown, he's in a strong enough emotional state to handle whatever they attempt to throw at him and to make the wedding weekend is an upbeat, pleasant experience he'll be able to look back on with a smile.

Chances are, you've experienced a toxic relationship in which you're required to interact with that person. These can be extremely stressful, especially if they're work or family relationships. A mother separated from an emotionally abusive husband is court-ordered to work out custody arrangements on a regular basis. A law associate not only has the stress of his job, but he has to deal with a boss who can never be satisfied and constantly threatens him with his job. Both the mother and the associate can build up their resistance against the negativity and thrive. It just takes intention and patience with themselves.

Visualization

This sounds a bit "out there," but if practiced before stepping into a potentially negative environment, it can serve you in fantastic ways. Take time when you're alone to sit or stand quietly and envision a protective sphere around your whole body. Imagine anything that's bothering you as particles floating around in your safe space, then imagine them moving out of it. Once your safe space is clear, focus on your breathing: six seconds to inhale, six seconds to exhale. Do this for a minute several times a day. Your own energy will begin to shield you from negative external influences. When you've got this weapon in your arsenal, you can take it and use it anywhere.

Tokens

A token is a physical object that you can keep on your person and touch to help you remember to be present in your body and maintain your energy. In the film Inception, Leonardo DiCaprio's character Cobb keeps a top that he would spin to determine if he was awake or still dreaming. Other tokens, or totems as they are called in the film, were a weighted red die, and a golden bishop chess piece that is hollowed out to feel different than others. A token for an empath could be a rosary, a scarf, a foreign coin, a crystal, or a piece of jewelry.

Let's return to Ana and her sister Maria from chapter three. Nearly a decade into their estrangement, their father passed away. Ana knew that Maria would be present at the services, and she knew that her own energy was at jeopardy just going into the day. That morning, Ana dressed very deliberately. Once her black dress was in place and her shoes on, she carefully selected two necklaces: one her father had given her, and a longer pendant featuring a happy unicorn that her daughter Paloma had gifted her. She tucked the unicorn pendant into her dress and went about the other preparations for the day.

As soon as Ana arrived at the funeral site, she found Maria already in singular histrionic form. Ana navigated the services that day gingerly, giving her sister a wide berth. Maria tried to make a scene a few times, even falling to the ground as they walked away from the burial mound. Ana didn't react except to reach up and touch the unicorn, then to tuck it back into the top of her dress. The simple act of responding physically to herself via something with a pleasant memory attached to it, like the unicorn pendant, helped Ana to stay within her own energy so that she could support her mother and other family members during a particularly trying time. She had maintained enough positive personal energy that their grief did not have negative effects on her.

Move Something

If you are assaulted by negative energy in a certain place, say your office at work, it can help to rearrange things drastically. If you usually reach up to your left to get a piece of tape, put the tape dispenser on top of the cabinet to your right. If small items are cluttering the top of your desk, get an attractive container to corral those things and put the container somewhere new. The act of reaching in a different way should act as a prompt for you to remember that your office isn't what's different, but your mind is. Use it as a reminder that you are making new, better decisions for yourself.

Declutter

Because empaths tend to spend a lot of time in their own heads, clutter tends to take over their workspaces. Take time to declutter those places. At home, the kitchen counter and sink may fill up with dirty dishes and foodstuffs. Your bedroom may not collect dirty laundry, but it may collect clean, unfolded clothing just the same. Taking the time to find homes for all of your belongings and creating clean surfaces will go a long way for your ability to deal with intangible problems.

Tap into Marie Kondo's wisdom and lovingly let go of things you don't have active use for or don't spark joy. For many empaths, hanging on too tightly to clothes and objects is intertwined with guilt. We feel ungrateful for giving away unwanted gifts. We feel selfish if we don't like a perfectly good sweater. We feel foolish for having bought something that broke too soon, and not either getting it replaced or fixed quickly enough. The best way to free up that emotional space is to take the time to downsize.

Recognize Threats

If a person walks into a convenience store brandishing a gun, they don't have to issue threats for the store's customers and employees to recognize a threat. People without special training to handle this sort of situation are likely to freeze up and want to get as far away from the threat as possible.

If a man is walking through the forest in the deep South and happens across a large snake in his path, he won't just continue walking. He will pause and assess the situation. What kind of snake is it? What are his routes of escape? Is there a better way to continue to his destination? He may weigh his odds and consider stepping over it. He may recognize it to be a non-venomous breed and feel comfortable either moving it or crossing over it.

The difficulty with most threats in an empath's daily life is that they're not easily identified. When it comes to toxic people, here are some things to look out for:

- After most encounters with the person, you feel drained of life.
- You experience signs of stress when their name is mentioned.
- When in a public place like a restaurant, you feel the need to check the door every time someone new comes in to be sure it isn't that particular person.
- You realize you're giving more than you're being given. Such a dynamic is not unhealthy if it's a parent caring for a child or an aging adult, but not in a friendship or romantic partner.

- You feel like you're walking through a field of land mines: you never know what's going to set the person off.
- When you have begun drawing away from mutual friends because you worry that they may report back to your toxic acquaintance.
- You often feel like you're being set up to fail with them.
- They employ triangulation, which is a tactic to keep you from someone else you enjoy being around. This can include the abuser telling lies to each party, so they think the other is the abuser.
- Gaslighting becomes common. They take your history with them and change facts, usually so well that you think there's something wrong with your own mind and memory.
- You feel as though you're literally bruised after an encounter with them, even if they didn't lay a finger on you.

- If they show no interest whatsoever in what's going on in your life.
- If you ask for help and they repeatedly drop the ball.
- They shift blame to you when you address an inappropriate behavior or action.
- Every encounter brings a new criticism, even if it's played off as "constructive criticism."
- If you make progress on a project or toward a goal, such as weight loss, they don't congratulate you but instead undermine you. "If you just cut out sugar, it would come

off faster." Or, "You can't expect to lose all that weight if you're not working out."

- If they're the victim or hero of every story they tell.
- They feel the need to be the center of attention when around other people. As the adage goes, "The bride at every wedding and the corpse at every funeral," as they say.
- If, when the attention or positive talk turns to anyone else, they seem to sour.
- Last minute change of plans with no good reason at a clear inconvenience to you. For example, they ask you to pick them up at the airport an hour away. You agree and when the day comes, are there with a few minutes to spare. You wait a while, sending a few texts to let them know you're there and where you're waiting, with no responses from them. You check their flight and see it landed twenty minutes ago. Finally, you call them. They answer and when you tell them you're there, they laugh. "Oh, I decided to have my sister come and get me. I thought you'd talk to her."
- They move goalposts: that is, they'll tell you they need one thing from you but once you give them that, they want something completely different and you never seem able to appease them.
- You become the joke at social events, as they love to tell stories about your failures without your consent.

- You go out of your way to look a certain way in hopes of avoiding a comment about your appearance.

- You catch them in small – or large! – lies on a regular basis.

- Your friends seem to pull away with you less now that you're associating with a certain person. Sometimes the people who love you see things you can't, even though you're an empath.

- You are afraid to miss any messages from them because you know you'll get an earful about how you're difficult.

- They can't keep a job for long. Their story about each employer focuses on everyone else's failing and it's never their fault.

- Everything must be on their terms and in their timing. If you ask them to call you at noon, they'll call earlier or significantly later. If you tell them you'll call at noon, they won't answer. If you say you'll help them with their project on Tuesday morning and not Tuesday afternoon, they get short with you and likely make a passive-aggressive comment about how it must not be important to you, so never mind.

- If you stop hearing your own voice first, and instead hear someone else's. It's normal to think about your child first, and even as an adult to weigh your own thoughts against what your childhood caregiver would say, but when you are so muffled that you forget what you think outside of a person, or are afraid to dive too deeply into your own needs and desires because it might result in conflict, you are losing your sense of self to the person.

- If you find yourself keeping secrets about your money you've spent on small, normal things to avoid getting "in trouble" or about entertainment choices you enjoy because you don't want to get mocked.
- If you remember who you were before you became entangled with that person and wish you could go back and be that version of yourself again because living like this is too uncomfortable.
- You find it pointless to tell the person "no." They've never respected your boundaries and instead pushed that their will be done.
- You've received any form of threat or ultimatum from you. This includes legal action against you, suicide threats, telling your family you have substance abuse problems, taking your kids from you, getting you fired, or refusing to finalize documents you need signed.
- You feel as though you're being monitored.
- Have you caught them in any sort of social media stalking?
- You feel the need to change your contact information or even move to escape their grasp.
- Blowing up your phone with calls or texts. This is a form of harassment.

- You keep thinking about the other person and their situation. Instead of being present in your own life, your mind seems to be with them too often.
- Do you internally rehearse dialogues you want to have with the person?
- Does your mood suddenly shift to worry, fear, or worse when that person makes contact with you?
- Do you feel the need to check all their social media accounts on a regular basis to ensure they're not talking about you behind your back?
- Do you feel the need to check in with them before you make decisions about your own life?

These things are all indicators of highly toxic relationships. If you ever feel unsafe with a person, please do what you can to remove yourself from that situation. There are support networks available free of charge, and many wonderful books about how to escape relationships with dangerous people. Having abusers in active roles in your life will at best slow down your progress toward health and at worst, turn into a life or death matter.

You have so much goodness to give. There is so much goodness to experience. Choose the energy you surround yourself with carefully.

Chapter Ten: Empathic Self-Care

Being an empath is a holistic thing. That is, your empathy is interconnected with every part of you as a whole. Just as you are not able to separate your blood from your body and expect function, you can't simply remove, or turn off, your abilities. Instead, you need to nurture them.

Some of us have been taught that self-care is indulgent and unnecessary. Probably, the same people who put that sort of idea into our heads are the same people who desperately need to exercise self-care beyond that exercised in daily hygiene.

Relaxation is somewhat of a beautiful, mythical beast in today's world. With demands coming from every side, rest takes a back seat. When we do find downtime, we tend to fill it with things that don't fill us up. Not only empaths and intuitives need time to decompress; we just seem to need more of it.

- **Open for Business**

You don't have to have a business license to create business hours. There is absolutely nothing wrong or weird about turning off your phone and any other devices that allow people who don't live with you to come inside your home at their will. Not long ago, it was considered rude to call someone past ten o'clock at night. This was a healthy boundary that was also a social norm.

It's almost impossible to stay completely away from social media, but it is possible to protect yourself from losing time or energy to it. There are social media influencers with hundreds of thousands of followers whose whole business is online, but they make a point to disconnect on weekends.

When it comes to texts and emails, most late-model smartphones give you the ability to auto-respond to messages with custom notes. These responses can explain your availability, and when your friend or client can reasonably expect a reply. The important thing is to also find a good time to follow-up.

- **Cut Down on Distractions**

Once you've tamed the telecommunications, think about other things that disrupt your day. This may take a bit of rearranging the items of your home to make things make sense. For example, if you pack a sandwich every day for lunch, then put all the things you use for preparation in one container in the refrigerator. It will be so much easier if you just pull out one bin that has the meat, cheese, lettuce, sliced tomatoes, and usual condiments in it. Another container could go in a cupboard, holding sandwich bags, chips, and bread.

You might want to add a mail station to your home. Keeping stationery, envelopes, seals or stickers, pens, and stamps together in one consolidated space will save you precious minutes that you might otherwise spend looking for one item.

If you have pets, schedule breaks to tend to their various needs. If you have older kids, arrange times where they do specific tasks without your supervision. Even better, engage in quiet activities with them, such as reading time, or a quiet craft or puzzle while listening to an audiobook you all enjoy.

- **Write Letters**

The act of handwriting letters is a lost art. Most of us only receive the occasional greeting card from an older relative at best, but imagine how you'd feel to receive a handwritten letter, even a short one, from an old friend you haven't seen in years? Don't get caught in paralysis because you don't think your handwriting is good enough, or that you don't have nice enough stationery, or because you made a few mistakes. The thing they'll remember twenty years from now is that you cared enough to write a letter. A real, actual letter.

- **Meditative Music**

The power of music is undeniable. Taking time to simply curl up in a comfortable chair, piping your favorite music through headphones, eyes closed can be incredibly freeing and energizing. Many empaths long for safe, fully immersive experiences, and music can offer that. You may want to explore sounds created with the intent to stimulate or relax parts of your brain, so search for phrases like "binaural beats" and "positive energy."

- **Solo Travel**

Traveling on your own may sound daunting or uncomfortable, but it's a wonderful way to engage cognitive and emotional functions that empaths tend to neglect. The need to focus on navigating a city that you don't know, then trying new food and a new form of entertainment can actually create energy, even if you're physically tired by the end of the day.

Can't get away for long due to responsibilities or financial reasons? Plan a day in your nearest big town and schedule something that focuses on your physical needs, like a massage, pedicure, or a haircut. Find a bookstore and splurge on something that looks engaging, then find a café where you can sit and read for a while. Get a meal at a favorite restaurant, and then get another at a restaurant you've never tried before. Take a walk in a nice park and learn to be comfortable hearing your own voice again.

- **Exercise**

It can be incredibly difficult for empaths and intuitives to keep their energy within their own minds and bodies. Engaging regularly in the favorite form of exercise can be the greatest tool in the highly sensitive person's toolbox.

- **Therapy**

Many empaths struggle to allow others to help them. This could be because we incorrectly assume that sharing our thoughts and feelings will burden others as much as those things burden us. The truth is that trained counselors are usually quite adept at separating their energy from that of their clients. If finances are holding you back, inquire at local social service agencies, libraries, hospitals, and churches for discounted or complementary programs.

- **Energetics Ministry**

Connecting with the right spiritual and energetics ministers can be difficult, but it's worth the time and effort. If you're unfamiliar with the types of energy healing, take some time and research the multitude of options available. You may find having your chakras properly cleared one month leads to polarity therapy sessions. From there, you may feel you need to explore Pranic Healing. Ultimately, it's you who knows what works for you and when.

- **Massotherapy**

From deep tissue massage to Reiki work, having some form of regular bodywork done is absolutely necessary for the highly sensitive person. These don't need to be expensive hour-long sessions three times a week. Even a twenty-minute session once a month will do so much to release negative energy and emotional pain. You are worth this and so much more!

- **Engage in Social Experiences**

It may sound contrary to the idea of introverted self-care, but being in safe environments with trusted friends can be one of the most energizing activities for empaths. If you can trust them with the story of your journey, explaining what brought you to this place and where you hope it will take you, you even find yourself releasing your hold on yourself and simply having fun and enjoying people again!

- **Sensory Experiences**

Take yourself on dates. Really, do it! Have you ever been to a movie alone? What about a concert, a play, or a sporting event? These places with energy not specifically directed at you can actually be revitalizing. Have you allowed yourself to get lost in a museum for several hours? What about an antique store?

Finding places to connect to something bigger than yourself can be daunting, but it can also be healing. Sometimes we need these activities to help us remember that the world is moving along— and doing it well—without relying so much on us as it often seems to. The best part about these things is that they create their own energy, so we can refill our own reserves. Since public places and events are designed for crowd enjoyment, we can find a sort of peace in the neutrality of it all.

- **Physical Care**

In the following two chapters, we are going to dip into the worlds of essential oils and supplements. Each body on the planet is affected by Nature, and Nature has given us a myriad of tools to use for our well-being. Diet, of course, is fundamental to emotional health. We're blessed to live in an age where we have quick access to oils and extracts from exotic locations. These oils and extracts each have many positive uses, but we will concentrate on those that help regulate empathic energy.

Chapter Eleven: Essential Oils

As of the early 2010s, there are many, many companies selling essential oils, blends, and related products. From Walgreens to the much-hyped multi-level marketing companies, essential oils come in just as many levels of purity.

Powerful organic compounds like sesquiterpenes, diterpenes, monoterpenes, ketones, aldehydes, alcohols, esters, phenols, and oxides are distilled from plants to create what is known as essential oils, which do not contain fat in the way we expect an oil to. They are, however, considered an oil because they are liquids not easily dissolved in water. They do not contain fat, which is why an oil applied neat or diluted with a dispersant like a witch hazel won't clog your pores.

Different composites comprised of the compounds mentioned above, derived from different parts of plants such as the root, leaves, and flowers. It is essential to understand a few things about essential oils before investing.

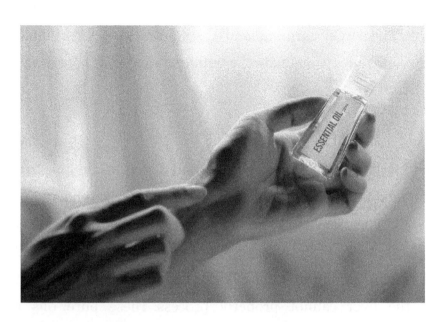

Essential Oils are not Regulated

While therapeutic claims made by those selling essential oils are monitored (and heavily enforced) by the Food and Drug Administration in the United States, the production and usage of oils are not. It is extremely important to do research on several different companies before beginning use.

It is standard practice for some companies to label a bottle of essential oils as 100% pure, even though only a small percentage of its contents may actually contain essential oils. The rest of the bottle is usually comprised of fillers, which are largely synthetic. The multi-level marketing or member-based companies may have a higher standard for their product, as they are targeted with great criticism by naysayers. These companies often have fairly transparent farming and distillation processes. Some of these companies even invite the public to view their operations at their farms.

A Warning about Ingestion

The internet is flooded with recipes and directions on how to use essential oils. There are three ways to use them: by inhalation, by topical application, and by ingestion. Not all essential oils are safe to ingest. Besides the industry's tendency to adulterate bottles with harmful additives, some have naturally occurring compounds that the liver cannot properly process. These pure oils are nonpoisonous when inhaled or applied topically.

Take wintergreen, for instance. While the leaf of wintergreen is not only pleasant to chew and perfectly safe, it has fantastic therapeutic properties when used properly. Methyl salicylate, a non-steroidal anti-inflammatory analgesic, is derived from wintergreen. Topically, wintergreen-derived salves, creams, and even essential oils are safe to use as directed. Methyl salicylate is also the active ingredient in aspirin.

When you have highly concentrated compounds like those in essential oils, a very small amount can go a long way to supporting the human body's many functions. It is integral that you follow the company's directions, just as you would a medication.

Outside of possible toxicity or overdose, another issue with the use of some essential oils is that they can be extremely painful when used undiluted. A single drop of a "hot" oil such as clove, cinnamon, and cassia can inflame the skin and be incredibly painful. Even a very cool oil like peppermint can be uncomfortable and irritating to the user.

Ingest essential oils only under the oversight of a doctor or licensed medicinal aromatherapist. The exception to this would be if the oil is labeled specifically for ingestion. In the case of the latter, be sure to follow the directions on the label.

Dilution Is Critical

Don't be fooled: proper dilution of essential oils has little to do with water. Essential oils are fat soluble. This means that they blend well with fatty oils, or carrier oils, such as almond oil, coconut oil, grapeseed oil, raw shea butter, and sunflower seed oil. These are perfect dispersal and dilution bases for most things that are going to be applied to topically. The lipids in the carrier base will absorb the essential oil's therapeutic compounds and disperse them evenly, with no effect on the oil's potency.

If you have a reaction to essential oil, do not flush the oil off your skin with water. Instead, use milk, olive oil, or another fatty oil to flush the skin. It will soak up the offending oil, and then you can wash the area with soap and water.

Also, remember water-based dilution liquids, even witch hazel, can develop microbes. If you're creating a spray to use on your clothes, bed linens, or skin, you should go with grain alcohol that is at least 120 proof. Essential oil expert Robert Tisserand suggests the 190 proof Everclear. ®

A safe ratio for spray bases and the like would be 25% of your grain alcohol to 75% distilled water, with essential oils added as desired.

If adding essential oils to bath water, first mix three drops to a portion of Epsom salts, then add the salts as directed on their package. The oils will attach to the salts and dissolve more evenly within the bath.

Other Notes

Do not store essential oil products in Styrofoam™ or similar foam products, or in any plastic that is not high-density polyethylene (HDPE, LDPE, or Specialty PE). Many essential oils can eat right through those materials. At best, we don't want to create a mess. At worst, you don't want your natural remedies to be contaminated by plastics that have leached into the product.
Keep out of the reach of pets and children. Essential oils are very powerful. Some are great for kids, and some are great for pets. Even so, children should never handle essential oils without a knowledgeable adult's supervision.

Citrus, rue leaf, angelica root, and cumin seed oils are photosensitive. You should avoid applying them to areas of the skin that will be exposed to sunlight or wait for 12 hours after application to spend time in the sun. Skin sensitivity varies vastly: some people have no reaction, while other people develop dark spots, redness, burns, and occasionally even blisters.

Remember that just about anything can be toxic in high enough quantities. Even clean water can kill a healthy person if there's enough of it! The rule of thumb when using essential oils is to start low, go slow.

If you have sensitive skin and are concerned about an application, please understand that inhalation is just as effective. Invest in quality oils and a good diffuser for your home or office. Car diffusers are affordable ways to keep both the scent and energy good while on the go.

If you are on blood thinners or other medication for blood pressure, do not use grapefruit, rosemary, sage, or thyme.

Keep away from sensitive areas, including eyes. If your eyes become irritated, flush them with milk, not water.

Finally, when selecting essential oils, it's important to know exactly which ones you're looking for. Cut down on confusion by knowing the Latin binomials. A chart of oils most used for empathic protection and growth is included on the next page.

Oil Name	Latin Name
Bergamot	*Citrus aurantium var.* or *Citrus bergamia*
Black Spruce	*Picea mariana*
Chamomile (Roman)	*Chamaemelum nobile*
Copaiba	*Copaifera reticulata*
Frankincense	*Boswellia serrata*
Hyssop	*Hyssopus officianlist*
Indian Sandalwood	*Santalum album*
Lavender	*Lavandula angustifolia* or *lanvendula officinale*
Lemon	*Citrus Lemon*
Lemon Balm (Melissa)	*Citrus limonum*
Myrrh	*Commiphora myrrha*
Palo Santo	*Bursera graveolens*
Rosemary	*Rosmarinus officinalis*
Rosewood	*Aniba rosaeodora*
Sage	*Salvia officinalis*
Valerian	*Valeriana wallichii*
Vetiver	*Vetiveria zizanioides*

Bergamot

Bergamot essential oil comes from the rind of the citrus fruit of the same name. A staple ingredient in black tea, bergamot essential oil is not steam distilled like many oils, but cold-pressed. Bergamot is used by aromatherapists as an antidepressant and an anti-anxiety aid. The flavonoids in bergamot oil can play a part in the stimulation of serotonin and dopamine. Note: One of the components, bergaptene, becomes toxic if exposed to sunlight.

Black Spruce

A North American evergreen with higher concentrations in Canada, black spruce's needles are steam distilled to extract a lovely warm, clean-smelling dark green-blue oil. The scent itself is comforting, and even if you've never had the pleasure of holing up in a cozy cabin, you'll feel like you have. Used for emotional clearing and healing, black spruce is an oil you'll be glad you added to your home apothecary.

Chamomile (Roman)

There are two types of chamomile flower-based essential oils in heavy circulation: Roman chamomile and German chamomile. While German chamomile has many wonderful properties, Roman chamomile is used for mood stabilizing and recharging energies and calming anxiety at the same time. The

Latin binomial name Chamaemelum Nobile can be translated to ground apple and was thus named for its fruity scent.

Copaiba

Steam distilled from resin of the South and Central American copaiba trees, copaiba essential oil is loved for its powerful anti-anxiety and anti-inflammatory properties. High in the terpene beta-caryophyllene, a non-cannabinoid that effectively triggers the human body's cannabinoid receptors, copaiba is a potent pain reducer.

Frankincense

An incredibly powerful resin and oil, frankincense comes from the gum of olibanum trees, which grow in the Horn of Africa, Yemen, and Oman. There are several different varieties of frankincense available, but the one we are focusing on goes by the Latin binomial of Boswellia serrata. Certain religions frequently use frankincense in their worship services. Depending on your background with the balsamic fragrance, usually related to church experience, this could trigger positive or negative feelings, so bear that in mind before you begin using this oil or resin. Frankincense is an extremely powerful oil with many uses but is particularly helpful in respiratory support and stress relief.

Hyssop

The flowers and leaves of the Mediterranean shrub, hyssop, are steam distilled to make its essential oil. Hyssop is used to regulate the nervous system: if you're feeling nervous, scattered, or overwhelmed to the point of panicking, it will soothe. It also can stimulate the nervous system if you need an energy boost.

Indian Sandalwood

Central to many Hindu ceremonies, Sandalwood plays a part in many lives from birth until a person's passing. Medicinal practitioners worldwide have found it effective in the treatment of hypertension, as a sedative, and as an anti-inflammatory.

Lavender

Not to be confused with lavandin, lavender essential oil is steam distilled from the beautiful, soft purple flowers of the Lavandula angustifolia plant. It's clean, the bright scent is ideal for refreshing cars and living spaces. It is also especially good on fabric, so many people add to wool dryer balls when doing laundry and spritz it onto their pillows and bed linens. In 2018, the Western University of Health Sciences reported that their research showed lavender oil was excellent for relieving anxiety issues. It has also been proven to improve the quality of sleep and improves the function of the circulatory system

Lemon

It's important to note that many citrus essential oils are not derived from the highly acidic internal parts of the fruit, but cold-pressed from the nearly neutral rind. If you are adding high-quality lemon to your food or beverage, you needn't worry about the enamel of your teeth being eaten away! You should, however, take caution with most plastics and plastic-based products, aside from high-density polyethylene (HDPE) plastics. A single drop of undiluted lemon oil can eat completely through the wall of a thick

Styrofoam® cup within a few seconds. A natural antidepressant and anti-anxiety remedy, lemon essential oil's scent is uplifting and cleansing to the respiratory system and the spirit.

Lemon Balm (Melissa)

Lemon Balm, also known as Melissa or Bee Balm, is an herb with many culinary and medical uses. Part of the mint family, the leaves are steam distilled to create an essential oil that stimulates serotonin production. Lemon balm is also being studied for its compound citral's role in Alzheimer's treatments.

Myrrh

Egypt is home to the Myrrh tree and referenced consistently throughout the Bible. The essential oil produced from its resin is used to stimulate the functions of the nervous and circulatory systems, is anti-spasmodic and can expedite healing. In the book of Exodus, it was one of the oils used for spiritual cleansing as part of a synergy called the anointing oil.

Palo Santo

Palo santo, literally translated to Holy Wood, is native to a coastal region of Ecuador. This prized oil is steam distilled from the wood of decaying trees, which makes it unique in the aromatherapy world. Traditionally used for spiritual purification, palo santo is also used for the removal of and protection from negative energy, chakra cleansing, and easing anxiety.

Rosemary

An evergreen herb, the fine silvery leaves are like needles, and pastel flowers of the rosemary are packed with nutrients and is a favorite for seasoning pork, chicken, and beef. Its steam-distilled oil gives off a bright, distinct scent. When rubbed into the scalp, it's refreshing and invigorating, offering the user a boost in focus and productivity. This clean, floral scent boosts mood and reduces cortisol, which is known as "the stress hormone."

Rosewood

A Brazilian native, this beautiful tree is under strong legal protection due to deforestation. If you can find a legally obtained source of rosewood oil, you'll be in for a rare treat. A powerful mood-stabilizing treatment, rosewood essential oil also serves as a gentle stimulant and is used to enhance memory.

Sage

Sage is a favorite for cleansing negative energies from a place or object. Sharing a large amount of the same chemical compound as rosemary, sage is akin to being rosemary's darker, earthier sister. Sage is also used to boost brain function and reduce inflammation.

Valerian

Originating in India, the roots of the valerian flower are steam distilled to create a deeply woody, musky scented essential oil. Used in sedative supplements and organic anti-anxiety elixirs, the valerian root soothes the nervous, respiratory, endocrine, and cardiovascular systems. Valerian has a moderately high viscosity level but blends well with other oils.

Vetiver

The roots of this grass are steam distilled to create a rich, sweet, almost sticky essential oil with a higher level of viscosity than most other essential oils. Its thickness can make it difficult to pour out of its container, so if you get a bottle that won't release the liquid easily, exchange the silicone spill guard for a cap with a medicine dropper attached. You'll want to use this oil, so don't be discouraged! Studies have shown that vetiver has a positive calming effect on the mind and has been used successfully in schools to help children with attention difficulties focus and perform better. A powerful tool for the relief of the results of stress and trauma, vetiver is one you'll want to keep in your toolbox.

Chapter Twelve: Supplements

Simple actions get much more difficult when we are carrying around other peoples' emotional baggage all day and night. Having to sort through everything can be debilitating. When we absorb so much, our natural instinct is usually to disengage and numb. Empaths, intuitives, and highly sensitive people need to support their systems from the inside out by filling up on pure foods without excluding pleasurable ones.

Eating whole foods and largely avoiding processed foods, going for organic when possible, and staying properly hydrated (read: water, not coffee!) are integral. We are often far more sensitive to foods than we think, and yet empaths tend to have a strong addiction to caffeine, processed "convenience" foods, and yes, even alcohol.

Notice the term "largely avoiding." For those who are prone to withdraw or get stuck inside their own heads, looping through what they've received from other people, experiences, or things, it is also highly important to engage—and reward—our first five senses. Food is never the enemy. The ability to enjoy favorite dishes is not something a highly sensitive person should deny themselves entirely, but we do need to regulate them.

A high-carb meal like macaroni and cheese with a favorite soda could certainly be an occasional reward, but not standard fare. If you feel the need to further assist your system in the proper ways to retain good energy, look for organic supplements with these ingredients. Before beginning any supplement regimen, consult your health care provider and read all the literature associated with the products.

5-HTP

5-Hydroxytryptophan is a naturally occurring chemical that stimulates the creation of the "happy chemical," serotonin. Serotonin plays a crucial part in pain reduction, sleep, mood stabilization, and contentment.

Ashwagandha Root

Also called Indian ginseng and Indian winter cherry, ashwagandha root is a staple in Ayurvedic medicine. A powerful anti-inflammatory and anti-anxiety herb, ashwagandha is also known to improve brain function and support the endocrine system.

B Vitamins

Although it may seem obvious that vitamins are an integral part of healthy body function, their effect on a highly sensitive person's ability to deal with outside energy is often overlooked. In particular, B vitamins improve the dispersal of oxygen throughout the bloodstream, improve brain health, regulate the nervous system, and stimulate the digestive system. Know that the human body cannot store B vitamins, so they need to be restored daily.

Boswellia Serrata

You may know boswellia serrata as frankincense, but in the supplement form, it's usually not incorporated as an essential oil, but as a resin extract. Used for many physical ailments, boswellia serrata is also known to enhance the feeling of well-being. You have an aversion to the scent of frankincense essential oil but want to use it; you'll be glad to know that the gel capsule form is usually tasteless.

GABA

Naturally produced in the brain, Gamma-Aminobutyric acid is a neurotransmitter. Rather than heightening the speed of which the brain receives information, it actually works to slow things down. When information is delivered at a pace at which the brain can process more naturally. This supports an overall sense of security, well-being, and the ability to make good choices without feeling overwhelmed.

Iron

A vital mineral for many of the body's functions, iron is naturally available in a wide range of foods, yet most people require more than they consume daily. In 2005, the "Journal of Nutrition" published a study that showed that iron-deficient mothers who began taking iron supplements showed a 25 percent increase in both depression alleviation and stress management. Iron is also crucial for the maintenance of proper energy levels.

L-Theanine

A central element in Chinese culture, green tea is also heavily present in its traditional medicines. One of its many beneficial elements is L-theanine, an amino acid connected to GABA production and brain wave activity. A single cup of black or green tea contains enough of a dose to calm the mind while not causing any drowsiness. It also can elevate levels of dopamine, glycine, and serotonin.

Magnesium

Once plentiful in the human diet, magnesium and other minerals integral to proper health are now depleted in much of today's soil. Magnesium aids in the production of energy in cells. It can successfully combat muscle cramps and seizures, anxiety, headaches, depression, and mild behavioral disorders such as irritability, restlessness, apathy, and moodiness. Magnesium has effectively treated patients with insomnia, traumatic brain injury, post-partum depression, and even cocaine cravings.

Omega-3 Fatty Acids

Found in fish oil, oysters, flax seeds, chia seeds, walnuts, some seaweeds, and soybeans, omega-3 fatty acids are wonderful anti-inflammatory compounds that also attribute to muscle and joint health, heart health, and brain function.

Probiotics

Good bacteria in the gut are responsible for healthy skin, the processing of cortisol, and proper digestive function. The strains known as Bifidobacterium and Lactobacillus have proven effective in the improvement of depression, anxiety, and other mental disorders.

Vitamin D

A nutrient every person at every age can benefit from, Vitamin D plays a vital role in human health. While it is rarely present in food, our skin readily produces it when triggered by ultraviolet sunlight rays. Fortunately, it is available as a dietary supplement. Vitamin D aids in healthy bones and teeth, healthy energy levels, and the processing of insulin. Many inhabitants of the northern United States report varying degrees of Seasonal Affective Disorder, which is likely due to the many months that are spent indoors because of unfavorable weather. Some doctors in sunnier parts of the country haven't even heard of Seasonal Affective Disorder, because they have access to plentiful sunlight and a climate that accommodates outdoor activity year-round.

The symbiotic link between plants, animals, and human wellness is undeniable. Regardless of your ability to understand the energies of plants and animals, our lives are clearly dependent on theirs.

If supplementing your diet with all of these recommendations seems like an overwhelming task to undertake, start small. Research one supplement and see if it looks like it's what your body needs. Many companies produce supplements that combine several of the components listed here and at reasonable costs. Do what you can, create the habit, and notice the positive changes that will come.

Chapter Thirteen: Affirmations and Permissions

Most people talk to themselves on a regular basis. Whether it's to replay a discussion we had with another person or to remind ourselves what to do when we get to work, a dialogue of one sort or another walks us through various parts of our day.

For some personalities, it's easy to keep a fairly neutral, matter-of-fact tone in these intimate communications. They don't take things too seriously, and if they get frustrated or angry, they don't spend much time in those feelings. At the same time, they don't blow off their mistakes or leave messes for others to clean up. They learn from their mistakes and keep moving forward.

Others appear to be happy-go-lucky, devil-may-care, free as a bird about things. One imagines that their self-talk leans heavily toward the optimistic side. Perhaps it normally does, but when they are in distress or unhealthy, whatever isn't going well is enough to throw them into panic. When the panic fades, they're appear deeply depressed for a long time.

Another personality type seems to keep records of every good thing and every wrong thing in their lives. They blame themselves for any problem they're having at work or in friendships, and they appear stressed out almost all the time.

While some people can take disappointments, failures, and setbacks in stride, the rest of us tend to fall away into self-hatred mode. We propagate lies about ourselves when we speak negatively about ourselves. When we say, "I'm so stupid" or "Of course they don't want me around, who would?" we're doing more than just damaging our resilience. We're inviting negativity right into our homes. In some cases, we're holding the door wide open for abusers and misfortune.

Where do those words come from?

Gianna came from a good family. Her father worked hard to keep not only a roof, but a very nice one, over their heads. His mother made sure meals were on the table at 6:30. If she had problems, she knew she could talk to them. She had many good friends, and she was involved in activities that were pleasurable and not stressful or highly competitive. She made above-average grades, read books for fun, and helped out at several volunteer organizations throughout high school. Her parents were supportive and available. They all loved to travel, so they'd seen a good percentage of the United States and some of Europe's most influential cities.

In her junior year, something changed. Gianna began writing negative things about herself in her journal. She wrote about her frustration for her lack of deep relationships. She wrote about her weight even though she was not heavy. She began backing off from most of her friends. Her parents had never spoken negatively to her, but words began to attach themselves to her without any known causes. Words like worthless and burden.

Gianna had never experienced verbal or physical abuse. She'd never been bullied. Sure, she'd had a slight mutual dislike for some people, but it didn't affect her much, and it was always mild. She wouldn't have been able to pinpoint anything as actually wrong or causing trauma. But here she was, in high school, writing unkind words about herself in her notebook.

Her mother, on the other hand, had experienced verbal abuse. As a child, she had been bullied. She was all grown up now, beautiful, and by all means, successful.

Gianna began to self-harm the summer before her senior year. She withdrew further and didn't pursue the relationship with her parents much. They no longer pursued one with her, either. Her dad stayed busy at his office, and her mother stayed busy taking care of the house. She later found out that her mother had begun having flashbacks of her own trauma. She also found out that her mother was suffering depression on deep levels. It took years for Gianna to realize it, but she finally understood that she had taken on this negative self-talk because those were the same words her mother was saying inaudibly to herself.

The heart knows more things than the mind can decipher. Gianna picked up on this deadly habit of negative self-talk without hearing her mother say a single word about depression or feelings of worthlessness.

It doesn't take trauma or vicarious trauma for us to be downright awful for ourselves. Is it so hard to speak positively about ourselves instead?

Affirmations and permissions are a great way to begin to change the way you think about yourself and the world around you. Below are lists that may or may not resonate with you. You may not quite be ready to open up your world to some of these things. You may not want to give permissions to an abusive person. That is all completely fine! Go at your own pace with these. Some of them may be manifestations you don't want for yourself. You have permission to choose who you are and who you become. Read through these lists and see what you do agree with and what does meet you where you stand right now.

I Am

I am strong.

I am balanced.

I am able to give generously of myself to my passions.

I am sensitive to those who can genuinely benefit from my energy.

I am unavailable to those who want to abuse my energy.

I am allowed to say no.

I am responsible for my actions and attitudes with my spouse.

I am released from the responsibility of my spouse's actions and attitude.

I am resilient.

I can disagree with another and keep my energy at the same time.

I am unashamed of what happened to me.

I am more than my abuse story.

I am healed from irrational fear.

I am healed from rational fear.

I am healed from cynicism.

I am healed from festering anger.

I am healed from separation anxiety.

I am successful.

I am open to learning new skills.

I am open to new realities about myself.

I am open to new realities about others.

I am content, regardless of my circumstances.

I am good with money.

I am open-handed with my resources.

I am ready.

I am able.

I am joyful.

I am playful.

I am kind.

I am patient.

I am disciplined.

I am honest.

I am gentle.

I am fierce.

I am calm.

I am smart.

I am a quick thinker.

I am easy-going.

I am organized.

I am grateful.

I am warm.

I am trustworthy.

I am determined.

I am supportive.

I am loving.

I am friendly.

I am perceptive.

I am thoughtful.

I am optimistic.

I am athletic.

I am healthy.

I am hopeful.

I am ambitious.

I am ethical.

I am unpretentious.

I am fair.

I am aware.

I am responsible.

I am sincere.

I am mature.

I am conscientious.

I am self-reliant.

I am well-spoken.

I am a defender.

I am a good leader.

I am a protagonist.

I am a good mother.

I am a good father.

I am a good friend.

I am a good worker.

I am worthy of friendship.

I am worthy of love.

I am aware of my surroundings.

I am in communication with my body.

I am respectful of my senses.

I Am Allowed

I am allowed to nap.

I am allowed to cry.

I am allowed to be angry.

I am allowed to enjoy this moment.

I am allowed to celebrate.

I am allowed to grieve.

I am allowed to be alone.

I am allowed to ask for a company.

I am allowed to dance.

I am allowed to eat this food.

I am allowed to make good dietary decisions.

I am allowed to eat food I enjoy.

I am allowed to dream.

I am allowed to see beyond the physical world.

I am allowed to be spiritual.

I am allowed to speak.

I am allowed to share my story.

I am allowed to say, "No, thank you."

I am allowed to embrace who I am.

I am allowed to embrace who I was.

I am allowed to be excited about who I am becoming.

I am allowed to disagree.

I am allowed to take my time before making a decision.

I am allowed to embrace others.

I am highly intuitive.

It Is Safe

It is safe for me to see.

It is safe for me to feel.

It is safe for me to speak.

It is safe for me to think critically.

It is safe for me to create.

It is safe for me to be intuitive.

I Control

I control what I feel.

I control how I perceive things.

I control what I accept in my life.

I control who I accept into my inner life.

I control what media I let into my mind.

I control my time.

I control when I tap into my intuition.

I Am Open

I am open to goodness.

I am open to the light.

I am open to those who need my goodness and light.

I am open to my intuition's guidance.

I Attract

I attract those with whom good energy flows to and from.

I attract abundance in all things.

I attract

I Have

I have access to a well that does not run dry.

I have integrity.

I have enough.

I have enough experience.

I have enough knowledge.

I have enough discernment.

I have good discernment.

I have a good sense of humor.

I have good intuition.

I have enough energy.

I have gifts to share.

I have overcome negative self-talk.

I have good things to say about myself.

I have good things to say about others.

I have blessings to give others.

I have blessings to accept.

I have a good mind.

I have the ability to learn.

I have the ability to master a new skill.

I have good time management.

I have the authority of my body.

I have good intentions and make good plans.

I have the ability to carry out those plans.

I have been given the capacity to use the gifts I have been given.

When I

When I laugh, I am healed.

When I engage with nature, I am healed.

When I tend to my own home, I am healed.

When I connect to my loved ones, I am healed.

When I partake in physical activity, I am healed.

When I do something alone, I am strengthened.

When I do something difficult, I rejoice in my success.

When I take care of others, I feel at peace.

When I fulfill my promises to others, I gain energy.

When I learn something new, I am excited.

When I take the time to do something right, I make my future easier.

When I share my time with someone, I am rewarded beyond imagination.

I Make

I make good choices about how to support my body.

I make good choices about how to support my mind.

I make good choices about how to support my spirit.

I make good choices about how to serve others.

I make good choices about how I share my time.

I make wonderful friends.

I make good meals.

I make a beautiful home.

I make choices that improve my life.

I make choices that improve the lives of those I love.

I make other people feel safe.

I make animals feel safe.

I make other people feel powerful just as I am.

I Know

I know what my gut needs for health.

I know what my muscles need for health.

I know what my liver needs for health.

I know what my brain needs for health.

I know when someone is genuine.

I know I can trust my senses.

I know what is right.

I know what is good.

I know how to love others and retain my energy.

I know how to filter my negative energy out of my body for release.

I know how to use oils to improve function.

I know how to use supplements to improve function.

I know how to use movement to improve function.
I know how to use silence to improve function.

I know how to use social activity to improve function.

I know I am loved.

I know I am accepted.

I know I am valued.

I know I am a pleasure to be with.

I know how to add value to every situation I am in.

I know how to focus my energy to meet my own present needs.

I know how to deflect other peoples' energy.

I know the difference between other peoples' will and my own.

I Am at Peace With

I am at peace with my spouse.
I am at peace with my partner.
I am at peace with my mother.
I am at peace with my father.
I am at peace with my brother.
I am at peace with my sister.

I am at peace with my daughter.

I am at peace with my son.

I am at peace with my neighbor.

I am at peace with my co-worker.

I am at peace with my past.

I am at peace with the future.

I am at peace with where I presently am.

I am at peace with my own voice.

I am at peace with my history.

I Live in

I live in abundance.

I live in joy.

I live in peace.

I live in awe.

I live aware of my surroundings.

I live in touch with my senses.

I live open to my intuition's guidance.

I live in the present.

I live with goodness in my future.

I live with appropriate disassociations.

I live with appropriate associations.

I live in peace with nature.

I live with fearlessness.

I Can

I can filter out bad energy and receive good energy.

I can trust myself.

I can trust my friends.

I can trust my instincts.

I can live in the present.

I can forgive.

I can be humble and strong at the same time.

I can learn.

I can love without expecting anything in return.

I can be in a space I normally would feel unwelcome in.

I can make friends.

I can enjoy my work and be fulfilled by it.

I Am Able to

I am able to heal.

I am able to improve my grade.

I am able to meet this deadline.

I am able to advance in my career.

I am able to finalize this separation.

I am able to pay my bills.

I am able to create a safe place.

I am able to create an organized home.

I am able to be comfortable in my body.

I am able to enjoy the company of others.

I am able to take a time out.

I am able to protect my space.

I am able to create the correct goals for myself.

I am able to attain those goals.

I am able to get quality sleep.

I am able to remember important things from my sleep.

I am able to recognize my intuition clearly.

I am able to trust the information gathered by my intuition.

I am able to interpret the different things that come from my dreams.

I Love

I love the body I have been given.

I love nourishing my body.

I love nourishing my mind.

I love nourishing genuine souls.

I love forgiving past mistakes I have made.

I love forgiving past mistakes others have made.

I love letting go of the injuries that others have caused me.

I love spreading happiness.

I love being a source of peace for others.

I love listening to my friends.

I love laughter.

I love abundance.

I love leadership.

I love community.

I love my empathy.

I love my intuition.

I love my senses.

I love to share my knowledge with those seeking.

I love knowing what is worthy of my attention.

Take one of these affirmations and repeat it aloud to yourself several times today. Do the same thing tomorrow. Write it down. Dissect it. Journal about what it can mean, what these new manifestations will look like.

5 x 55

The 5 x 55 exercise is one that many people have seen success with. The idea is to write one positive affirmation or manifestation statement 55 times a day for five days in a row. The idea is to rewire your brain to integrate a truth that you had forgotten or hadn't yet learned, such as I am safe. By intentionally building our new narratives, you will begin to see positive energy coming your way.

Chapter Fourteen: Developing Your Gifts

Go ahead and raise your hand as high as you can.

Can you get it another inch?

Perhaps one more?

Did you stand up?

If you didn't, why not?

You may be reading this in a bookstore or at work on your break, or perhaps you're in a park. What limited you from standing up and pushing onto your toes and trying to get just another inch?

The chances are, it was a social construct.

In most places, it would be perfectly admissible to raise up high on your toes, hand over your head. It just wouldn't be normal. If you're reading this on a plane and the seat belt sign is still on, sure, it wouldn't be prudent to follow those physical directions.

Limiting beliefs are experiences or attitudes that keep you from trying to do something that could be positive for yourself or others. Sometimes these are based on past experiences when you tried to do that thing or something similar. Sometimes these are based on things we've been told by our parents, peers, or employers.

Empaths and intuitives are often guilty of absorbing others' limiting beliefs and taking them as their own. Worse, we tend to imagine scenarios where failure or heartache is the only option. The thought of doing something can be so negative that we bow out and don't even try.

Think about how much we miss out on when we create a worldview around these common limiting beliefs:

Common Limiting Beliefs

- I'm not good enough to...
- I'm not in good enough shape to...
- I don't know how to...
- I don't have the skills to...
- I'm not worthy of...
- I can't talk to people.
- I'm irresponsible.
- I'm a bad parent.
- I'm a bad romantic partner.
- I don't make good choices.

- They will never forgive me.
- I will never be successful...
- There's no money in doing what I love.
- I'm an imposter...
- I deserve these bad things.
- I can't change.
- I'm not lucky.
- My dreams are selfish.
- Life is not going to get any better.
- I am weak.
- That will hurt.
- I'm too weird for anyone to care about.
- I can't.
- I'm stuck.
- It's not worth the trouble.
- I'm not good at math.
- I'm not a good employee.
- I will never have enough money to feel safe.
- I will never be safe.
- I'm disposable.
- I will have a panic attack.
- They will talk about me behind my back.
- I won't fit in.
- I don't have enough money to...
- I don't have the time...
- I don't have the resources...

- I don't know anyone there.
- I don't like being by myself.
- I don't know how to get around there.
- I am not disciplined enough to...
- I'm too fat to...
- No one else is going to...
- They're not going to listen to me.
- What do I know?
- I'll be far too uncomfortable to...
- I don't have the confidence to...
- I'll mess up.
- I'll fail.
- I'll embarrass everyone.
- I'll embarrass myself.
- I don't have the energy.
- I'm not loveable.
- I'm not worth...
- I'm not worthy of...

Now, let's go back and take a few of those examples and flip them. Instead of I am not disciplined enough to create an online store and keep up with the paperwork, what would the world look like if you found out that I was able to create an online store and I have kept up with the paperwork.

In order for the positive future to become a reality, action needs to take place. Maybe the positive future version of you has learned how to do all the website design and accounting. But maybe it hasn't.

Maybe, instead, you have teamed up with a fantastic website designer to get your online storefront up and running, and you figured out how to do the accounting yourself. Perhaps you've figured out the website design end but knew that the bookkeeping would be an ongoing source of stress and anxiety. You asked friends for references, and one name came up several times, and your friends were right! The accountant they recommended is fantastic!

In any of these scenarios, you've won. When we outsource some of our workload, it's not a mark of failure. In fact, it builds community. You're supporting other people, and this way, we share in each other's successes.

Let's try flipping another limiting belief. I'm not in good enough shape to... In this case, Beth plans to take her husband and twelve-year-old to Disney World for their first visits. She's saved the money, and she's planning the trip when she realizes that they'll be walking in the Florida heat and humidity for an average of ten miles a day. With her desk job and fairly inactive lifestyle, Beth begins to worry that she's not in good enough shape to keep up with her family. Her instinct is to plan for them to have more of the fun, so she doesn't slow them down, but deep down, she really wants to experience those things with them.

She decides that the experience is absolutely worth conditioning herself for. The trip is three months away, so she begins by waking half a mile around her neighborhood. She builds her way another block at a time. Some days she takes a longer walk, others she keeps it to just a mile.

According to her tracker, the family racks up thirteen miles on the first day! By the time they make it back to their hotel, everyone is reasonably tired, but they still have enough energy to cool off in the pool. By morning, they've recovered well enough to hit the next park! With the exception of a little fatigue and some quickly cared-for blisters, the trip turns out to be a success! On their way home, they're already planning their next visit.

In this case, Beth understood what her limiting belief would cost her: precious time spent with her quickly growing daughter, and the ability to see her husband come alive as a kid again, going on rides, getting photos taken with characters, and singing along at the live shows. She wasn't willing to give up the future memory because of her own restrictions, so she lifted those restrictions.

Removing a limiting belief can require effort. For Beth, it was a matter of taking twenty minutes out of her day at first, but some days it was a full hour. She was careful to not fall into any secondary limiting belief traps, like what the internet had to say about what weight she should be, what condition she should be in, or how quickly she should walk. Instead, she kept her eyes on her goal: she wanted to condition herself just so that she was comfortable ambling around theme parks all day.

Stop Lying

In order to increase your abilities and evolve into someone who can use their abilities at will, you need to stop lying about yourself and about others.

When you say I am not smart enough to learn this skill, it's a complete lie. No matter who you are, whatever setbacks you may have, you still have the capacity for learning something. It may come easier to others, but when growing intuition, there is no room for comparing one's self with another.

Comparison is the thief of joy, true. But it's also completely at odds with your evolution. It's tempting to say; I'm only competing with myself! This attitude isn't conducive to your fine-tuning your empathy or intuition, either. Your unique sensitivities will change your personal needs on a daily basis, and sometimes even hourly. You may have been able to push yourself at the gym for an extra hour yesterday, but today your energy may be directed toward something completely different, like helping your son through his first romantic breakup.

You may say something like. I'll never be a good leader. No one listens to me. They're going to think I'm stupid. This is a lie of omission. What you're omitting from this equation is your potential audience. If you feel a call to lead even a small group of people, then you need to do the work to learn how to communicate clearly. For some, it will be even harder to learn to speak up simply.

You may not have found the correct audience yet. You may have found the correct audience, but they're not ready to listen. But if you haven't tried speaking in the way you feel led to because you assume something about another person's character that may very well not be true. It's as if you're saying, I have something that will help you, but you're not worth the risk.

Failure Isn't a Possibility

Many speakers and authors have emerged in the past few years with messages that incorporate the idea that the real failure is to stop trying. This is especially true when it comes to mastering your individual gifts. Another thing to keep in mind is that failure is never permanent, but neither is a success. Both come and go, and neither is better than the other. It's very important to learn from your failures, but also not to give up because of them. Be as grace-filled with yourself as you are with other people.

Hone Your Senses

Extraverted sensing is the use of your five main senses: touch, sight, smell, sound, and taste. Extraverted intuition is the ability to gather information about their physical environment and decipher connections between tangible and intangible things. In activating both functions, you can give your gift opportunities to grow. Engage in activities and focus on being fully present at the moment.

Giving words to the actions and objects around us helps ground us at the moment. Rather than just passively acknowledging that the person you're with is pleasant, create a narrative in your mind as if you were writing a story.

She laughs when I quote Friends. Then, she returns with "Pivot!" We get into a quote war as we work. I notice that she favors her right hand but does any heavy lifting with her left side. After an hour, we pause, and she takes ibuprofen. I ask if she is okay. She says she is, but that she injured her right shoulder as a teenager. I ask how she did it. She explains how she had been a competitive showjumper. She was riding a horse, and out of the blue, it stopped right before a jump, and she was thrown. She tells the story movement by movement. It's still fresh in her mind, as if it happened only yesterday and not twenty years ago.

By creating a running narrative in your mind, you are connecting to that moment in time. Once you've connected in this manner, go deeper.

At lunch, we go to Burger King. I check in with myself before I order a burger: will my body be able to process it today? I think it can handle a fast food meal, so I order my favorite. The first soda I get from the machine isn't mixed right. It's too syrupy and thick, and there isn't much fizz. I try again and have the same experience, so I report it to one of the employees and get an orange soda instead. It's been a long time since I had an orange soda. I had forgotten how much I like it and how refreshing it can be. They're playing pop music on the speaker system, but it's so quiet that we can only make out the choruses.

We get back into James's car. It's very clean and smells like piña colada, due to the small vent clip air freshener on the passenger side. My headache has gone away with some food, so I'm not regretting the fun meal. On our way back to work, we see a double rainbow.

It's okay to not hyper-focus on the present narrative all the time but try to do it a few times during the day. Once you begin doing this comfortably, carve out time to jot down some notes in a journal. A few weeks into journaling these narratives, read back over your entries and see if any patterns or new thoughts start to emerge.

Take this exercise up a notch by taking field trips like the ones below:

Visit a thrift shop or an antique store.
- Visit an animal shelter.
- Visit a restaurant that serves a cuisine with which you are unfamiliar.
- Write at a coffee shop on the campus of a college or university.
- Take a gardening class.
- Attend a church service.
- Take a cooking class.
- Go to a new library or bookstore.
- People watch at the mall.
- Attend a lecture and pay attention to those around you.
- Offer to help a parent of young children with chores or errands.
- Volunteer at a domestic violence or homeless shelter.
- Sign up for an art or home improvement class.
- Invite a friend you don't usually spend one-on-one time with out for coffee or lunch.

- Attend a yoga class. If you are an advanced yogi, take a beginner yoga class and focus on yourself first, then the vibrations on those around you.
- Walk a mile into a state park or nature reserve.
- On foot, explore a small town you've never visited before.

Give yourself time to journal your narratives onsite when the situation permits, or directly after. This writing session doesn't require a large amount of time: if you only have ten minutes, embrace those ten minutes. The things that want your attention will float to the top. You can always dig into things at a later date.

Chapter Fifteen: Increasing Your Positive Energy

The beautiful thing about positive energy is that it never ever runs dry. We may have difficulty accessing that fountain at times, but it is always there, always ready to light our paths and give us comfort and strength. Now that you've begun work to release negativity within you and have begun to protect yourself from the absorption of toxic energy, you're ready to connect to positive things.

Intention

First, choose three relationships you'd like to improve. For example, we'll go with a relationship with a demanding, toxic co-worker, a disorganized home, and a cherished friend who's going through a series of very demanding trials.

Write out your intention and desires for each:

I intend to protect my workspace from negativity. I want to go to work and be able to do my job with minimal distractions, no drama, and not feel fried by noon. I want to enjoy my other co-workers, and I want to exceed our clients' expectations. I want to leave feeling accomplished and have enough energy to make a good meal, take care of things at home, and play a game with the kids before they go to bed.

I intend for my home to feel like a safe harbor with no chaos. I want to come home and have a place to put everything. I want to feel welcome. I want to be able to relax the minute I step onto my property. I want to have enough food and household supplies that I don't have to go to the store on a work night. I want to be able to take care of our basic chores within an hour every night. I want to set us up for success in the mornings by having things ready before we go to bed. I want to laugh more and get irritated less.

I intend to support Naomi in practical ways without hurting myself in the process. I want to see her once a week over coffee. I want to be emotionally available for a quick call whenever she needs to chat. I want her to know how much she means to me. I want her to know I value her friendship even when she's not at her best. I want her to feel seen and validated. I want to give her good energy and help her release the negative.

With these intentions in writing, begin to speak them. There is power in your voice; your voice matters more than you know. Speak to them in the morning as you get ready to start your day.

Avoid negative statements, such as I do not want to engage in gossip. I don't want to have to nag. Instead, find a positive way to put your desire into the universe. I want to mind my own business and wish others well. I want my children to see what needs to be done and feel powerful enough to do it happily on their own.

Cause-Effect Journal

Begin a cause and effect journal. Set it up by drawing a line down the center of each page you'll use. Whenever you have an emotional response to something, write the cause in the left column.

Chris said he didn't want to have the party after all.

On the left, write the effect it had on you or others.

I felt that, because the rest of us wouldn't be able to stay late on Wednesday like he wanted, he wanted to punish us by canceling Jeri's going away party.

Fill pages this way.

Got home and the dishwasher had leaked. None of the dishes were clean. // Spent an hour cleaning and washing dishes. Feels like no matter how hard I try, I can never get ahead.

Naomi posted a goodbye to Uncle Case. // It was sweet and gentle and very respectful to him and to the rest of us. It made me feel like there can be healing after all of this.

Boundaries

After you've journaled for a few days, you may see patterns starting to emerge from your Cause-Effect lists. You may see that Chris's mood always shifts after a phone call with his wife. If that's the case, then begin thinking about what a boundary could be. Even just being armed with the knowledge of his trigger can help: now you know that anything he says or does after he talks with his life will come off as aggressive.

Sometimes the boundary needs to be your expectation of a situation. Life happens; things happen in life—dishwashers leak. Sometimes you have to do things the old-fashioned week. It's not a punishment. It's just a thing that happens. I need to accept that inconveniences are not always assaults on my energy.

Sometimes you can allow things past your usual boundaries because you know the spirit behind them is good. I called Naomi and talked through things while I hand washed all my dishes. She's finding bits of peace, even though she's sad.

Enforcement Brainstorming

When it comes to people like Chris at work, you may need to take action to avoid his attitude. If, on a break, he approaches you in the break room and begins complaining and making unkind comments about another employee, what are your options?

Look him in the eye and say, "I wonder why you feel that way?"

Or, "That's not true at all."

You could perform a grey rock. It's not a style of stadium music, but it is a fantastic way to deal with people who are so painfully self-centered. Look them in the eye, make it clear that you heard them, then make a small sound or say, "I accept that you're talking, but I don't accept what you're saying."

Or, you could just walk away from him.

There are many more options to consider in this scenario; don't limit yourself. Choose the one that you know you can most easily perform if you're feeling stressed out.

Create Your Transformation Plan

Finally, begin experimenting with the ways you've been shown to release negative energy and protect yourself from it. Practice self-care regularly. Create a physical toolbox of supplements, oils, even gift certificates for when you know you've been absorbing others too much!

Continue to log your progress and revelations in your journal. There will be times that you get stuck in a rut, so to say, and it always helps to go back and read over what you found worked in the past. You are the expert of your own experience. When things get to be too much—and they will from time to time—and you feel overwhelmed and overloaded by other peoples' energy, go back to this beautiful, difficult road you've already traveled.

You know the way out, and you'll be all right.

Resources for Escaping Abuse

If you or someone you know is in an abusive relationship, please contact an appropriate organization.

In the US:

RAINN Rape, Abuse & Incest National Network	1-800-656-HOPE www.online.rainn.org
The National Domestic Violence Hotline	1–800–799–7233 *or TTY for the deaf:* 1–800–787–3224.
Crisis Text Line If you're concerned your computer may be monitored by an abuser, this may be a safer alternative.	Text HOME to 741741

Empath Survival Guide:

A Beginner's Guide to Protect Yourself from Energy Vampires: Understand Your Gift and Master Your Intuition. Learn How Highly Sensitive People Control Emotions and Overcome Fears.

Introduction

Congratulations on purchasing *Empath Survival Guide and* thank you for doing so. Empathy is a word that is often used, yet many people miss the definition of the word. I will walk you through empathy, being an empath, and how to deal with energy vampires. The world needs more empathy, and this book is the first step you can take to understand the importance of empathy. And if you are an empath, you would know how to utilize your gift for the betterment of the world. The information you find in this book can be put to practice as soon as one wants to.

Matters of the heart are also challenging for empaths. There are those who, when they see a natural giver, they approach these empaths with the sole purpose of receiving, without intending to give anything. You will feel that the relationship is not right, yet you'll feel guilty about leaving. You'll be afraid of offending the other person. Before you know it, you'll be a sacrificial lamb stuck in a relationship that is doing nothing for you. Here, we outline ways to keep that from happening and to ensure that you receive as much in a relationship than you give.

We also delve into the issue of mental health. As an empath, you're highly vulnerable to mental health issues. Dealing with a mishmash of emotions every single day is no easy task. You have to be deliberate about self-care. To begin with, learn as much as you can about your personality. Going through this book is a good place to start. Self-awareness helps you recognize what is happening to you, and why you react the way you do. You then learn to anticipate certain reactions, so that you're not overwhelmed.

If you discover that your empathy level is high or advanced, you will also find many tools, practices, and guides here to help you manage intense emotions and maintain your energy reserves, shielding your essence from psychic vampires and toxic relationship dynamics. From the realms of western medicine, neuroscience, psychology, and metaphysical healing traditions, you will learn strategies for managing empathic power that can be combined and tailored to suit your individual needs. You'll be steered first towards the goal of finding joy and gratitude for your empathy, though it can indeed be challenging to manage. Secondly, your goal will be to find inner peace, a form of energetic balance that provides enough stability for you to weather whatever emotional storms life might throw at you.

The following chapters will discuss more empathic nature, the many gifts that empaths possess, the possible effects of empathy in the society, the relationship between empaths and narcissists, narcissistic abuse and how to avoid it. It will also focus on the best strategies that empaths should have to defend themselves from being manipulated, and the grounding for empaths. You will get to know why you need time alone as an empath and the best strategies you can apply when restricting yourself from going back to a narcissistic relationship.

There are many books on this subject on the market, thanks again for choosing this guidebook! Every effort was made to ensure it contains as much valuable information as possible. I am sure you will enjoy it!

Chapter 1: The Science of Empathy: (the Mirror Neuron System)

The words "empath" and "empathy" both stem from the Ancient Greek term "Empatheia," which is a hybrid of the words "en" meaning "in" or "at" and "pathos" which means "passion" or "feeling" but can also be interpreted to mean "suffering." This is etymological root is perfectly illustrative of empathy as a double-edged sword. Humans crave deep interpersonal connection and often find joy in shared passions, but when we open ourselves up to the blessings of those around us, we also open ourselves up to their sorrows, fears, and furies.

Within the past few decades, the fields of psychology, neuroscience, and many others have made enormous strides in research towards understanding the minds of those who do not display the "normal" amount of empathy. There are some conditions, such as autism or Asperger's syndrome, wherein a person seems able to detect the emotional energies of those around them, but simply lacks the necessary cognitive tools to interpret them or determine an appropriate reaction. These people often feel attacked or overwhelmed when the emotions of others resonate within them—which is a form of empathic sensitivity—but they often react by shutting down or self-isolating rather than trying to find a way to harmonious coexistence. It is not a struggle for these people to put their own needs first in interpersonal connections, even if it is at the expense of other people's feelings, but this isn't a malicious sentiment; it is primarily a self-preservation instinct in hyperdrive.

Alternatively, there are empathy-deficient personality disorders, such as narcissism, sociopathy, and psychopathy, wherein a person is capable of recognizing the emotions of others but feels personally detached from them. This is why we often describe psychopathic criminals as "cold" or "calculating." It is unsettling to imagine that a person could decide to take action, knowing that their behavior will cause pain or suffering in others and that they might remain unbothered by that fact or actually derive pleasure from it--but that is the thought process of an empathy-disordered individual. The feelings of others are considered unimportant because they do not impact their personal emotional sensations.

The general population holds a lot of misconceptions about people with these personality disorders, which are most evident within the criminal justice system. Many of us convince ourselves, for instance, that these people commit crimes of passion, temporarily losing their sense of right and wrong in the blinding heat of rage, or alternatively, that they are so mentally skewed as to be incapable of understanding how much pain and suffering they are causing. Unfortunately, neither of these possibilities proves true for these individuals. They do understand the impact of their actions and are capable of determining right from wrong, yet they choose to ignore these factors, hurting other people to serve strategic needs or for the sake of personal gain. In fact, people with these personality disorders generally display impressive skill with cognitive empathy, which you might think of as theoretical empathy; this allows them to theorize or predict the emotional reactions of others and makes them masterful manipulators.

When discussing those who struggle to display or feel empathy, it's important to remember that empathic abilities are fluid, not fixed in stone. Anyone who is willing to put in the effort can improve their empathic capabilities, even those who have been diagnosed with an empathy deficient condition or disorder. Physical empathy is often accessible to those who do not display emotional empathy, which may be a function of evolutionary development. Humans can better protect their physical bodies by recognizing physical pain in others and are biologically driven to mimic pleasurable behaviors (whether that means eating good food or enjoying sexual stimulation) by watching others and empathizing with their enjoyment of such activities. Since this form of empathy is often observable in scans of empathy-disordered brains, we must embrace the notion that empathy exists as a complex and fluid and scale. It is not like a light switch that is either flipped on or off.

Empathy is important because it allows you to simulate the cognitive and affective mental conditions of other people. Neurobiological research studies have proved that empathy is a sophisticated encounter or phenomenon that can be explained in detail using a model consisting of top-down and bottom-up processing.

Top-down processing is also called the theory of mind or cognitive perspective-taking. This is a phenomenon where you fully imagine and understand the feelings of other people. It is centered on inhibition and control mechanisms. Available evidence shows that empathic brain responses are usually affected by distinct modulating factors.

I hope you are still with me! Researchers have come up with a new model that provides an explanation of the origins of empathy and other things such as contagious yawning and emotional contagion. The model demonstrates that the origin of a wide range of empathetic responses can be found in cognitive simulation. The model shifts attention from a top-down approach that starts with cooperation to one that begins with one cognitive mechanism.

According to a post-doctoral researcher in Max Planck Institute called Fabrizio Mafessoni, standard models of the origin of empathy concentrate on situations in which cooperation or coordination are the favorites. Michael Lachmann, a theoretical biologist, together with his co-author, looked at the possibilities that cognitive processes have a wide underlying range of empathetic responses including contagious yawning, emotional contagion, and other feelings such as echopraxia and echolalia. Echolalia is a compulsive repetition of other people's speech, while echopraxia is the compulsive repetition of other people's movements. Echolalia and echopraxia can evolve in the absence of mechanisms that directly favor coordination and cooperation or kin selection.

Lachmann and Mafessoni asserted that human beings and animals could participate in the act of stimulating the minds of other people or animals. You cannot read other people's minds because they are like black boxes to you. But as Lachmann put across, all agents have the same black boxes with members of their species, and they constantly run simulations of what other minds may be doing. This ongoing process or as-actor simulation is not always focused on cooperation. It is something that animals and human beings do as a result of a sudden impulse or in other words without premeditation.

A good example of this process can be shown using mirror neurons. It has been discovered that the same neurons that take part in planning a hand movement are also responsible for observing the hand movement of others. Lachmann and Mafessoni tried to figure out what would happen if the same process of understanding would be extended to any social interaction. After modeling outcomes rooted in the cognitive simulation, they discovered that actors responsible for as-actor simulation produce different systems typically explained in terms of kin-selection and cooperation. They also realized that an observer could once in a while coordinate with an actor even when the outcome is not beneficial. Their model is of the opinion that empathetic systems do not evolve only because animals or people simulate others to envision their actions.

According to Mafessoni, empathy must have originated from the need to understand others. For Lachmann, their discoveries have completely changed how people perceive and think about human beings and animals. Their model is based on a single cognitive mechanism that unites a wide set of phenomena under a single explanation. It consequently has theoretical import for a broad range of fields such as cognitive psychology, evolutionary biology, neuroscience, anthropology, and complex systems. Its power emanates from its theoretical interest and unifying clarity in the limits of cooperation.

Electromagnetic Fields

The subsequent finding depends on the way that both the mind and the heart produce electromagnetic fields. These fields transmit data about individuals' musings and feelings. Empaths might be especially delicate to this info and will, in general, become overpowered by it. Correspondingly, you frequently have more grounded physical and enthusiastic reactions to changes in the electromagnetic fields of the earth and sun.

Enthusiastic Contagion

The third discovering which upgrades everyone's comprehension of empaths is the wonders of the enthusiastic virus. Research has shown that numerous individuals get the feelings of people around them. For example, one crying newborn child will set off a flood of weeping in a medical clinic ward. Or then again, one individual noisily communicating nervousness in the work environment can spread it to different laborers. Individuals generally get other individuals' emotions in gatherings. Ongoing research expressed that this capacity to synchronize states of mind with others is vital for proper connections. What is an exercise for empaths? To pick constructive individuals in your lives, so you are not brought somewhere near pessimism. Or then again, if, state a companion is experiencing a hard time, play it safe to the ground, and focus yourself.

Expanded Dopamine Sensitivity

The fourth discovering includes dopamine, a synapse that expands the action of neurons and is related to the joy reaction. Research has demonstrated that contemplative empaths will, in general, have a higher affectability to dopamine than extraverts. Fundamentally, they need less dopamine to feel cheerful. That could clarify why they are increasingly content with alone time, perusing, and reflection and need less outer incitement from gatherings and other enormous get-togethers. Conversely, extraverts long for the dopamine surge from happy occasions. Indeed, they cannot get enough of it.

Synesthesia

The fifth discovering, which is very convincing, is the original state called "reflect contact synesthesia." Synesthesia is a neurological condition wherein two unique faculties are combined in the cerebrum. For example, you see hues when you hear a bit of music, or you taste words. Be that as it may, with mirror-contact synesthesia, individuals can feel the feelings and impressions of others in their very own bodies as though these were their own.

This is an excellent neurological clarification of an empath's involvement. "Sympathy is the most valuable human quality."

During these upsetting occasions, it is anything but difficult to get overpowered. All things being equal, compassion is the quality that will get you through. It will empower you to regard every other person, regardless of whether you oppose this idea. Sympathy does not make you a wistful softy without wisdom. It enables you to keep your heart open to encourage resistance and comprehension. It may not generally be successful in breaking through to individuals and making harmony but always believe that it is the most obvious opportunity you have.

Where Does Empathic Power Come From?

The question of where empathic powers come from, or how people come to possess them, is one that science still does not have a solid answer for. But there are a few theories. There is certainly plenty of evidence to suggest that a "normal" degree of empathy is accessible to most all of us in early development. Newborn infants in neonatal units display an inability to distinguish personal feelings from those around them. If one infant begins to cry, usually most others will follow suit very quickly as they are not yet aware that this pain or anxiety isn't theirs to own. Most infants who receive a healthy amount of care and attention will continue mimicry and emotional enmeshment throughout the first few years of life. This is how children are able to learn speech and movement. Some children, raised in especially tight-knit families or communities, may struggle at first to understand the function of pronouns that distinguish between the individual self and the group, posing questions like, "Mama, why are we sad today?" when they observe this emotion in another person.

Those who believe in the supernatural possibilities of empathic power also tend to believe that certain individuals are fated to receive these gifts and that empaths feel as they do in order to serve some greater purpose as determined by cosmic or holy design. This belief often coincides with the notion that empaths are born special and not shaped by their surroundings. While the level of power they possess or the manner in which they channel energy may fluctuate throughout their lives, their heightened sensitivity is considered an innate trait.

Conversely, there are those who believe empathic abilities come from the environment or circumstances in which a person is raised, as a function of nurture rather than nature. Many psychologists note that children raised in volatile, neglectful, or dangerous households learn early on to detect subtle changes in their parents' behaviors as a necessary coping skill and defense mechanism, allowing them to predict, avoid, or even prevent traumatic episodes.

Parents may not necessarily be nefarious or malicious in raising a child who develops extreme empathic sensitivity. Some theories posit that the only environmental factor needed to trigger such a development is an older authoritative figure in the child's life, who requires the child to empathize with them frequently. For example, a parent who is grieving the loss of a loved one might, without ever intending to, compel their child to empathize with a level of emotional pain, which they haven't yet been prepared for, and can hardly even comprehend at such a young age. A child who is put in this position frequently enough may never learn to distinguish their own emotions from those of others and might even struggle to feel that they are real, solid, or whole without the influence of another dominant personality. They become hyper-focused on caring for the parental figure in their life, and never learn how to receive care without guilt, shame, or anxiety, as most children do.

Once a child develops this ability, it is only natural for them to continue using it outside the home, amongst friends, colleagues, lovers, and even strangers. There are also those who note this same skill of hyper-sensitivity emerging for the first time in full-grown adults when they are romantically involved (or otherwise closely bonded) with an abusive personality type, like a narcissist.

It is worth noting that many empaths first become aware of their heightened sensitivity during relationships with those who are empathy deficient. Furthermore, whether they are aware of their abilities or not, empaths are so frequently involved with narcissists, sociopaths, and psychopaths. This makes many wonder if empathic power functions as a sort of invisible beacon to those who have these personality disorders. This theory—that empaths and empathy deficient types are drawn to each other like magnets—begs the question, which typically comes first? The empathic power, or the abusive environment in which it becomes a necessary skill for survival? While it makes sense that empathic abilities develop as a response to abuse and trauma, it is also certainly possible that abuse and trauma would always exist anyways, and empaths are simply drawn to these environments more than most people. An unfortunate reality of life for the empath who has not yet fully awakened to their power is that they will often feel compassion for those whom everyone else has abandoned, failing to see that these souls have been left alone for a good reason and are not worthy of the empath's care or attention. This could indicate that abusive circumstances and relationships are like traps which empaths are particularly vulnerable to falling into, rather than the cause or catalyst for heightened sensitivity.

Thus far, science has not been able to provide proof one way or the other, but some recent findings may allow for both possibilities to coexist. The study of epigenetics concerns the way in which our genetic material is impacted by our experiences and surroundings, meaning that we pass on more to our children through our DNA than simply a blueprint for the body. With the discovery of epigenetics, we are now able to theorize that trauma can have an intergenerational ripple effect, leaving a lasting mark on the descendants of victims, whether those descendants are fully aware of the trauma or not. This would allow a soul to be born with empathic abilities which are at once innate and a developed response to abuse.

There are many possible sources of empathic ability, and new information is constantly surfacing to expand our understanding of it. Likewise, the scientific field has yet to firmly define the source of empathy-deficient personality disorders, nor that of conditions like autism and Asperger's syndrome. Some believe these emotional states or conditions feed into one another, like two species sharing a symbiotic relationship, or an active embodiment of yin and yang energies. Others still believe there are purely biological explanations for conditions that fall on both ends of the empathy scale. Then, of course, there are those who see the empathy scale as a circle rather than a line, believing that a person with an overabundance of untrained empathic ability can evolve into a narcissist or vice versa.

Whatever you believe, one thing is clear: Empathic ability must be understood, trained, and balanced in order to be part of a healthy, happy lifestyle.

Chapter 2: Types of Empathy

Empathy is defined as the capacity to understand or feel the emotions of others. It can also be described as the ability to share the feelings of others. Empathy, for the most part, is a beautiful attribute. It's one of the finest qualities a human being can possess. It is associated with goodness, charity, compassion, care, and self-sacrifice. Empathy makes it easier to identify with those who are suffering, and consequently, take action to remedy the situation. The world can always do with a little more empathy.

Empathy is mostly classified into three groups:

Emotional Empathy

Here you experience the feelings of other people: sadness, anxiety, joy, pain, and so on. An emotionally empathic person catches the sensations of others, which strengthens relationships with those around her/him. Emotional empaths can do well in fields like medicine, nursing, and counseling since they deeply identify with the suffering of others and go out of their way to alleviate that.

The downside to emotional empathy is that your emotions fluctuate up and down, depending on the situation of those around you. That can be exhausting. In other instances, you feel the pain of others so deeply, yet there's nothing you can do to change their situation, and you're left suffering as well. In the following chapters, we will explore measures that empaths can take to protect themselves from such extremities.

Cognitive Empathy

This is the ability to know the thought process of other people, and in the process, understand their perspective. It mostly involves thoughts, intellect, and understanding. Cognitive empathy helps you appreciate different viewpoints. You're able to accommodate people who hold different opinions and beliefs from those of your own. This ability also comes in handy during discussions since you understand the thought process of others and engage them appropriately.

Compassionate Empathy

In this case, you do not only identify with the suffering of others, but you're also moved to take an extra step and lend your help. This is the ideal form of empathy, where you actually take action to make a difference.

However, precaution should be taken so that you do not run yourself dry, trying to donate to every cause. A donation here refers not only to finances but also time, expertise, skills, goodwill, and so on.

Empathy isn't just towards people. It applies to situations as well. An empath will be drawn towards the state of the environment, economy, politics, international relations, animal welfare, and such other matters that eventually affect the quality of human life. People without empathy find it easy to look away, especially when others are suffering.

First, all empaths are born with the ability to experience what other people are going through, either through emotions or even their feelings. Secondly, no empath is born already skilled. They all have to learn the skills, and if not, they are prone to suffer a lot. This should not get you worried if you have no skills yet, this book will help you learn some new skills that you need to know as an empath. To your surprise, you might even be more than one kind of an empath, so if you find yourself falling into various kinds of empaths, count yourself talented. These types are also referred to as the many gifts of empathy.

Physical Intuition

These are the kind of empaths who are able to know what exactly is happening in another person's body. For example, this type of an empath can easily tell when you have a stomachache or a headache. Being a skilled empath will make you able to help other people through this correct knowledge.

Physical Oneness

The way these empaths get information is always personal. These are empaths who can feel other people's physical way of being in their own body when around or with them. For instance, this kind of empath, when with Betty, they will always develop a stomachache, like this stomachache belongs to Betty. This is a confusing type of empath, but if you are a skilled one, you will be able to assist those around you with the messages you get into your body. You ought to be skilled to avoid confusion or any form of suffering.

Intellectual Empath Ability

These types of empaths are able to get into people's intellectual abilities. For example, they might find themselves using long words while speaking to Joy, but then later, they come to realize that Joy also likes using long words.

Emotional Intuition

These types of empaths are able to tell what is going on in someone's body, specifically their emotions, even when other people are trying to hide or fake their emotions. For instance, an empath will note that Betty is always cheerful, but she is hiding worries behind her smiles. Skilled empaths will know how to cut through the fake and real emotions since they all have the ability to differentiate what is real and what is fake. This helps you become a better friend since your friends get to realize you know them better.

Emotional Oneness

This is the type of empath where you get to learn the reality about what is cooking in other people's feelings. The difference of this kind of empath with the Emotional Intuition is that an empath in emotional oneness is able to feel what others are feeling. Your emotions and those of your friends will tend to merge. And as a skilled empath, you should not be carried away by the absorbed emotions since most of them are always negative. Instead, you should help your friends come out of this negative emotion or feeling, for instance, worries or anger. Being skilled means, you will have a stable emotional foundation to help out.

General Types of Empaths

Spiritual Intuition

This is a kind of empath where you get to experience how someone else connects to God or other spiritual beings. For instance, accompanying Betty to church and getting to hear what her pastor preaches about God, you get to feel the flavor that Betty gets from the teachings about God. This can happen in the case where you know nothing about your friend's religious views. Skilled empaths use this chance to know the many faces of God and even develop interests for religions and spiritual lives.

Spiritual Oneness

This kind of empath is different from that in Spiritual Intuition in that, in Spiritual Oneness, an empath will experience directly how their friends are connecting to their Supreme Being. This can be through the hymns that are being sung and relating the inspiration behind them. This helps skilled empath grow more spiritual in various ways.

Animal Empath

An animal empath will experience what it feels like to be a certain animal. A skilled animal empath is totally different from an animal lover in the sense that an animal empath is able to tell the difference between two animals that an animal lover thinks are identical. A skilled empath will help animals locate their groups or even help pet owners.

Environmental Empath

Environmental empaths are able to tell the difference between landscapes in certain environments. To them, each landscape is scenery. Skilled empaths enjoy walking through forests, and this can even make them emotional.

Plant Empath

Plant empaths get to feel what it is like being a certain tree, leave, or even flower. Skilled empaths use this gift in their agricultural farms or even in gardening.

Mechanical Empath

Mechanical empaths experience what it is to be a certain machine and their needs. This can even make them fix machines without the necessary qualifications due to the increased interest in machines. As a skilled empath, you are advantaged because you will not need a mechanic to identify what your machine needs, you will be able to tell it yourself. It may lead to more research into machines and technologies.

Medical Empath Talent

This gift helps identify any sickness or anything about your own or other people's health matters. Skilled medical empaths help give support, can even end up developing professional skills and become nurses, or even help in preventing any burnouts.

Empath Talent with Astral Beings

These empaths have direct experiences with astral beings such as angels and fairies. Skilled empaths will use the experience to grow themselves or enjoy more of these adventures.

Chapter 3: The Traits of an Empath

Most empaths have a hard time getting hold of their emotions. Can you imagine how much more challenging it is for a child? If you're an empath yourself, then you'll feel that your child is an empath. Most parents are not, so at first, they'll simply notice that their child is different. Here are some traits of child empaths:

- **They are Overwhelmed in Crowds**

While other children are happy to interact with others and jump around in crowds, empath kids will be fussy at best. Yet you can't blame them. All their senses are alert. They can hear every sound and smell every scent. Above all, they feel the emotions of those around them. They have a combination of feelings inside them: joy, sadness, anger, fear, and whatever else those around them are feeling. This is overwhelming for anyone, much less a child. The children will be uncomfortable and probably ask to leave. If you've not understood their personality, you'll be wondering why they can't enjoy the gathering like everybody else. If you cannot leave, then let them take breaks. You can have them sit in the car or in an isolated corner for some minutes. This helps relax their minds and emotions. With time, you should be able to identify the triggers and avoid or at least minimize them.

- **Cry when Others Are in Pain**

As soon as others are in distress, they will be in tears. This includes animals. They will offer to soothe those who are crying and end up crying as well. These kids can't stand to see others being bullied. They will cry along and try to beg the aggressors to stop. You know how it goes in these bullying cases. The kid supporting the one being bullied also ends up in the same boat. If your child comes home complaining about bullies, seek to find out the details. Perhaps your kid is being targeted for standing up for others. If you notice such a trend, chances are, you're raising an empath. Such kids should be encouraged. Those are the activists of the future. Assure them that they're brave to be standing up for others. They will only be picked on for some time, but once they prove their resilience, no one will dare bully others in their presence.

- **Excess Feelings**

Children have shallow feelings. If you upset them, they'll only be sad for a couple of minutes before something distracts their attention. That's why sometimes a child will get spanked then offered candy. The sadness evaporates in a minute. If your child seems to have intense feelings, especially the negative ones, you could be dealing with an empath. You may have spotted a video clip that was doing rounds online of parents pranking their kids. For most of them, they got upset for a moment when they realize they've been pranked. Then a moment later, they are giggling and promising to prank back. But there was this one kid that fell into a fit of rage. He shouted and cursed even as the dad explained that it was supposed to be a funny joke. That is definitely not normal for a child. A child will hardly ever be upset for hours. If you're dealing with such a case, chances are you're raising an empath. As a parent, help them acknowledge their feelings and walk through them.

- **Readers and Deep Thinkers**

Young empaths often have their faces buried in a book. They're seeking for information. They mostly read books that are beyond their age. They're interested in the real world, as opposed to fairly-tale stories. They think deeply about issues. They ask a lot of questions, the kind you would not expect a kid to ask. They question things that other people may not; like religion. *Who created the world? God. Who created God? He was always there. Everybody has to have come from something. And how could one person create so much?* The questions may irritate you, yet they will not relent. If you can't answer them, direct them to someone who can. If you always react with irritation, they will feel guilty and end up suppressing their curiosity. This curiosity ought to be fanned, not deflated. Such children could be grand researchers in the future, and who knows what they might come up with.

- **Sensitive to Media**

Empathic children get extremely upset at certain scenes in the animations or movies that they're watching. These are not a 2-minute frowning, but a complete change of mood that may even be accompanied by crying. They stay upset for a long time. The scene is likely to be one of a person or animal getting assaulted in a way. The kids feel deeply for the victim, never mind it could be a work of fiction. Since they cannot do anything to help, they release their emotions the best way they know how; by crying or sulking. Other kids might laugh at the empaths. To them, it's all fun and jokes, and they don't see why anyone should take it too seriously. If you notice that your child is highly sensitive to the media, monitor what they watch. Let them avoid content with intense scenes. Let them know that there's nothing wrong with what they feel, and their emotions are valid.

- **They Love the Outdoors**

This lot loves to get their hands dirty. They want to be out there exploring the outdoors. Since they feel with all their senses, they see so much where others don't. Your simple backyard feels like a nature trail to them. They will play 'fetch' with the dogs, build tree houses, dig around for worms, and plant a garden and pretty much anything else that crosses their mind. They will observe, feel, smell, touch, and basically have a blast out there. To you as a parent, you see them getting dirty. But they feel refreshed in those activities. The best you can do is let them explore safely. Buy books that teach them more about nature. Referring to the point about their sensitivity to the media, the outdoors becomes a great alternative.

- **Often Stay Alone**

Children normally reach out to others to play. Empathic children want to spend a lot of time alone. They will be in their room reading, exploring something, or just having a quiet time. If they have to share a room with a sibling, they will make an effort to carve out their own private space by forming an enclosure with a bed sheet or something similar. If you have playhouses, they will crawl in there and stay for hours. And no; they're not upset. In fact, they leave their little private spaces feeling better than before.

Do not force them out of their quiet sessions. Let them stay until they're ready to come out. Do not force them to play with the others either. If they seem reluctant, leave them alone. Given their deep thinking, child empaths often feel like they don't belong with their age mates. Their activities and conversation don't spark their interest. They may prefer to hang out with older kids or even adults.

- **Animal Lovers**

This trait begins very young. You will notice an intimate attachment even with stuffed/plastic animals. They will carry them everywhere, and even attempt to feed and bath them. Should they break or tear, they will be beside themselves with sadness. They will put a bandage on the wounds.

When they come of age, and you buy them a pet, the bond will be even deeper. They will spend the most time with the pet; showing reduced interest in people. Their caregiving properties will begin to manifest. They will attend to every need of the pet. Should the pet get sick or injured, get ready to drop everything and run to the vet? The child will be so affected to the extent of interfering with schoolwork.

As they grow older, child empaths show interest in animals on a larger scale. They could want to know what goes on in animal shelters. They could start talking about adopting an abandoned animal. They also gain interest in wildlife and love to watch National Geographic and other such programs. Buy them books that teach them more about animals. This interest can be nurtured into a career or into advocacy for animal rights.

- **Artistic**

They gravitate towards one form or another of art. It could be painting, drawing, playing an instrument, singing, and so on. They see things in multiple dimensions. When they look at a drawing, they see aspects that a normal child may not. As a parent, whether you share this ability or not, you should encourage it. Buy them materials to practice the craft that they're interested in. Once in a while, you can sit with them and have them explain the motions behind their pieces. You may not get it, but that's fine. You can also enroll them for classes to perfect their art.

Art offers a noble outlet for their emotions. When they're feeling overwhelmed, they can turn to art to express themselves. In their drawings and paintings and sculptures will be an outpouring of emotions, and that's what makes them so unique.

- **They Feel Your Energy**

This is probably the most unnerving bit of raising an empath. These children mirror your emotions. If you're sad, so are they. If you're going through a rough patch where you're experiencing mostly negative emotions, you can imagine the suffering the poor kids are going through. If there's strive in your family, such as a strained marriage, the children can feel it. You will try to act all fine in their presence, but they can feel every single emotion going through your body.

This makes them very sensitive. Children should be protected from adult challenges. If you're having a spat, you can send them to a relative for a few days. Do not let children suffer over an issue which they can do nothing about.

Their ability to feel also implies that you cannot lie to your children. In most cases, this happens the other way around. It is children who cannot lie to their parents, as they can see right through them. Here the roles are reversed. You cannot lie to your child that all is well between you and the other parent. They can feel the strain. You can't claim to be okay when you're sick; as parents often do to keep their children from worrying too much. They can feel your emotions, and in some cases, they can feel your symptoms in their own bodies.

The solution here is to tell them the truth. Tone it down to a language that they can understand. If you keep insisting on bending the truth yet their intuition is telling them otherwise, they will have a problem trusting you even in the future.

Raising an empath is no mean feat. It takes a while to understand what is happening to your child. You could even end up thinking that something is wrong with him/her, especially due to the time spent alone instead of playing with the others. The first step is to familiarize yourself with what being an empath is all about. Now that you're already reading this book, you're definitely on the right track on getting the relevant information.

That your child feels your energy means that you have to hold yourself to high standards. If you're plagued by sadness, anxiety, fear, and so on, your child will experience the same. These emotions are tough to handle even for an adult. Imagine how much more a child will struggle to try to manage them.

If you're going through a tough period in your life, for the sake of your empathic child, get help. Unfortunately, you do not have the privilege of handling your issues quietly. The moment you feel it; it's out there.

After working on yourself, concentrate on helping the child understand the unique personality. Many empaths will tell you how confusing it was as a child to be highly sensitive, yet not understand why they were feeling the way they were. Now that you're enlightened, your child should have better luck.

If children do not get this information in good time, they think that something is wrong with them. They suppress those emotions and numb their intuition in an effort to be normal. They suppress the urge to stand up for others, fearing they will be teased by their peers. With time, the gift goes to waste.

Let those around your child know that they're dealing with an empath. Start with the siblings. It can be challenging to have one child who is an empath and another who is not. They'll be wondering why they're so different and why they're not interested in the same things. Teach them about personalities as soon as they're in a position to understand.

Empaths are the minority in society, and if you have one in your hands, then you're one of the chosen few. Help that young empath to nurture that gift, accept it, and utilize it to the highest levels.

Chapter 4: Understand Your Empathic Nature

Empathy plays a key role in the functioning of society. It promotes our needs, sharing experiences, and desires between people. Our neural networks are set up to connect with the neural systems of others to both see and comprehend their feelings and to separate them from our own, which makes it feasible for people to live with each other without always battling.

Empathy is quite vital as it helps us be able to comprehend and understand the feelings other people are going through so that we can be able to respond appropriately to their situations at hand. To a greater extent, it has been associated with the social behaviors with research supporting it, arguing that the more empathy then, the more one tends to help. Notably, an empath can also be able to inhibit social actions or even go to the extent of having an amoral behavior. For example, someone who sees a car accident and is overwhelmed by emotions witnessing the victim in severe pain might be less likely to help that person.

Importantly, having strong empathy can also lead to negative causes. Such strong feelings towards our family members; social or racial groups can lead to hatred between one another brought about by insecurity. Also, people who are skilled in reading other people's feelings can start using this opportunity for their own gains by deceiving the victims. They include the manipulators, fortune tellers, and psychics.

Interestingly, people with higher psychopathic traits show more utilitarian responses in events where there are moral dilemmas, like, footbridge issues. In this experiment, people have to decide whether to push a person off a bridge to stop a train about to kill five others laying on the track.

Measuring Empathy

Quite often, a self-report questionnaire is used in measuring empathy. Such types of questionnaires include the Interpersonal Reactivity Index (IRI) or Questionnaire for Cognitive and Affective Empathy (QCAE). In the process of measuring empathy, the person is asked to indicate how much they accept the statements that are set to help measure the different types of empathy that one might be having.

One will find statements like, "It affects me very much when one of my friends is upset," which QCAE test uses to measure the effect of empathy. QCAE plays a key role in the identification of cognitive empathy by the use of statements such as "I try to look at everybody's side of a disagreement before I make a decision."

With the use of this method, it was discovered that people scoring higher on affective empathy have more grey matter. Grey matter is said to be a collection of nerve cells in the anterior insula, which is an area of the brain.

This zone is regularly associated with directing positive and negative feelings by coordinating ecological stimulants—for example, seeing an auto crash with instinctive and programmed in essence sensations. Likewise, individuals utilizing this strategy to gauge compassion found that high scorers of sympathy had a progressively dark region in the dorsomedial prefrontal cortex.

The activation of this particular area takes place when there are more cognitive processes, and this included the Theory of Mind. The theory is the ability of one to attribute the mental beliefs to oneself and another person. The theory also accepts the fact that one has to understand that the other person has desires, beliefs, intentions, and perspectives different from theirs.

Can Humans Lack Empathy?

Several cases have proven that not all humans have empathy. For instance, walking down Minnesota, you bump into a homeless person shivering in the cold. You will notice that few people will express sympathy, empathy, or compassion for the homeless person. Most of the time, we have seen people expressing outright hostility towards such people. So, what could be the cause of us expressing empathy selectively? Various elements assume the role. How we see the other individual, how we characterize their practices, what we fault for the other individual's difficulty, and our very own past encounters and desires all become an integral factor.

Further, I have come to find that there are two main things that contribute to human beings experiencing empathy— and these are socialization and genetics. Going back to age and time, we get to understand that our parents have the genes that highly contribute to personalities, and this includes our propensity towards matters, empathy, sympathy, and compassion. Notably, our parents spent enough time with us socializing, we chat with peers, the society, and the community at large and this is enough to affect us. The interactions have so much to do with how we treat others, our feelings, and beliefs as they are a reflection of our values and beliefs instilled in us while at the early stages of life.

A Few Reasons Why People Sometimes Lack Empathy:

a. We fall victim to cognitive biases

Cognitive biases are said to play a key role in the way we perceive the world around us. For instance, attributing the failures of other people to internal characteristics and blaming our shortcomings on external things or factors. With this type of biases, then it might be difficult or rather challenging to be able to see all the factors that contribute to a certain situation, and that means we won't be able to see the situation from another person's perspective.

b. We dehumanize victims

Quite often, we are trapped in the thought that people who are different from us have different behaviors and feelings from us. This is evident when dealing with people who are different from us. A good example is a time when we watch conflicts, fights, disagreements, and calamities from a foreign land. Then, we end up having less or no empathy with the thought that those suffering are fundamentally different from us.

c. We blame victims

It happens that people start blaming a particular situation or suffering on the victim for his or her circumstance despite them undergoing a terrible experience. Many times, people ask what the crime the victim had committed to provoke an attack. This tendency stems from the belief that the world is a fair and just place.

We can't brush away the fact that empathy at times might fail, but people usually figure out how to identify with others in an assortment of circumstances. This capacity to see things from someone else's point of view and identify with another's feelings assumes a significant job in our public activities. Sympathy completely permits us to be able to take our time and understand others and compels others to go ahead and take an action that will help the person who is suffering. Empathy is all about minding about another person.

Can Empathy Be Selective?

Previous researchers have found that human beings tend to be more empathetic for members belonging to their group, like the ones from their ethnic groups. For instance, one researcher checked the cerebrums of Chinese and Caucasian members while they watched recordings of individuals from their ethnic gathering in agony. They likewise watched individuals from an alternate ethnic gathering in torment.

A study by other researchers has also found that brain areas involved in empathy are quite less active when we are watching people undergoing pain for acting unfairly. When a person is watching a rival sports team failing, we can be able to see activation in the brain areas which are involved in the subjective pleasure.

It is good to note that in such times, we never feel empathy for the people who are not of our group. When giving rewards to members who aren't in our group, the brain involved in such activity was very active when rewarding the same ethnic group, but when watching people of other groups being hurt, the mind activeness remains equal.

At times, it is advisable to be less empathetic to be successful. To put this into perspective, when in a war, a soldier should have less empathy, especially towards the enemy who might want to kill them. From the explanation, it emanates that humans tend to have an implicated brain when they are harming others and have a less active mind if the act is justified.

Assessing If You Are an Empath

Here is a simple test that can help you know whether you are an empath or not. Go through it, providing a simple yes or no answer to each question.

- Have I at any time been labeled as sensitive, introvert, or shy?
- Do I get anxious or overwhelmed frequently?
- Do fights, yelling, and arguments often make me ill?
- Do I often have the feeling that I don't fit in?
- Do I find myself being drained by the crowds, and by that then do I mostly need my time alone so to revive myself?
- Do odors, noise, or nonstop talkers get me overwhelmed?
- Do I have chemical sensitiveness or low tolerance for scratchy clothes?
- Do I prefer using my car when attending an event or going to a place so that I will be free to leave earlier?
- Do I use food as my source to escape from stress?
- Do I feel afraid of being suffocated by relationship intimacy?
- Do I easily startle?

- Do I have a strong reaction to medications or caffeine?
- Do I have a low threshold for pain?
- Do I tend to be socially isolated?
- Do I get to absorb the stress, symptoms, and emotions of the other people?
- Am I mostly overwhelmed by doing several things at a go, and do I always prefer handling one thing at a go?
- Do I replenish myself generally?
- Do I need a long time to recuperate after being with difficult people or energy vampires?
- Do I always feel being in a better place while in small cities than the big ones?
- Do I always prefer having one on one interaction and small groups and not the large gathering?

You can now try to know who you are by calculating your results.

- If you agreed to at least five of the questions, then you are partly an empath.
- If you agreed to at least ten questions, you are at a moderate level.
- If you agreed to eleven or fifteen questions, then you are a strong empath with strong tendencies.
- If you have agreed to more than fifteen questions, then it's without a doubt that you are a full-blown empath.

The determination of your degree of an empath is important as it will make it easy for you to clarify the types of needs and the type of strategy you will need to adapt in a bit to be able to meet them. With the determination, then you will be able to find a comfort zone in your life.

Chapter 5: Merits and Demerits of Empathy

Are you that person who gets bored easily, disliking commitments and routines? Do you tend to feel like the stability and repeating the same thing over and overweighing you down? How about having issues in respecting the people who try imposing their will on you? A person who does this quite often may be made to feel guilty by being given names like a selfish and troublesome person. Do you always have dreams of visiting new places and doing new things? This is thanks to your creativity and having high levels of energy generally.

A person who is not aware of their status could find a day to day interactions with others being a source of stress to them. Empaths, who are not aware of the abilities they possess, might be inclined to start using alcohol, food, and drugs to cure their emotional stresses.

Due to the positive impacts that the empaths bring, I tend to believe that they are the medicine that the world needs. They have a profound impact on humanity with the understanding and compassion they possess. In the process of learning and understanding your talents, you will realize that you may enrich not only yourself but also the people around you. You will need to understand that it is an important skill to fully understand how to be able to take charge of sensitivities and also get to understand the specific strategies that you need to use in a bid to prevent empathy overload.

Merits of Being an Empath

Being empathic has inconceivable advantages, for example, more prominent instinct, sympathy, innovativeness, and a more profound association with other individuals. In any case, living in this condition of high sensitivity likewise accompanies its difficulties, for example, ending up effectively overpowered, over-invigorated, depleted, or engrossing the pressure and pessimism of others.

I cherish being an empath so much. I thank God for the gift of sensitiveness bestowed on me. I have a strong liking on being intuitive, having a feeling of the flow of the world's energy, getting to read people, and also having an experience of the deep feeling the life offers.

I came to realize that God has given us so many marvelous traits that we ought to use on our day to day lives. You will need to understand that God gave us a huge heart and wonderful instincts that allow us to be able to help our society day in day out and those who are less fortunate. Empaths are said to both idealists and dreamers. Other character traits that define us include being creative, deep, passionate, compassionate, being in touch with our emotions, and can always see the bigger picture. Empaths can be friends with other people due to their ability to appreciate their feelings. They are quite spiritual intuitive and can always have a sense of energy. They highly have much appreciation for nature and feel it as their home. They highly resonate with nature, forests, plants, and gardens and have a deep love for the water.

Empaths get energized by the water, may it be warm or cold, taking a shower or even if they live by an ocean. They do feel a solid bond if they own animals, you can find them talking to the animal as they are just humans. With such a strong bond to animals, then such people might end up being involved with the rescue of animals or animal communication.

Being an empath is a blessing as they are natural healers with the ability to gift healing energy to their friends just via the hands, voice, or having to play a musical instrument.

Being an empath is an advantage given that these people only need their sense of smell for them to enjoy food, flowers, beverages, essential oils, etc. An empath who works harder and manages to increase his or her sensitivity can even smell death or disease from a person or an animal. With such ability, it means that many lives will be saved.

Empaths have an advantage of sensing danger before it hits; this is done using their sixth sense. Isn't that amazing? Notably, empaths enjoy feeling greater highs than the other people who don't have sensitivity. This is despite them being prone to feeling low due to the much energy they get from other people. Empaths have greater enthusiasm towards life; they do experience joy and life itself with greater intensity. They are advantaged as they are always kind, compassionate, caring, and understanding as compared to the other people who are not sensitive.

Even though the people who are not emphatic feel quite uncomfortable for not spending time with others, the case is quite different for the empaths as they do love being alone as this is the time they need to balance and de-stress. Empaths use this time to recuperate, and this makes them much aware due to the time they spent alone.

As discussed earlier, this kind of people do have high levels of creativity in their lives, and this is not only in the art field but also in situations, experiences, and possibilities. They can see things prior and hence being at a point of conceptualizing. Many people might label this creativity of thought and processing as wrong, but you won't need to worry about that, it's a capacity of yours.

Empaths enjoy the advantage of being able to read emotional cues, and this makes them be able to understand other people better since they can understand what that person is feeling and how it will affect the person if their needs aren't met.

Due to their sensitiveness, they are said to be very good at sensing all kinds of nonverbal communication and indicators of physical needs and emotions. With this ability then they can be said to be having a talent for intuiting the unconscious mind as well as for being able to sense the need the plants, animals, human body and those unable to speak.

Empaths have the advantage of being able to understand the thoughts of people, their feelings and emotions, and this ability enables them to sense a lie from someone. They can easily understand when something is a matter despite the person insisting that he or she is fine but hurting from inside. Because of our heightened awareness, we can see through the false facades people up.

Empaths have an advantage when it comes to loving as their degree of love is said to be on another level. It is believed that coming up with a mutual understanding in a relationship has proven itself to be a very hard thing. Empaths try as much to explain their feelings to the other person but unfortunately, they don't understand their feelings as the empaths do. It can take someone a lot of time for them to be able to place themselves in the shoes of the other person.

Through this, an empath can cultivate that high level of love and compassion difficult for the other people to accomplish despite the much time they might have at their disposal. With deeper levels of love, understanding and relating with people becomes quite easy, even those you are most likely to disagree with.

Empaths enjoy the advantage of being very creative. This is part and parcel of all empaths as through their emotions, and they can express their levels of creativity. Empathic can channel their feelings into a piece of art. If you are in the space, you need to be in, and then your creations will be touching other people around you.

Let's say, for instance, and you are an older adult who is unable to dance or paint; creativity will be able to teach you more about yourself. I came to realize that I am so much creative, and it is then when I started having an open book near me. This has assisted me in understanding so much about who I am, the meaning of life, and the patterns.

Empaths do receive insights naturally. Every creation allows an empath to be much happier, and further allow pure essence to explore itself fully. You can consider commencing with 20 minutes every week and believe you me that you will never want to stop.

Another benefit enjoyed by empaths is the ability to find and understand their true selves. This means that they are quite authentic and always speak their hearts and minds out. In my career, I came to notice that so many people face challenges when it comes to this. More so, in the current generation, many people see authenticity as a norm. Most of my clients have expressed themselves to me, saying that they would find it quite hard to be themselves. We do build a substantial prison around us as a society. You will need to make use of the facts that you quickly feel to your advantage. Empaths can connect to the deepest parts of themselves if they allow themselves to be very free. Some of the activities that you can engage in when alone include writing journals, having a new hobby, and dancing to be able to realize your true self. The main point behind this is to help you explore the depths within you. After feeling comfortable about it, you can then share with your friends by being authentic.

Therefore, when having a conversation with someone, you should always state yourself out comfortably, and don't shy from saying it if you feel the need. It is always advised to be polite to others and not attar statements that might leave them hurt. This becomes easier when you decide to share what in the heart freely. Understandably, it becomes quite caring and loving when people do speak their hearts out. And if the truth from our hearts becomes offensive to the other person, then it indicates that their ego has interpreted the message as an attack. However, you have the responsibility to say what matters to you and do it lovingly and openly.

Empaths are said to be peacemakers. This is because they have the ability the outside surroundings more than the inner surrounding. And it is due to this that leads them to be able to forego their needs and focus on the other person's needs. Generally, these people are said to be less violent, less aggressive, and they always tend to lean more toward being a peacemaker than a troublemaker. They are always filled by an uncomfortable feeling the moment they are in a surrounding filled with disharmony. If they find out that they in the middle of a confrontation, they will seek ways in which they can resolve the matter as within the shortest time possible or avoid it altogether. When harsh words are thrown to them in defense, they tend to resent their lack of self-control. They will always opt to handle the matter and resolve it promptly. Have you ever been in a similar situation?

Empaths sensitivity is a gift and not a curse. These people have the advantage of having creative thoughts, and through them, they can become something great. Therefore, before you start cursing your heightened awareness, you will need to remember that some of these advantages you possess, and you will need to uncover them. It is high time you start majoring on your benefits and advantages as an empath as this will enable you to create a life in which you will be able to benefit greatly from your gift and not drain you.

Demerits of Being an Empath

The most and common challenges I've known and seen with my patients and workshop participants include the following:

a) They struggle with anxiety and depression

Anxiety, depression, and doubt have been known to stumble the life of empaths. I am not surprised by this if I consider how they are embarrassed by our society, given all sorts of negative feedback. Besides, most of the empaths have been brought up in unstable homes, places where emotional welfare is raged daily. It is from this point that most empaths have resorted to addictions in a bid to be able to cope with the emotional overwhelm.

b) They attract narcissists and are energy vampires

We will agree that being an empath hurts because it does. These people do sense everything that every other person feels. They become greatly affected by other people's emotions. They can feel the loss and pain the other person is going through. They can feel their tears and the tone soul hence being quite hurt. But people won't understand them.

The empaths will act as an emotional sponge as they attract all manner of emotions when they are in the bank, grocery store, office, and from the surrounding people. They get to absorb the energy of the people who have the same energy signature.

Even though they are quite active in intuition, once in a while, we all get into the trap of the toxic people. This is the time when we give room to narcissists and other energy vampires to take advantage of your kind and compassionate nature. They find it hard to detach themselves from such relationships. They are highly disadvantaged because they never let many people in their lives, but when they do, they tend to give their all, of which the other person might take advantage of their character.

c) They feel too much but may not know why

With so many emotions and information hitting them from all corners, it is quite easy for them to be confused at the end. They may be unable to differentiate what issue belongs to them and what they collected along the way belonging to other people. They are also disadvantaged by the fact that their moods get tampered with by the physical environment. A very lovely-looking home might instead their levels of anxiety due to inexplicable reasons and factors. Because these people spend a lot of time going through subtleties around them, they end up spending a lot of time out than in their bodies. There is a dire need for an empath to take time to center and be fully in their bodies, and thoughts as this is quite important. By doing this, they will be able to establish boundaries in their life.

d) They have jellyfish boundaries and get stung

One of the main things that empaths hate is to disappoint others. This is brought about by the reason that they always feel the emotions in them and firmly, and it's the thought of hurting the other person is what makes their anxiety levels soar. They will feel quite guilty if they have to say no. It is for this reason that they might tend to have jellyfish boundaries something which might be taken for granted by other people, hence hurting the empath.

Also, if a person is seeking help from an empath, and the situation is quite dire, the helplessness behind the plea will highly affect the empath triggering them to accept the request even if it would mean personal misfortune to themselves. For an empath to stop being disadvantaged, then they will need to learn how to turn people away by saying no to requests that might cost them so much.

e) They face challenges when winding down

Empaths go through a hard time as they try to transition themselves from high stimulation to solitude. Brains never stop buzzing after a very involving and busy day at work. It is due to this that the empaths won't be able to focus easily. It is for this reason that we get a sad mood, or we feel a strange feeling after we get home from work, event, or a party despite it being filled with fun.

Have you been a victim of any of the above challenges? Then it is good to understand that nearly every empath has felt the same. There is no need to be ashamed of your sensitivity. Your empathy has much positive than detrimental to the world, and it brings to light more so when you get to learn the skills to learn and cope.

f) System Overload

Empaths are much wired to notice all the happening around them; hence, they experience a lot just before they get overwhelmed. Every empath should build up a tolerance because they relate quite differently, and this helps them be able to be quite aware when their sensory are being overloaded, and due to awareness, they can then have time to release and discharge.

Sometimes you can't tell if an emotion or sense of bodily discomfort is your own or someone else's. Taking on other people's energy can cause a variety of physical and emotional symptoms in you, from pain to anxiety

g) Sustaining Intimacy challenge

Empaths do face real challenges when in a relationship. Look at this scenario: an empath will have that time he or she will want to connect with their partners deeply, both body, mind, and spirit. Yet, still, there are times he or she will be feeling like blowing up yarning for time alone so to refresh and breathe. They are generally neutral at giving but what about receiving?

h) Becoming overstimulated

Empaths can quickly feel like they do possess a raw nerve something which can make them burn out quickly, and this is caused by the fact that they think not to be having the same defenses as the other people possess.

Failing to have enough time for oneself every day will lead to them to suffer from the toxic effects caused by being overstimulated and also sensory overload.

i) They Feel things intensely

Empaths have a challenge when it comes to anything seemingly brutal. They actually can't be comfortable when watching a violent or upsetting movie may it be about animals or humans because they will be badly hurt in the process. These people can even find themselves carrying the weight of the world on their shoulders as they can be suffering from the pain they took after watching the news or feeling the pain of a loved one.

j) They experience emotional and social hangovers

If you are associated with many people on a day to day activities, then you might be quite overloaded by the end of the day.

k) They have a feeling of being isolated and lonely

Because the world might appear to be quite overwhelming, you might find yourself keeping yourself a distant away from the rest. In the end, people may view you as standoffish. Like many empaths, you may be hyper-vigilant at scanning your environment to ensure its safety, which others can perceive as a signal to stay away. Some empaths prefer socializing online to keep others at a distance, so there's less of the tendency to absorb their discomfort and stress.

l) Experiencing emotional burnout

The fact that people will be flocking to you to share their disturbing stories will surely be emotionally distressing. I used to wear a sign written "I can help you" ever since I was a small child. And this clearly explains why empaths will have to set boundaries in their life if they want to stop being drained.

m) Coping with increased sensitivity to smell, light, smell, touch, sound, and temperature

Empaths find loud noises and bright lights being quite painful. They do react with our bodies, penetrate and shock us profoundly. All the time an ambulance passes-by, I have no option but to hold my ear. Could this be the same situation as you? What are your experiences when visiting your friend who has a home workshop and maybe with a loud machine? I have come to realize that I can't withstand the explosive blasts of the fireworks. They do startle me so much hence reacting similarly like a frightened dog.

Scientists have resulted that empaths have an enhanced startle response because they are super-responsive when it comes to intense sensory input. Empaths do feel queasy if they are exposed to strong smells and chemicals, such as perfumes and exhausts. Could this be a similar experience to you? Empaths are also susceptible to temperatures extremes and even dislike air-conditioned places. Scientists have proven that our bodies as empaths can also be depleted or energized when in quite intense weather, the likes of gusty winds, thunderstorms or snowfall. Empaths get much energized by a bright full moon whereas, other empaths with feel agitated by the same.

Chapter 6: A Deep Dive into Empathic Listening

One of the most profound qualities of an empath is listening. What makes it so special; yet we all listen to people on a daily basis? How do they do it that the rest do not? Here's how to listen like an empath:

❖ Attentive Listening

Dedicate your full attention to listening, without doing anything else on the side. Stop scrolling on your phone or computer, typing, eating, or playing music in the background. Turn your body to face the speaker and maintain eye contact. Nod as necessary. Observe the facial expressions, gestures, and general body language.

It is not enough to listen; it is just as important to let the speaker know that you're listening. This assurance makes it easier to open up. Have you had one of those conversations where the listener turns attention to something else midway, such as replying to a message? You then pose to give him/her time to finish the task. But alas; they tell you to proceed. 'Go on. I'm still listening.' In most cases, this will be someone senior to you, so you will have no choice but to oblige. You attempt to carry on with the conversation, but you're deflated. You don't speak as well as before. It turns out the quality of listening affects the quality of speaking.

In this regard, attentive listening encourages the speaker to open up fully. This is what separates counselors from the rest of us. No wonder they manage to get people to open up on issues they've kept inside for years.

Attentive listening in the workplace encourages productive communication. Workers know that they can go to their bosses and express exactly how they feel. Customers can also give their honest feedback.

❖ Non-judgmental Listening

Following the point on attentive listening, try to listen without forming an opinion on what is being said. Listen to understand— not to answer. If you let your mind wander, you'll begin to critique what you're listening to mentally. This changes your perception and affects your listening.

It is natural to lean towards judgment. We often do it subconsciously. You have already set standards in your mind regarding how people should behave when faced with various situations. Everything is in black and white; right or wrong. While you're listening, you're also trying to classify the decisions and actions in the story as either right or wrong. How much can be achieved with such an attitude? Not much. You will even miss out on some bits of information as you're busy adjudicating.

Be cognizant of your thoughts, so you can catch them whenever they turn away from the conversation. Instead of labeling actions as right or wrong, seek to know the circumstances leading there. Ask follow-up questions. The answers will help you identify with the speaker and understand why they chose to act the way they did. While at it, don't interrupt. It can be hard to get back to a line of thought once interrupted.

❖ **Rephrase**

We often judge because we feel the need to say something in the conversation. We end up saying something like, 'how could you take him back after all he had done to you?' which is just plain judgmental. Instead, you can rephrase what has already been said. Repeat what you have understood from the conversation in different words. 'So, he convinced you that he had gone for counseling and was now a changed man?'

Rephrasing keeps your thoughts from straying. You remain attentive so that should you have to reword something, you'll have gotten it right. Restating assures the listener that you're attentive and encourages the conversation to keep going.

❖ **Moments of Silence**

Silence in a conversation does not have to be awkward. In empathic listening, moments of silence are not only allowed, but also encouraged. Opening up about sensitive matters takes a lot of energy. The speaker may have broken down and cried at some point. The listener also needs time to absorb what has been said. In moments of silence, both catch their breath.

Observe the speaker during the silence. If a hand of comfort is needed, you can offer a pat on the back or a rub on the back of the hand. Ask a follow-up question when ready to continue.

Silence does not make you a bad listener. Resist the temptation to barge into 'salvage' the moment. Silence is actually a healthy part of communication.

❖ See Things Their Way

Non-judgmental listening encourages empathy, where you put yourself in the shoes of the listener and feel the emotions. Picture listening to a 20-year-old who is pregnant and the boyfriend has left her. From your point of view, it is easy to wonder how she fell for such a common mistake. *What's wrong with these young girls? Couldn't she wait until she was married? Or at least use contraceptives?*

That's your narrative. But what's her story? That she met someone she truly loved. And he looked responsible enough to start a family. She was certain that they would eventually get married. She had always looked forward to being a mother, anyway. And she made her decision on the backdrop of these assumptions. As soon as you look at the situation from than angle, you can feel her pain of betrayal, and guide her appropriately.

If you allow yourself to trivialize their issues from your point of view, you'll be quick to assert how many others have gone through those situations before. Chances are they've already heard that before. And most importantly, it does not make their pain any less. Stepping into their shoes allows you to empathize with your situation, no matter how minor.

❖ End on a Positive Note

No matter how awkward the conversation was, it should end on a positive note. Find something good that can come out of the situation. If you're speaking to a lady who has just come of an abusive relationship like in the conversation above, point out something constructive about the episode. For instance, she can now tell the signs of an abusive partner from the onset. She can share such information with others to help them avoid such relationships. She can also help those in abusive relationships or those who have just quit. In short, the experience equips her with the knowledge that she can use to impact society.

The conversation should not end when the two of you part ways. The talk should be the beginning. A problem indeed shared is a problem half-solved. What about the other half? It comes in what is done after the problem is shared. Here we're referring to a case of counseling where someone comes to you with a problem. You might have made some recommendations on how to move forward. Were they implemented? Was there any noticeable change? Does the burden feel any lighter? Monitor the situation so you can know how to proceed from there.

Merits of Empathic Listening

How do you feel when someone listens to you attentively, patiently, and without judgment? You feel valued and appreciated. In a world that is so quick to judge, knowing that you'll not be judged will encourage you to speak your mind and heart.

Listening in this way also strengthens relationships. True bonds are formed between people who can talk about anything. It is a lonely world. Even with hours spent on social media talking to friends and strangers, many people do not have someone whom they can open up to about the issues going on in their lives. Setting yourself apart as an empathic listener will draw people to you, and you'll be a treasure to those you interact with.

Finally, empathic listening ensures that communication actually takes place because someone is actually listening. Very often, we have someone who is talking, but the would-be listener is either distracted or disinterested. The communication chain is broken midway. Follow the tips above to become an empathic listener and watch the relationships with people around you shift for the better.

When You Don't Know What to Say

After listening, you feel compelled to say something. Often, you don't know what to say. You may result in these cliché statements:

- God will see you through
- He/she is in a better place
- This too shall pass
- I know how you feel
- Don't worry; things will be fine

These statements are said in good faith, but they rarely help. Essentially what these responses are saying is 'things are not that bad.' They're belittling the person's predicament. In any case, he/she has already heard these statements before.

Remember, empathy is all about connecting with the other person's pain and emotions. You cannot show empathy by downplaying the situation.

Start by acknowledging their pain or struggle. This shows that you understand what they're going through; or at least that you're trying to. You can say something like 'I see how difficult that is' or 'that must be really challenging.'

Then, appreciate their step of courage in opening up. It takes a lot of guts to do so, especially if they've tried to open up before and received a negative response. Talking to you means that they trust you, and it pays to acknowledge that faith in you. 'Thank you for choosing to share this with me' would suffice.

Ask questions to prompt further information. People often begin to open up then stall midway, either due to emotions or just afraid that they've already revealed too much. Assist them to go on talking. 'How did that make you feel?' 'How have you tried to cope?' 'Anything else that you can mention on this issue?'

Finally, show support. You can't fix everything, but you can be there. Offer to listen whenever the need arises. Reinstate your love and care. Affirm them by reminding them that they're brave and strong enough to go through the situation. Such an empathic response will leave those who have the privilege to speak to you feeling better and boost their ability to deal with their situation amicably.There is no blueprint for empathy. You just have to follow your intuition, which is something that you're good at as an empath. Deal with each case as your inner voice leads. You will leave people feeling better, and you'll gain fulfillment from utilizing your gift of empathic listening.

Chapter 7: Protecting Yourself through Energy Healing

The way to self-care is to rapidly perceive the primary indications of encountering tactile over-burden or when you begin engrossing pessimism or worry from others. The sooner you can act to lessen incitement and focus yourself, the more adjusted and ensured you will be. At whatever point you begin to feel depleted or overpowered practice the accompanying five security tips.

❖ Shielding Visualization

Protecting is a snappy method to secure yourself. Many empaths and touchy individuals depend on it to shut out lethal vitality while permitting the free progression of inspiration. Approach it consistently. The moment you are awkward with an individual, spot, or circumstance, set up your shield. Use it in a train station, at a gathering on the off chance that you are conversing with a vitality vampire, or in a pressed specialist's lounge area. Start by taking a couple of, deep, long breaths. At that point, imagine an excellent shield of white or pink light encompassing your body and expanding a couple of crawls past it. This shield shields you from anything negative, distressing, harmful, or nosy. Inside the security of this shield, feel focused, glad, and invigorated. This shield squares out cynicism, and yet, you can, in any case, feel what is absolute and cherishing.

❖ Define and Express Your Relationship Needs

Knowing your needs and having the option to affirm them is a reliable type of self-security for empaths. At that point, you can be in your full power in a relationship. If something does not feel right, raise the issue with your accomplice instead of enduring quietly. Discovering your voice is proportional to creating your capacity; otherwise, you may end up depleted, restless, or feel like a doormat seeing someone where all your fundamental needs are neglected. Your accomplice is not a mind peruse. Talk up to shield your prosperity.

Ask yourself, "What do I need in a relationship that I have been hesitant to request? Okay, incline toward all the more alone or calm time? Okay, prefer to rest without anyone else's input at times? Would you like to play more or talk more or engage in sexual relations more? Or on the other hand, might you want to move under the full moon together? Give your instinct a chance to stream without judgment. Reveal your actual emotions-no motivation to be embarrassed or to keep down.

❖ Set Energetic Boundaries at Work and Home

Empaths frequently endure in their condition when they ingest the worry in their environment. The work environment mainly can be loud and over-invigorating. To ensure your vitality level in a sincerely requesting or swarmed condition, encompass the external edge of your space with plants or family or pet photographs to make a little mental obstruction. Sacrosanct articles, for example, a statue of Quan Yin (the goddess of empathy), the Buddha, hallowed dabs, precious stones, or defensive stones can define an enthusiastic limit. Clamor dropping earbuds or earphones are likewise helpful to mute discussions and sound.

❖ **Prevent Empathy Overload**

When you are retaining the pressure or side effects of others, and you have to discharge the negative vitality, breathe in lavender essential oil or put a couple of drops halfway between your eyebrows (on your third eye) to quiet yourself. When you are capable, invest energy in nature. Offset your alone time with individuals time. For you, time the executives are vital to your mental stability. You should make an effort not to plan patients consecutively.

In your own life, you do not design such a large number of things in a single day. You ought to have likewise figured out how to drop plans when you get over-burden. This is expertise. All empaths must adapt, so you do not feel obliged to go out if you are worn out and need rest. Set clear cutoff points with vitality vampires and dangerous individuals. Keep in mind, "No" is a complete sentence. You do not need to continue accounting for yourself. You are brave about abstaining from depleting individuals, especially when you are over-burden at long last practice self-empathy. Be sweet to yourself at whatever point conceivable refrain from pummeling yourself. In the wake of a monotonous day, let yourself know, "I did as well as could be expected. It is alright nectar."

Activities That Can Help You Thrive as an Empath

❖ Express Your Thoughts and Feelings

Get into the habit of consciously expressing yourself when you feel something. It gives you the power to handle your emotions more effectively. This does not mean throwing a fit of rage or yelling at people or crying all the time. However, when you feel something, open up at least with people whom you can trust.

Do not get aggressive or act increasingly submissive. Gently stand up for your feelings without resorting to belittling or pulling down others. Assertiveness is taking charge of the situation and your emotions in a more constructive and calm manner, without doing things that will further damage the situation.

If you want to become more emotionally intelligent, start getting into the habit of taking control of the situation in a balanced and assertive manner without resorting to aggression or passivity. Present your stand in a clear, non-offensive, and sure manner. You will eventually start becoming more confident, develop better negotiation/problem-solving skills, and manage anxiety efficiently.

❖ Identify Feelings without Judging Them

Tune into your deepest feelings and emotions without being judgmental about it. For instance, when you identify that you are experiencing pangs of jealousy towards another person, do not automatically term yourself or your feelings as bad or wrong. Simply acknowledge that there is a feeling of jealousy and try to tackle it more positively.

❖ Take Responsibility for Your Actions

Accepting complete responsibility for your actions is one of the first steps towards developing a higher emotional quotient. Emotionally intelligent people do not feel the need to shift responsibility on someone else, justify their wrongdoings, or defend themselves aggressively. They shy away from putting the blame elsewhere and completely own up to the mistake.

You acquire the ability to control your emotions, manage negative feelings, develop more fruitful interpersonal relationships, wield better decisions, and influencer your actions more positively. You are not relying on others or external circumstances for determining your emotions but taking charge of how you feel.

❖ Use Generous Doses of Humor

That thing about do not take life too seriously, no one gets out alive anyway is true to an extent, isn't it? We increase our stress levels by viewing every situation with seriousness and conflict.

Get away from that mindset consciously and start seeing things with a more light-hearted and humorous perspective. View the positive or optimistic side of every situation to keep the atmosphere more upbeat. Spread joy and happiness wherever you go. If the situation seems slightly tense, try to crack a joke to lighten the mood a bit.

❖ Master Empathizing with People

Emotionally intelligent people are adept in the art of feeling other people's feelings. They place themselves in other people's shoes to understand the other person's perspective. When you develop empathy, you learn to consider every situation from other people's point of view, too, before coming to a decision that benefits everyone. This understanding paves the way for less conflict and greater stability in relationships. Connecting with others becomes effective and more fruitful when you learn to acknowledge the feelings of others.

The next time you find yourself getting angry with someone, stop in your tracks, and try to understand why they may be compelled to behave the way they do. Is it related to their childhood experiences? Is it related to issues related to low self-confidence or self-esteem? Has an incident deeply impacted them? Try and pin down their behavior to underlying factors to gain a more holistic overview of the situation. This will help you handle the situation more intelligently rather than succumbing to impulses or thoughtless actions.

Chapter 8: Empaths, Insomnia, Exhaustion, and Adrenal Fatigue

As an empath, one should remember that his/her presence is a blessing; the sweetness and tender application of the gift of empathy on people make all the difference in the world. The special intuition and refined sensitivity are a healing platform for self and others. Empathy comes with loving, kindness, and compassion.

However, as seen in previous topics, empathy has a list of challenges. These challenges include; absorbing the negativity and stress of others, Becoming overstimulated, experiencing social and emotional hangovers, emotional burnouts, feeling things intensely, feeling lonely and isolated, the need for space even when in a relationship, and dealing with heightened sensitivity to light, taste, smell, temperature, touch and sound.

These challenges can hinder the performance of an empath, both physically and emotionally. The spiritual gift of empathy tends to become a challenge once a person forgets or fails to understand that the true purpose of this ability is to heal. Empaths might find themselves absorbing all the energy instead of using it to understand the situation without hoarding it. Consequently, the empath becomes overwhelmed by the emotions and in worse cases; he/she becomes physically and mentally ill. Uncontrolled empathy has been linked to conditions such as body aches, difficulties thinking clearly, adrenaline fatigue, insomnia, and exhaustion. It is important for an empath to remember that his/her energy source is not without a limit. Energy is finite; therefore, if an empath keeps giving without taking care of oneself, he/she will eventually run out of energy.

Empaths are like sponges that absorb the emotions, feelings, and conditions of those around them and as such, they can absorb an array of health problems, including physical conditions. This sharing of emotions leaves the empath very tired such that they need a lot of sleep/ rest in order to repair what has been affected. Unfortunately, many of the empaths find it hard to sleep and toss in bed all night. Consequently, these empaths do not get healed completely, and instead, they become broken down and depleted. Researchers say that many of the empaths are misdiagnosed when they seek medical attention because there is little understanding of the empathy phenomenon in the medical field. People often say that if the world had fewer guns and more hugs, we would be living in a better place.

The society has been made better by empathy and empathetic people. As seen in previous chapters, empathy is one of the main keys to survival for both humans and most animals. We have lived through the centuries witnessing the kind acts of people such as Mother Teresa and Mahatma Gandhi. These people are considered empaths because they have gone beyond and over what other people can do for the world. We can say that without these people, the world could not be as bright as it is today. However, the energy it takes for one to give their heart, soul, and strength to another comes with a high price, and as such, most of the empaths find themselves dealing with burnouts and adrenalin fatigue.

Empaths can experience an unexpected onset of chronic fatigue because of the significant crash of different energy levels.

Mostly, this crash is a result of having an array of emotional responsibilities. Empaths leak their energy so furiously that it is almost impossible to remain grounded, consciously aware, and balanced. These people will mostly feel drained when they have spent too much time in the presence of others. Interactions with people can lead to emotional exhaustion for the empath. As such, the people with the gift of empathy need a whole deal of alone time to recharge their energy levels.

The thoughts, feelings, and emotions of empaths can play havoc on the internal systems, thereby causing devastating consequences that debilitate the people involved. IF THE empaths have regular moments of solitude within the day, then they get the time to process emotions and feelings, avoiding exhaustion. Taking some alone time facilitates better emotional, physical, and mental conditions because the empath is able to let go of the bad energy that might play on the mind and weigh him/her down.

If the empath does not get enough time to retreat and reenergize, if he/she lacks space during the day, then the mind will react at night. One might wonder why the mind chooses to overreact at night; it is because the night is still and quiet, meaning that there are no distractions from external stimuli. Consequently, these reactions make the empath unable to relax and allow sleep to take over.

In other cases, the empath may be able to sleep but will keep waking up throughout the night. The interrupted sleep sessions are as a result of the mind trying to process the information it over absorbed during the day. As the empath attempts to make sense of the occurrences that took place during the day, insomnia crops up. The consequences of insomnia include daytime sleepiness, irritability, low energy, and depressed moods.

The hyperactive mind brings about fatigue on the individual by continuously hurling an overwhelming amount of stimuli at the empath, not allowing him/her the chance to replenish rest, and recharge. Consequently, the empath will have erratic sleep patterns whereby some days he/she will need only two or three hours of rest while other days require ten or more hours of rest, depending on the amount of energy that is attached to the energy field and is pulling the person down.

If one does not find time during the day to figure out the internal thoughts, emotions feelings and commotion taking place within the mind, it is essential that he/she engages in meditation before sleeping in order to clear the mind enough to rest. Allowing thoughts to come and go lightly without paying too much attention to them allows one to get some closure without igniting a psychological response that is hormone-induced.

Our experiences and memories are linked to emotionally charged feelings that tend to provide emotions such as resentments, fear, anxiety, paranoia, and panic. Consequently, the human mind is convinced that the owner is under some form of genuine threat. This belief makes the brain to send signals to the adrenal glands to release hormones that facilitate a surge of energy.

When someone experiences prolonged or intense stress or anxiety, the lifestyle becomes very unhealthy. For instance, one might get into substance abuse, too much/ inadequate sleep, poor diet, overworking, stressful relationships, family challenges and general life crises-consequently, the individual places excessive continuous demands on the adrenal glands.

What are adrenal glands? They are small endocrine glands shaped like kidneys, approximately the size of walnuts that are placed in the area just above the kidneys in the lower back. These glands are essential and beneficial when one is under stress because they release hormones that keep the individual focused, alert, and creates increased stamina to facilitate better handling of stress.

However, when the adrenal glands are overstimulated, they keep producing energy which results in conflict, especially when we try to sleep or get some rest. Consistent overstimulation of the adrenal glands makes one feel like they are permanently wired on high alert. If a solution is not found in time, the adrenal glands experience excessive stress, and they might eventually malfunction and burn out.

As the energy levels get drained quickly, empaths are tempted to top it up with instant solutions; therefore, they will settle for quick fixes such as highly refined foods with high levels of sugars and salts. These foods burn energy very fast, giving an instant boost of energy. However, this move initiates a vicious cycle whereby the refined food burns energy very fast, leaving the person in need of more junk to fuel the body. When people feed the body with the refined products found in most quick fixes, the body only craves more sugar and salt because it thought it what it needs to keep it going. People should be having unrefined salts and sugars because these have high nutrition value, and when consumed in healthy doses, it can replenish and nourish the adrenal glands.

People might again try to raise energy levels by taking products that are high in caffeine, for instance, coffee and energy drinks. What they fail to understand is that caffeine just irritates the glands further. As a result, the consumer will experience regular lows and highs as the energy levels drop and hike throughout the day. When the adrenal glands are not working as they should, the affected person will feel constantly fatigued, anxious, irritable, overwhelmed, dizzy, and run down. Again, one might experience sugar and salt cravings, heart palpitations, low blood pressure, high blood pressure, and a harder time when dealing with stressful situations.

If one is well balanced, he/she thinks positively, eats well, sleeps and gets enough rest and as such, the adrenal glands are not easily overwhelmed. During sleep, the levels of cortisol in the body rise naturally and peak just a few hours before we wake up. This increase happens so that a person can have a good start once he/she wakes up. It is also referred to as circadian rhythm, and it elevates and reduces energies accordingly so that the body can function effectively by staying awake when it is daytime and sleeping when it is dark.

When the adrenal glands are exhausted, an empath and any other person for that matter wake up feeling tired and disturbed even if he/she has had a long and otherwise restful sleep. This person will feel drowsy for the better part of the day, and then the cortisol levels will rise in the evening. The late peak will result in a lack of sleep or difficulty resting at night. It is very hard for anyone who has overrun the adrenal glands to get them back to a normal state. It can take a lot of time, but there are some changes that one can make and have an immediate positive effect on the glands.

For an empath, the most critical initial thing to do is to listen attentively to the body and take note of how it feels. If one pays attention to the feelings of the body, then he/she will stay aware of how the energy levels within are rising and falling throughout the day. This will help in noting the hours during the day, which one feels exhausted than others; therefore, make the right moves to alter the patterns.

It is important that an empath understands why he/she is placing too much energy pressure on the glands. Once he/she identifies the root cause of the stress, emotions, and feelings, it will be easier to ensure that a heightened state of alert is brought down, therefore removing the pressure from the adrenal glands.

In some cases, the empath may have to use medication to help focus on the body in order to identify any sensation that is taking place. Medication can also help one to soothe the mind and become calm so that he/she does not keep repeating the negative thoughts that will trigger adverse chemical reactions.

Another method that can help one to regulate the level of cortisol is spending time with friends, family, and outside, doing social activities. Scientists have found that cortisol levels increase if one spends too much time alone. Loneliness, separation, and isolation trigger feelings that we associate with negative experiences; therefore, empaths should learn how to balance alone time with social time. Consequently, cortisol will not be such an issue.

Other factors that affect the cortisol levels include diet and exercise. The regime that one uses for exercise and feeding determines the amount of stress placed on the adrenal glands. If one pushes the body too much, then he/she places too much demand on the adrenal glands, which then results in an overproduction of stress-related hormones. Bad practices such as skipping meals, intense workouts, and eating junk foods force the glands to overwork. In the event that the person has food allergies, then the glands get additionally stressed. As such, it is vital to be attentive to the food that one tolerates.

An empath can keep the adrenal glands nourished and balanced by sticking to a healthy diet and getting enough exercise. An organic, nutritious, and well-balanced diet with healthy levels of proteins, and vitamins A, B, and C can go a long way in ensuring that the glands are functioning properly. It is also important to allow time for the body to absorb the nutrients before a person can engage in any physical activity. The empaths can also avoid large consumptions of alcohol and eliminate the intake of refined products and caffeinated foods.

If the unrest and sleeplessness occur due to disturbances in the mind at night, then we can create an environment that helps rebalance the glands. For instance, one can create stability, security, inner peace, joy, and optimism just before going to bed. The aim is to get a restful night's sleep, and sometimes we can be startled by the thought of going to bed and failing to drift off as expected. Anxiety develops just before getting to bed when one realizes that he/she is going to stay awake for hours without getting to the highly desired delta state. The anxiety only makes matters worse.

When the adrenals are exhausted, empaths tend to wake during the night on high alert and to make matters worse, high stimuli dreams can add to the overanxious state of mind. Sleepless nights are particularly common for the empaths after they have endured an anxious and stressful period. When they enter sleep, they can keep waking up at intervals during the night because of the hormones circulating through the body even when they cannot understand the cause.

Disturbances in sleep are in most cases linked to biochemical reactions resulting from the flashes of high levels of stress hormones occurring throughout the body system between 2:00 AM and 4:00 AM. The high spike of these hormones affects the body so dramatically that it becomes impossible to remain calm; thus, the ability to stay asleep is interrupted. These disturbed sleep challenges can be rectified by making a therapeutic potion that consists of unrefined salts and organic honey. Mix one teaspoon of unrefined salt, for example, the pink Himalayan salt with five teaspoons of raw organic honey. The salt has healing properties, while the honey supplies the body cells with energy. One can take a teaspoon of the mixture about 20 minutes before sleeping; it will help to relax the mind and naturally regulate hormones. Consequently, one will be ready to drift into a restful place of rest.

Summary of Techniques to Deal with Adrenal Fatigue, Insomnia, and Exhaustion

It is easy to understand how being empathetic can lead to constant exhaustion, insomnia, and adrenal fatigue, especially if the person is frequently around a big crowd. After empathizing, socializing, and taking in all the emotions and feelings in situations such as this, most empaths need time to recuperate and recharge their energies. They will require a quiet environment to heal.

If the person cannot identify a time during the day to sort out the thoughts and feelings, he/she will be forced to deal with the issues at night while trying to sleep. The quietness and calmness of the night make it easy for the mind to keep analyzing things it took in during the day.

Consequently, the empath will wake up unrested and fatigued; therefore spend the day worn out. This will definitely become a vicious cycle because in the evening again, the mind will start to drift. The adrenal glands will be producing hormones when they are not needed and failing to reach the expectations when needed. The crash of energies makes the empath more confused, tired, stressed, fatigued et cetera.

However, the empaths can help their bodies to get the rest they need by taking a few positive steps. For instance, they could use more natural sources of salt and sugar which will supply the body with long term energy, therefore, breaking the cycle of the need for instant energy from refined products. Again, becoming more active helps one to replenish the adrenal glands. If possible, one should gain and maintain a positive attitude towards life; the benefits will increase mentally, physically, and emotionally. With these simple practices, an empath and any other person should start to notice an increased amount of sleep and proper rest, revived levels of energy, and overall happiness in life.

Balance the time spent alone with the time spent with family and friends. It is very beneficial to balance socialization. Get into activities that make you happier; for instance, ride a bike, nature is good. Watch an inspirational movie. There is always something to learn. Follow a nature trail. Fresh air helps to open up, unwind, and get clear thoughts. Boundaries are also very essential for dealing with fatigue and exhaustion. One of the main challenges of empaths is that they will always want to help; thus, they forget that their energy has limits. Boundaries will help one to avoid the manipulation of energy vampires. It is okay to say no and also to rest.

Meditation has also been noted as one of the techniques that makes life easier for the empaths. Meditation makes one check into their bodies and minds and heals the things that are broken. For empaths, meditation also helps to identify and eliminate the emotions absorbed from others. One can meditate for about ten minutes in the evening to release the stress collected during the day, therefore creating room for sufficient sleep and rest.

Exhaustion, insomnia, and adrenal fatigue are bad for the health of any person, regardless of whether they are empaths or not. Good adrenal health is essential for everyone; therefore; we should share the information about the glands with everyone. Wearing out the adrenal glands leads to a lot of health issues. Although empathy is a gift that should be shared as much as possible, one should find time to take care of him/herself. And to keep going, it's important to pick the habit of practicing a positive mentality. This means patting oneself on the back for achievements and not beating oneself up with negative thoughts.

Chapter 9: Enjoy your empathy

Regardless of our empathic abilities or lack thereof, we all aim to fill our lives with as much joy as possible. Using the tools and strategies outlined in previous pages, the empath should find that their overall level of happiness generally increases. As it becomes easier to recognize and manage the different types of energies that surround them, it will also become easier to be selective and make consistently positive choices.

Still, even for those who have mastered these skills and choose to focus all of their energy on positivity, constant and everlasting joy is an unrealistic goal to strive for. We all have our blind spots, vulnerabilities, and weaknesses. Sooner or later, the empowered empath will encounter a source of negativity that they cannot (or simply do not wish to) ignore, compartmentalize, or remedy.

It is in those moments, where joy is not accessible, that the empath must learn to find a way to inner peace instead. Imagine, for example, that someone you love and deeply respect has passed away. It would be ludicrous for anyone, even an empowered empath, to expect to find their way to true joy during the funerary services, or at any point within the mourning period. Whatever your views on death and the possibility of an afterlife may be, a loss of this magnitude is always painful. If the empath wishes to attend a wake or funeral, they'll certainly need to prepare themselves for the experience. They have to utilize whatever strategies they need to avoid taking on the pain of other mourners in the room. However, the empath who is focused exclusively on seeking joy may run the risk of ignoring their own genuine feelings of pain, thereby distancing the self from emotions and feelings that belong to no one else. This is a dangerous practice for any empath to grow accustomed to, as it can be seductively pleasant at first. But much like the alcoholic who avoids the pain of a hangover by consistently consuming the hair of the dog that bit them, the empath will find that they can never outrun their own emotions. Even if they aim to shut them out the same way that they shut out the feelings of negative people, the emotions almost always find their way back to the empaths.

Balance, ultimately, is a superior goal. An empath with a strong sense of inner balance can attend a funeral, commiserate with others, and honor their own sadness and process feelings of grief without being consumed by them. Their balance allows them to recognize that sadness is not an opposing force to happiness, but rather that it is a functional part of joy; that without misery, we would never feel bliss or perhaps anything at all.

Over time, the empath will learn that this state of equilibrium is indeed their most heightened state of being and the place where they will find their truest self.

Learn how to deal with discomfort

Here's a revolutionary idea that can take your yoga, tai chi, or mindfulness practice to the next level: discomfort is just an emotion. It isn't real. It isn't a threat, but it is a motivator.

Embracing discomfort isn't the same as numbing yourself to it. When you accept cognitive dissonance or moral injustices, you numb yourself to discomfort, embracing apathy, and encouraging the distortion of the truth. When you allow yourself to experience discomfort without immediately reacting, however, you can learn to make empowered choices, overcome fears and anxieties, and reach towards emotional growth. For empaths, discomfort is often a sensation of uncertainty or anticipation of conflict. If you can learn to recognize the feeling without letting it trigger your fight or flight response, you can instead focus on taking productive action, making yourself the true master of your own universe.

This is an enlightened position that very few humans take. If you can start to use your discomfort as a tool, rather than avoiding it at all costs, you may find yourself able to overcome challenges that leave others destroyed. Once you've mastered this technique, do your best to pay it forward to another empath.

Live a comfortable life

One thing that can throw any empath off balance and block the pathway to inner peace is a lack of authenticity in your lifestyle. Empaths often carry lies or dishonesty inside for long periods of time, haunted by them, even allowing the memory of them to block their throat, heart, and solar plexus chakras. This being the case, it's best for empaths to avoid lying whenever possible--even white lies can cause disruptions in your energy field.

You can work towards this goal through both addition and elimination. In addition, make a point to invite positive energy flow into your life by aligning your career, personal relationships, eating habits, and hobbies with your value system. For example, if you have come to realize that environmentalism is deeply important to you, then pursuing work in green planning would be a fantastic first step. You could also reach out to foster new friendships with people who are passionate about the same causes. You might alter your diet to favor organic, locally sourced produce, and make a heightened effort to buy from environmentally conscious companies.

For elimination, you'll want to start purging anything from your life that puts you in a position of moral conflict. If your job or social circle is not environmentally conscious, you'll be under constant pressure to swallow your truth and project dishonesty, which will ultimately leave you feeling dissatisfied and ungrounded. Any relationship wherein you feel the need to lie to keep everyone happy is a bad relationship for you, and you should feel free to let go of it.

You'll also want to stop using your money to support brands whose values contradict your own, and give up any habits that have a negative impact on the things that matter most to you—for instance, if you love poetry, song, and other forms of vocal expression, it's may be time to quit smoking cigarettes once and for all. You might be pleasantly surprised to notice your physical body and metaphysical energy shift in a tangible way once you release the cognitive dissonance you once held inside yourself. You'll feel lighter, taller, more dynamic, and more capable.

I'll include another reminder here to be careful with social media use. Sometimes, these applications can do a lot of good to bring people together and inject dynamic momentum into progressive movements—but most often, they are cesspools of inauthentic energy. Aim to use these platforms sparingly, if at all, and to post honestly and responsibly.

Choosing Humility and Respecting the Unknown

No matter how empowered one may become, and regardless of how well one has honed their empathic power, it is important to embrace humility and keep the mind open for unexpected possibilities. The self-righteous empath who develops a hermetic view of the world, unwilling to entertain ideas that do not strongly resonate with their interior knowledge, is likely to be deeply discontented or anxious, and struggle with communication and loving relationships, as others will perceive them to be arrogant and standoffish.

This type of attitude is also likely to weaken your empathic powers. Truth is multifaceted and always changing. In order to grasp even a sliver of it, the empath must maintain a balanced connection between their interior and exterior worlds. Shutting either out, or favoring one over the other, will eventually lead the empath to receive misleading messages, or lead them to misinterpret messages that would otherwise be clear and easy to decipher. Empaths are privy to knowledge that often goes unseen, unheard, unacknowledged, but from time to time, they can be flat out wrong, especially if the information they're receiving from the exterior world is limited, it can be skewed to support an incomplete hypothesis.

There is an ancient Indian parable, of possible Buddhist origin, that has become popular in discussions of philosophy and religion, spreading to cultures throughout the world and retold in several different versions, about a group of blind men who encounter an elephant in the jungle. (Perhaps this parable is due for a modern update to include an equal number of blind women. Please bear in mind, men are not the only gender susceptible to the pitfalls this proverb warns us against.) In this story, each of the blind men must use only their hands to try and comprehend the elephant's size, shape, and overall nature; however, one man's hands find only the elephant's tusks, while another finds only the rough skin of a hind leg, and another still can only feel the animal's wide, thin ears. When they compare their experiences, they are each convinced that the others are wrong or insane; in some versions of the story, this inability to agree on their sensory perceptions leads the men to resort to violence. Ultimately, the point of the story, which only the audience can see, is that each of the blind men is right, describing his experience accurately and honestly; the only problem is that they fail to acknowledge the perspectives of others as equally valid.

This is human nature, though the parable aims to inspire us to evolve past it. The truth can never be fully comprehended from one fixed vantage point. It is far too vast for any single person to hold alone. Still, the enlightened empath will be more successful than most at gathering contrasting perspectives and finding a way to incorporate them all into a single philosophy or belief, untangling knots of cognitive dissonance and drawing connections between seemingly disparate concepts. If, and only if, they are willing to stay humble and open to uncomfortable experiences, that is. This pursuit should be handled with care—again, there is a difference between mild discomfort and decisively negative energy. And it's important for the empath to stay guarded against the latter. Don't force yourself to endure an experience that is depleting rather than charging you, but don't let yourself fall into the habit of avoiding the challenging and unpredictable opportunities life offers you, either. As an example, many empaths learn early in their journey to self-empowerment that large crowds can quickly cloud or drain their energy fields. They may have had one particularly difficult or painful experience at a party, concert, funeral, wedding, or rally, and quickly decide that it would be best to avoid large gatherings from that point on. This might be a mistake, though, as joining large groups that are unified in honest intention (a faith-based service, or performance that is effective at steering the emotional path of every audience member, for example) can be one of the most positive and energizing experiences available to the empath.

Though it may be tempting to stay cocooned in whatever emotional spaces feel safest, the empath must make a point of continuously expanding their perspective by trying new things, meeting new people, and seeking out challenges for the sake of growth. The most important thing for any empath to know is just how much the universe has yet to teach them.

Chapter 10: How to Protect Yourself from Energy Vampires

An energy vampire is quite a harsh phrase here. It is used to refer to people who always want things their way while disregarding everybody else's feelings. These are toxic people who do not care about the emotions of others, provided their interests get served. Energy vampires are bad for everyone, but particularly for empaths.

Empaths are ready givers, while the energy vampires are ruthless takers. If you're not careful, they'll drain you dry, and you'll have no energy left to take care of anyone else, including yourself. Common symptoms of energy vampires include:

- Insecurity makes them feel disadvantaged. They complain all the time, outlining their perceived challenges in great detail. You're forced to walk on eggshells around them, to avoid making their situation any worse. Having such a person around you is like having a fussy baby, just without the sweet face.

- They demand attention by claiming always to have a crisis. Even when good things are happening, they find a way to turn the situation around and see a problem there. And you don't dare claim to be having a problem as well. Yours will be promptly be declared trivial. Theirs is always the most

284

serious issue in the room. They thrive in the 'poor you' attention every single day, whether the problem is real or imaginary. Playing victim demands that other people lift them with their energy, which can be tiring.

- They never take the blame for anything that happens to them. It's always other people's fault. If they're flagged for non-performance at work, it's not anything that they did wrong. It's their coworkers who don't like them. Or the boss that is picking on them. If their relationship goes wrong, they won't point out what they could have done better. It's always the other person. Or other people who are jealous of the relationship. If there's no one to blame, even the good old universe is not safe. 'No one likes me.' 'Nothing good ever happens to me.' Here they're trying to say that the universe has conspired against them. How convenient?

- The spotlight always belongs to them. Should anyone else try to occupy it, especially with a happy story, it is instantly grabbed back. They will pour cold water on your happy news. You could have just gotten engaged, but instead of celebrating with you, they will talk about divorce statistics. They will remind you that 60% of all marriages end up in divorce. They will tell you of their peers who got engaged in glamorous weddings and didn't even last long enough to celebrate their first anniversary. These statistics may not even be true. They're simply intended to bring you down. Alternatively, they'll turn the story around to be about them; how they were once engaged, but so-and-so left them heartbroken. Now the attention turns to the sorry story. They never embrace joy and thrive in deflating the joy of others.

- They guilt-trip you into doing what they want. They will make you feel like it's your fault that they're miserable. They will say things like 'it seems I'll just have to go through this on my own. Everyone treats me like crap. You don't have to invite me. Nobody invites me anyway.' You will feel sorry for them, which is exactly what they want. You will then go out of your way to accommodate them, even when that means jeopardizing your own welfare.

- Their opinions are made to sound like facts, and in their usual character, it will be negative. They will say something mean about your hair or clothes, with zero regard to how it makes you feel. 'You're going out wearing that?' The question will be asked in a sneer. You will be left feeling judged, mocked, and ridiculed. They will expect you to go right back and change; that's how highly they think of their opinion. Be ready for the second round of scrutiny even when you change, the alternative might not be good enough either for their taste. Or something will be wrong with your shoes this time. They also criticize things that you cannot change—your height, the shape of your nose, or your personality. They leave you feeling miserable and are too self-absorbed to care.

- They speak of worst-case scenarios to spread fear. They can't stand positivity, so they'll always bring up those things that make people anxious. *What if we lose our jobs? What if the economy crashes? Do you know how much toxins are in these packaged foods? Have you checked the statistics on cancer cases?* If there is nothing bad happening, they will bring up that possibility. And that sight of your frightened faces will further cater to their twisted egos.

Dealing with Energy Vampires

Energy vampires are well amongst us—friends, family, colleagues, and peers. You can't avoid them completely. Your paths will cross at one point or the other. As an empath, keen to share goodness with all and sundry, you may be tempted to play the bigger person. You may even look for a way to help them change their ways. But remember that these people are thieves of energy, and of joy. They will leave you so deflated that you'll not have the strength to serve others, much less yourself. They will waste your gift. You have to engage them with caution.

Are energy vampires intentional, or do they do so by chance? There are those whose character is flawed by experiences. They grew up among energy vampires. They don't know how to be happy. They're accustomed to misery. They simply treat people how they were treated. This lot has a chance of changing if somebody points out the negative effects of this habit on others.

Then there are those who are vampires by choice. Life has dealt them a few rough cards. They're not happy, and they don't want to see anyone else happy. Instead of focusing on working through their situation, they choose to make others miserable so they can ride in the same boat. They know what they're doing, and they know they're hurting others. But they don't care.

Here's how to deal with energy vampires:

➢ Set Time Limit

If you're obligated to deal with them, set time limits. These are people who can engage you for hours if you let them. And the conversation will be dominated by their sorry stories the entire time. It's normal for people to have challenges, but you can't have this one individual claiming to be in crisis all the time. Set a time limit and let them know. For instance, you can say that you only have one hour to listen, after which you'll have to attend to something else. Be firm with your time limit; they will try to manipulate that too.

➢ Avoid Arguing

Contradicting an energy vampire yields nothing. They will come to you whining about a failed relationship claiming always to be innocent. You will try to make them see the part they played in the failed relationship. As usual, they will not accept any responsibility. They will only insist that they're innocent. Don't argue; otherwise, the conversation will carry on till kingdom come. Just listen to what they have to say. They're happy just to have your attention anyway.

> **Be Brief**

If you have to speak, stick to brief questions. Why? How? When? Such monosyllable questions will suffice. Here, keep your opinions to yourself. Voicing your ideas just keeps them going on and on, so they can discredit them and have theirs emerge as superior.

> **Minimal Reaction**

An energy vampire seeks to evoke an emotional reaction from you. They tell you their sorry stories, and they expect you to be sad for them. When they say degrading things, they want to see you angry and in despair. Do not give them these reactions that they're looking for. Remain passive. Listen with a straight face. Let them know that you're not moved by every whim. If your emotions fluctuate up and down as they engage you; they win. Don't let them 'win' at your expense. Nobody deserves that.

> **Avoid Eye Contact**

Empaths are good listeners and love to listen with all their senses. We have explained in a different chapter how empathic listening includes eye contact. If you're dealing with an energy vampire, however, this rule does not apply. Eye contact makes you more vulnerable to what is being said; just what we're avoiding here. Keep the eye contact to a minimum. Avoid sitting facing the speaker. Just glance at him or her occasionally. This does not sound very considerate but remember, you're dealing with a peculiar character here who is up to no good, and you have to protect yourself.

➤ Stick to Light Topics

We stated earlier that empaths thrive in deep conversations. Again, we have to make an exception here. You do not want to start speaking about the meaning of life with an energy vampire. They will do what they do best; water down your opinions, bring out their sad stories and create worst-case scenarios for everything. Make the conversation as light as possible. When they bring up issues of their own, just glaze them on the surface without going deeper. These are people intent on dragging you through the mud, and the closer you are to the surface, the better.

➤ Reduce Contact

Reduce the instances where you have to encounter such people. If they make a habit of popping into your home or office, let them know that they can only come with prior notice. What if they actually belong to your house or office? They could be your family members or workmates, you know. A bit tricky here; right? You still need to reduce contact. The last thing you need is an energy vampire siphoning your energy in the place where you spend your most time. If you have such a workmate, you're not obliged to hand out with them. If you go for lunch as a group, you can choose a different café, or carry a packed lunch. Do not entertain idle talk at your desk. If you have such a person at home, spend more time in your room. Distancing yourself from energy vampires is not selfish; it is a matter of self-preservation.

> ### ➢ Be in a Group

An energy vampire inflicts maximum damage when you're alone. Invite others into the conversation. If you have a workmate who singles you out to listen to sorry stories, you can request to involve the others, so they can also give their input on the issue. If they hover around your desk in the office, request them to bring up the conversation during lunch. You know the rest will be present, and you'll not have to suffer as much. In addition, someone in the group could have the courage to stand up to the energy vampire and call him/her out. Expect an argument, but the toxic character might just think about it afterward and makes some changes.

> ### ➢ Disengage Completely

Empath as you are; you can only take so much venom. Some energy vampires will be relentless, never stopping for a minute to think of the consequences of their actions. You will try to make them see some sense, but they'll be too self-centered to listen. You have a rare gift, which should be influencing as many as possible. You cannot afford to entertain people who will deflate you and makes it nearly impossible to serve. Feel free to cut off links. The world out there will teach them better.

Energy vampires deplete you physically and emotionally. You can actually feel changes in your body for every minute that you listen to them. You may feel sweaty, breath shallowly, have a faster heartbeat, and even experience a headache. Emotionally you feel anxiety, despair, and panic and even lose focus. You have that gut feeling that warns you that you're spinning out of control.

These effects could continue even after the toxic person has left. You keep replaying their words in your mind, and you feel drained all over again. It takes a while to detox from that feeling. Now imagine if you encounter several of these characters. You'll be so drained, with no energy left to attend to anyone.

You cannot afford to entertain this lot. What's worse; you won't even help them. Remember their goal was not to solve anything; it was to get attention. Their thirst for attention is like a bottomless pit. It's never enough. You do not have to suffer as a result. Remember, you cannot help everyone. The best you can do is hope that they decide to change, for their own good. Use these tips to tame them so you can go ahead and be of service to many others.

Chapter 11: How to Control Your Emotions with Meditation and Grounding

❖ **Returning to Earth**

As an empath, you have consistently been to some degree 'ethereal' in nature. Being ethereal can feel rather happy, far-reaching, and free – an invited alleviation from the power of being an empath. The ether is the space where unadulterated vitality thrives. It is the place life-power, chi, nourishment, widespread life vitality streams. Since empaths are about energy – feeling, detecting, transmuting and vibrating vivacious frequencies – the ether is somewhat an asylum for delicate creatures. It tends to resemble washing in an ocean of light. It is serene, quiet, and unlimited. Etheric vitality is a language that empaths get it. It just bodes well. It feels like home. For you, being ethereal ought to consistently be the simple part. Being encapsulated and grounded as a person, in any case, while feeling and detecting the majority of the energies around you is all that you need!

❖ **Gliding Around and Crash Landing**

Try not to be accustomed to being grounded by any means, frequently feeling floaty without a stay. You can be imbued with a mind-blowing feeling of softness, yet you could thump somebody over with a plume. This is the place the issue may begin from. It can bring about ceaseless 'crash arrivals' – back to earth! These unexpected, brutal shocks can even send you in turn. You may feel overpowered and thoroughly washed through with disorderly energies, an inclination that is so natural for empaths. Without being grounded, it tends to be hard to release the strengths that you had accepted. Without a firm ground to remain on, you cannot understand that feeling of steady quiet that usually happens when anybody is earthed.

There may be a moment that it occurs to you that without imbuing your experience of being an empath with an Earth association, you could be merely drifting around like a tumbleweed in the breeze; which is all great. However, it cannot generally fill a need. Your otherworldly encounters can be astonishing, with the most dominant of acknowledging; yet you could be floating. You may understand that your endeavors to acquire the heavenly and genuinely fill your need can be pointless except if you give it a firm ground to arrive upon. In this way, you ought to before long become familiar with the imperative significance of being grounded.

Why Is Establishing So Significant for Empaths?

One of the issues that empaths and exceptionally sensitive people face is feeling exhausted and fatigued because we take on an excessive amount of vitality from outside of ourselves. Here is the reason establishing is significant.

- Grounding offers a moment approach to release undesirable energies
- Grounding bolsters you enthusiastically
- Grounding reestablishes and revives your vitality field
- Grounding advances a moment feeling of quiet
- Grounding improves mental, passionate and empathic clearness
- Grounding gives your life's motivation someplace to arrive

❖ **The Mother Earth Association**

Even though you may feel the profundities of empathy for Mother Earth, being grounded does not work out efficiently for some Empaths. It is typically a procedure that must be educated. The brilliant incongruity for you could be, that regardless of your tendency towards the etheric domains, Mother Earth can be probably the best motivation. With the unlimited love of a genuine Mother, she can continually be close by, controlling you through this manifestation. You could not need to request a superior instructor. She addresses each individual, managing individuals with her antiquated shrewdness – all you have to do, is tune in.

Physical bodies are made of similar stuff that Mother Earth is. In this sense, individuals are all likewise offspring of the Earth (regardless of were known to humanity individuals feel they may have recently originated from). When you go out into nature, your vivacious recurrence starts to sway a similar recurrence as the Earth. This breathes life into you. It inhales everybody. It reestablishes and revives your vitality field. The reappearance of Mother Earth is amazingly mending. It is superbly designed for an ideal person.

❖ Getting to be Earthed

Studies have since found numerous methods for establishing. The best is regularly the most basic. Strolling in nature is fantastic, just as anything that encourages you to feel your bodies (that is, moving, development). You may find that being shoeless and touching the ground underneath your feet, in a split second revives your proclivity with the Earth. You may love to invest energy interfacing with anything familiar; communing with the trees; venerating untamed life; feeling the loftiness of the moving slopes and mountains.

Basic Hints for Establishing

- Acknowledge the significance of creating for yourself
- Commit to intentionally interfacing with nature at whatever point conceivable
- Use a reflection to enable you to ground and interface with Mother Earth

An Establishing Reflection

(While regarding your etheric nature)

Here is a straightforward technique for establishing any place you are – regardless of whether you are not out in nature. In this reflection, individuals additionally respect your unique ethereal quality as well. Preferably, locate a particular spot, associated with the Earth, in any case, if you cannot do that where you are at the time, envision your association with the ground.

Close your eyes and carry your attention to your association with Mother Earth.

Feel your vivacious 'roots' sink into the Earth, through your feet (if standing) or base chakra (whenever situated).

When you feel associated, get a feeling of Mother Earth unadulterated vitality ascending through you. Enable her spirit to stream up through your base, permitting the implantation of Earthly energies all through your body.

Feel the completion of your body as you feel grounded and associated with Mother Earth.

Allow your ethereal self to imbue into your body while keeping up your feeling of 'groundedness.'

Your ethereal and natural energies will start to move together and inject.

Carry on with your day feeling the completion of your groundedness. Feeling alert, associated, present, and mindful.

As an empath, this will keep up a feeling of yourself, without getting excessively lost in other individuals' energies.

Grounding Methods to Help You Center Yourself

These days, with the consistent assault of negative energies, it is a test for the Empath to remain grounded. Notwithstanding when staying at home, inside their asylums, their empathic radio wires are continually exchanged on, getting passionate vitality from the outside world. Along these lines, they effectively become depleted, overwhelmed by disregard, and diverted from their actual Empath jobs. To battle the consistent overpower, the cutting edge world engravings on an Empath, they have to secure themselves and work to remain grounded. Everybody is extraordinary, and what works for one Empath won't generally work for another. Be that as it may, it must be stated, the best type of assurance and approach to remain grounded for any Empath is to make a flexible, solid body, calm personality and solid vitality field. The following are probably the ideal approaches to accomplish this:

❖ Water

The body is comprised of seventy-five percent of water (somebody tissues have ninety-five percent), so it should not shock anyone this is far up there on oneself mending scale. Numerous individuals are unconscious of exactly how got dried out they are. Lacking supply of water makes issues with the working of the enthusiastic and physical bodies, influences general prosperity and quickens the maturing procedure. Water is a fantastic defender for the Empath, and they need loads of it, both inside and outside of their bodies. Most ought to drink in any event eight glasses of unadulterated water multi-day to recharge what the body usually loses through perspiring or pee. The heavier you are, the more water you need. There is an old religious saying that: 'Neatness is an underdog to righteousness.' Water washes something other than earth away; it can rinse the animated body and evident cynicism. If you are doubtful, when you get back home from a hard day at work attempt this: rather than going after the wine, bounce straight in the shower and see what an elevating and clearing impact it has. Or on the other hand when feeling genuinely fatigued beverage a half quart of lukewarm crisp water and perceive how it weakens the effect.

❖ Diet

Perhaps the best thing an empath can do, for establishing as well as for all-round equalization, is to incorporate all the more establishing, nutritious sustenance to their eating routine and evacuate any medication like nourishments. Wheat is one of the most exceedingly awful guilty parties. Stopping a long story: grain acts as a medication in the body. Empaths respond more to medicate like nourishments than those not of a delicate sort since they are profoundly receptive. High reactive are sensitive to various vibrations of vitality. Everything is vitality vibrating at multiple frequencies, and that incorporates sustenance, medications or liquor: the quicker the wave, the higher the recurrence. Empaths are contrarily influenced by anything of a low vibration. Most drugs and alcohol have low vibrational vitality and cut the Empath down quick. Wheat is not classed as a medication, even though it demonstrations like one, and in this manner conveys a similar mark. You may not eat bread but rather still devour loads of grain. It is covered up wherever for a reason it keeps everybody swallowing a more significant amount of it.

❖ Sea Salt

It is said that the 'father of drug,' Hippocrates, was among the first to find the, practically otherworldly, mending capacity of ocean salt, after seeing how rapidly seawater would recuperate injured anglers' hands. In addition to the fact that sea is salt an incredible restorative healer, it is additionally profoundly decontaminating. It can draw out and break up negative energies from the passionate and physical body. This is particularly useful if your day includes interfacing with others, where over and over again, you wind up picking their pushed or on edge vitality. Salt is not establishing, for the Empath, yet an immensely valuable vitality clearing apparatus.

How to Balance Your Energy

By adjusting your manly and female vitality, it works exceedingly well to help keep you grounded and enthusiastically steady.

❖ **Smudge**

Smearing helps clear your Empath vitality field of undesirable vitality and furthermore offers extraordinary insurance.

❖ **Exercise**

In the Western world, many go to practice for the advantages of weight reduction and a conditioned body. Be that as it may, the practice offers quite a lot more, particularly for the Empath. It discharges repressed feelings, evacuates debasements through perspiration, improves and elevates states of mind, stimulates, expands joy, assembles a ground-breaking vitality field, and is likewise establishing. With regards to exercise, do what you adore. If you do not care for guidelines, schedules, or set occasions at that point, go free-form. Make the principles yourself. Get the music turned up and move like no one is watching (which it is most likely best if nobody is while tossing shapes out). Move, stretch, and bounce your considerations away and get a sweat on.

❖ Meditation

This is an absolute necessity on the off chance that you have a bustling head with interminable personality gab and dreadful musings, as most Empaths do. A bustling disordered personality is un-establishing. Reflection encourages you to manage distressing circumstances and gives you a more precise understanding. There are numerous types of contemplation. It is only an instance of finding what suits you.

Example: The Jaguar Protection Meditation

When you need additional security studies to prescribe this reflection to approach the intensity of the puma to ensure you, you should utilize it when there is an excessive amount of antagonism coming at you excessively quick. The panther is a savage and patient gatekeeper who can ward off dangerous vitality and individuals. In a quiet, thoughtful state, from your most profound heart, approach the soul of the puma to secure you.

Feel her essence enter. At that point, envision this flawless, incredible animal watching your vitality field, encompassing it, ensuring you, keeping out interlopers or any negative powers that need to get past. Picture what the puma resembles: his or her lovely, wild, adoring eyes; smooth body; the agile, intentional way the panther moves. Have a sense of safety in the hover of this present puma's security. Give inward gratitude to the panther.

Realize that you can approach her at whatever point there is a need. Feel the intensity of that. As a touchy people, you should learn the way to manage tangible over-burden when an excess of is coming at you too rapidly. This can leave you depleted, on edge, discouraged, or debilitated. In the same way as other of us, you may feel there is no on or off switch for your compassion. This is not valid. When you think ensured and safe, you can assume responsibility for your sensitivities as opposed to feeling defrauded by them. To pick up a feeling of security, perceive some regular factors that add to sympathy over-burden. Start to recognize your triggers. At that point, you can rapidly act to cure a circumstance.

❖ Creativity

In a universe of standards and schedule, individuals only here and there persuade time to be imaginative; however, this is perhaps the most straightforward approaches to delight in the high vibe factor. When you feel great, you likewise feel grounded. When you make from your interests or interests, it has an inspiring impact on your mind, and when participating in something you adore, it wards off the brain from dull contemplations and sentiments which is an unquestionable requirement for all Empaths.

❖ Chakra Balancing

You have seven primary chakras which are a piece of your enthusiastic body. They are your focuses of otherworldly power that run the length of our organization, from the lower middle to the crown of the head. The chakras are spinning vortices of vitality lined up with the endocrine framework (organs which emit hormones, for example, adrenalin, cortisone and thyroxine into the body). At the point when any chakra is out of equalization, it can make infection (dis-ease) inside the body. Discovering approaches to adjust the chakras assists in being establishing just as being extraordinarily advantageous to the strength of the body and psyche.

❖ Yoga

Numerous individuals claim that yoga is not for them, yet it is the very individuals who get some distance from yoga who are the ones that need it most. Yoga is fantastically establishing. It takes a shot at the physical and lively bodies and serves everybody, regardless of what age or capacity. Yoga ought to be a staple in each individual's life. There is a yogic saying that: 'We are just as youthful as the spine is adaptable.' Because yoga attempts to make a supple spine, it could be classed as a mixture of youth. The very center of yoga is based on the breath. By taking all through stances, it stills and quiets the psyche, and makes a solid, supple body. Yoga is likewise classed as a moving reflection.

❖ Nature

Being outside in life has a recuperating and establishing impact on each Empath. As an Empath, on the off chance that you invest little energy in kind, you will battle to remain grounded or discover balance. If you work in a city, with no entrance to parkland, ensure you get out at ends of the week from autos and air contamination.

❖ Laughter

As adults' individuals invest a lot of energy being grave and genuine, and too brief period having a ton of fun (particularly in the present occasions). Do you recollect the last time you had an appropriate paunch snicker? Imprint this, 'You do not quit playing since you develop old; you develop old since you quit playing!' You hear youngsters snicker always. They do not have a clue how to pay attention to life; it is about play and fun, which helps keep them grounded. Everybody ought to endeavor to remain untainted. To see the world in surprise or more all have a ton of fun and chuckle. Anything that makes you giggle will make your spirits take off. It truly is a treatment.

❖ Crystals

The mending intensity of precious stones has for some time been known in various societies, from Atlantis to old Egypt. It is accepted that the people of yore had costly stone chambers they used to mend physical, profound or lively infirmities. Precious stones can be utilized related to the chakras to help balance them and expel blockages. Detecting their normal mending vibration, many Empaths are instinctually attracted to precious gems for their establishment and defensive capacities.

❖ Essential Oils

As with gems, the mending intensity of first fuels has been known through the ages. It is through the olfactory faculties that a large number of the advantages of essential oils are gotten. There is an organic oil to suit each Empath for either: assurance, establishing, re-adjusting, unwinding, and that's only the tip of the iceberg.

❖ Earthing

Even though this is a late expansion to the rundown, it is one of the most useful with regards to Empath establishing. Earthing includes setting exposed feet on characteristic earth or strolling shoeless! You may frequently underestimate the remarkable recuperating intensity of Mother Earth yet associating with her is perhaps the simplest ways for the Empath to discover balance. Blocking out the unwanted emotions of others

So how would you quit engrossing other individuals' vitality? How might you disperse negative life?

❖ **Discover Your Unresolved Issues**

You do not need to concentrate on what other individuals are doing. You need to focus on things that you need to fix inside yourself that other individuals feature in specific circumstances and conditions you face throughout everyday life. What happens when you get into a discussion with somebody, and you feel annoyed? They have hit a nerve which makes you need to lash out at them.

What have they done? They have gone about as an impetus to stir the dormant beast. It could have been some other individual in some other area. Indeed, you find that it is not so much the other individual as it is your uncertain issues. What is going to enable you to quit retaining other individuals' vitality, is to begin investigating those issues. Many individuals live from the outside in, so other individuals become their issues. In any case, when you start to live from the back to front, that is the point at which you begin increasing more exceptional lucidity. For some individuals, it is challenging to discuss uncertain issues since they would prefer not to assume liability. Everyone will be your concern until you begin investigating yourself and begin fixing your unpredictable problems, and start recuperating wounds to end up the total, and start reintegrating the divided pieces of yourself to turn into your most prominent adaptation.

❖ Express Yourself 100%

Convey what needs be without blame. What happens when somebody converses with you for quite a long time, and you need to state something; however, you would prefer not to be discourteous? You remain quiet. You become a wipe. You are presently retaining the majority of their vitality. By acting like this, you disregard your actual validness, and you quit liking yourself. In any case, when you can genuinely express 100% and expel blame from the condition, you build up a more noteworthy straightforwardness which will enable you to turn into your most remarkable form. Commonly the motivation behind why such a large number of individuals do not express how they truly feel is because they have been informed that their actual emotions do not make a difference. Growing up, individuals chipped away at the reward and discipline standards. On the off chance that you did things right, or regardless of whether you did what your folks needed, you would be compensated irrespective of whether you did not generally feel where it counts this is the thing that you needed to do. Everybody has a ton of quelled feelings.

Concealment is wretchedness, and once you can communicate 100%, you begin to decrease tension.

❖ You Are Not Responsible for Others

You have no power over how other individuals react to you, how they act to you, and how they feel towards you. In doing as such, you free yourself by the weight of conveying another person's conduct on your shoulders. Hence, you do not assimilate other individuals' vitality. It is not all that much.

❖ Find Your Environment

It is not about the external condition. It is mainly about the internal state. It is never where you are at, and it is the place you believe you are at. For what reason is nature so significant? The earth modifies an individual's DNA; however, correctly, it is your recognition that adjusts your DNA. The ground changes your state of mind. How you see yourself oversees what you become. You need to assume 100% liability for where you place yourself. Like never before, when you put yourself in a domain which supplements your vitality, the enchantment begins to occur. What you see with your eyes and what you have within yourself turns into an impression of how you feel. When you encapsulate congruity, you quit engrossing other individuals' vitality, and you begin engraving your energy on your general surroundings.

❖ Let Go of the Need to Be Validated

You need not bother with outer approval. You need support. Commonly along with your life, you look for outside endorsement, which is the reason you begin retaining other individuals' vitality. When you cherish yourself 100%, when you confide in yourself 100%, when you believe in yourself 100%, you start to approve yourself. To quit retaining other individuals' vitality, you need to remain consistent with yourself 100% and enable your legitimacy to thrive and bloom without other individuals' sentiments. Indeed, what others need to state does make a difference, and yet you should wind up mindful of how you respond to other individuals' perspectives. When you begin making a move and stay concentrated on your action; regardless of whether individuals state "frightful" things about you or your work, you are not in any case concerned. Why? Since you cherish what you are doing. The world is about the difference. Differentiation is basic. When you give up to distinction and comprehend that we need grating, you additionally understand that there are continually going to be individuals that will drive you up to the wall, except if you begin changing your point of view and know that these individuals are likewise serving a job on the planet. Remind yourself to associate with the individuals who remind you what your identity is. This encourages you to quit engrossing destructive vitality and to begin retaining progressively positive dynamism.

❖ The Invitation

No one can enter your domain without a welcome. You draw in everyone into your life. You are deliberately or unknowingly welcoming individuals into your life, and not consuming other individuals' vitality is to help yourself to remember this every day. You have the power inside to pick whether you need to welcome someone in particular in your sanctuary, which is basically inside yourself.

❖ Do Not Pay Attention

When you get up in the first part of the day, you have so much vitality. For the day you utilize that vitality by offering it to individuals and things around you, until the part of the bargain where it is not much, and you feel tired, and you rest once more. What you need to comprehend is that a few people fill you with vitality and a few people channel you of life. The individuals that direct you of energy are likewise called "vitality vampires." They can be your partners, your companions, or even close relatives. A vitality vampire is somebody who uses your vitality to endure. One of the significant activities is to truly distinguish whether they are transitory vitality vampires or characteristically vitality vampires.

A transitory vitality vampire is somebody who is experiencing a troublesome time in his life or somebody in the family has kicked the bucket, and for a couple of months, they are enthusiastically depleting. Be that as it may, on the off chance that somebody is intrinsically a vitality vampire, at that point, it is incredibly critical to observe that. That is a character attribute that won't change at any point shortly except if they are effectively dealing with it. Most vitality vampires would prefer not to take a shot at themselves at any rate.

Something to do now is to recognize these individuals. One approach to do it, is by asking yourself after you have invested energy with somebody, "Do I feel elevated, or do I feel depleted?" You would prefer not to feel depleted. You need to dodge those individuals. You have buckled down to inspire yourself and be a superior person. For what reason would you permit another person to come and deplete you? There is no motivation to feel regretful about it. Regardless of whether they are a dear companion or a relative, it is alright too, in the end, leave them since what you are doing is taking care of yourself. By elevating yourself, you inspire everybody around you. If you enable someone to pull you down, at that point, you are completing damage to all your different companions and all your other relatives.

By enabling one individual to pull you down, you are not allowing you to inspire the different loved ones that are around you who could be elevated by your quality. When you give somebody consideration, you are giving them vitality. You need to change your concentration to quit retaining other individuals' life. Whatever you center around develops. Is it accurate to say that you are concentrating on what you need, or would you say you are focused on what you dread? You make your existence dependent on considerations and emotions. You need to recall how to shield yourself from hurtful vitality. Make sure to have some good times and grin.

Chapter 12: Empathy and the World

From the news reports and things happening in our neighborhoods, anyone can see that humans are very capable of perpetrating unimaginable cruelty. The vicious nature of human beings knows no bounds; therefore, people result to insulting, bullying, criticizing, torturing, and even killing one another. However, if you ask the perpetrators of this horrible behavior if they would like the same things brought up them, they would say no. And yet, the evil deeds continue to happen every day. The disregard for other people and selfishness seems to be growing.

As conventional healers, empaths can sweep and peruse the vitality of the individuals, places, and articles around them. What's more, as the chakra outline features, the heart chakra is in charge of sentiments of adoration, pardoning, empathy, and confidence. Not at all like the individuals who are overwhelmingly aloof, empaths channel their energies through the heart chakra. They likewise have an unprecedented capacity to effectively direct the majority of the chakras, making them both empathic and mystic, which clarifies why one of the main characteristics of an empath is their inborn capacity to know specific things without being told. The adoration, association, and sympathy empaths radiate are the attributes the world needs increasingly at this moment. Since empaths have elevated affectability and sympathy, they make the best healers and can all the more likely help other people manage the inside feelings or torment they cannot process.

To make matter worse, people continually justify their wrongdoings based on their own small perception of the world without stopping to realize that there could be something wrong with the way they approach life. One of the main causes of the current societal distress is the diminishment of empathy.
In trying times, it is very essential that one considers the feelings of the people around him/her.

Everyone is in their own bubble with unique perspectives on the world, and as such, it is important that every person understands the experiences of the other person. This understanding will help in personal development. Trying to understand the experiences and feelings of the other person is what we have referred to as empathy. Of course, there are those natural reflexes that occur subconsciously without even thinking such as wincing when someone else gets hurt. In order to be truly empathetic, one must actively consider the needs and feelings of other people.

In real life, empathy is one of the essential skills one can apply and practice. Application of empathy in real-life situations will help a person succeed personally and professionally. The more one practices empathy constructively, the higher the levels of happiness. As exhausting as empathy can become for anyone, it has been identified as one of the primary drivers of success and good fortune. Everybody should explicitly work towards enhancing their ability to empathize with other people.

There is a wide variety of reasons why one should practice empathy in real life:

1. With empathy, one is in a better position to treat the people he/she cares about in a better way; more like he/she would want to be treated.
2. Empathy enables one to understand the needs of the people around him/her more clearly.
3. Empathy enables one to understand the perception he/she creates in other people with words and actions.
4. There is a lot of communication done in nonverbal ways. Empathy enables one to understand the non-verbalized parts of communication.
5. In work situations, the person using empathy will understand the customers, work colleagues, and bosses in a better way.
6. Empathy also enhances one's ability to predict and interpret the actions and reactions of people.
7. Once an individual learns how to use empathy, he/she is in a better position to influence and motivate the other people.

8. It will be easier to convince others about a particular viewpoint.

9. Empathy enables one to experience the world on a higher resolution; this is as a result of perceiving the world from a personal angle and the presumptions of other people.

10. Applying empathy in real life also enables one to deal with the negative energies of other people because he/she understands their fears and motives. Empathy enables one to calm down in a difficult situation, and it reminds one to accept things as they are.

11. The overall benefit of applying empathy in real life is that one becomes a better friend, a better follower, and a better leader.

As mentioned earlier, empathy can be a reflex action, but to be empathetic in this world, one must use critical thinking to understand, interpret and offer a solution to the challenges. In order to effectively apply empathy in real life, there are some practices that an empath should use to develop the gift.

Firstly, **Listen.**

Pay a lot of attention when people are speaking to you and to each other. Conversations tend to initiate a back and forth rhythm of speaking, especially when it is about heated topics. One party will start a point even before the other person gets to an end. You will also notice that you are prone to the same habit whereby you already decide what to say next even before the other person has completed his/her point. You feel that your point is too hot and too right to wait. It burns your throat and mind, waiting to be heard.

In conversations, it is important to slow down and wait for the other person to finish even before you can start on your opinion. Force yourself to understand the words you hear without rushing. Do not just consider the conversation and the fact that you want to prove a point; instead, consider the motivation that is behind the words of the speaker. Before jumping to conclusions, consider the experiences that might have forced the person to argue from a particular point of view.

Take time before responding and use visuals and sounds such as 'oh,' 'ah' and 'ya?' to indicate participation. Ask follow-up questions to facilitate a better understanding of the intentions of speakers. Make sure you know their true feelings before responding with a personal opinion. Such conversations will take a longer time because you have to focus on the speaker before you can think of an appropriate answer.

Secondly, **Watch and Wonder.**

In the current world, most of us have developed the habit of staring at the cellphones during every other free minute. While we are waiting for the bus, we are on social media. While we wait for the coffee to be served, we are reading articles online. While we are stuck in the traffic jam, we chat with people who are miles away using the cellphones. Consequently, we miss most of the things taking place around us. It is important that we put the phones and other devices down for a while and observe the people around us. Not that reading the news articles is a bad practice, but it is better if we can also read the faces and expressions of other people. Look at people and try to imagine what they are feeling the things they might be going through, and their next move. This watching and wondering bring about care. You will start feeling for the people around you and applying empathy.

Thirdly, **Know Your Enemies.**

In this context, the word enemy might appear as an exaggeration. However, the application of empathy in real life needs a little more than ordinary. Think of someone with whom you have an ongoing dispute or a tense situation; it can be a coworker who is always criticizing your work and giving you opinions on how it should be done or a family member you are in constant loggerheads with for some reason or the other. Whoever it is, you have already come to the conclusion that they are wrong and you are right. In fact, it gets to a point where you disagree regardless of the topic just because you have to be on opposite sides.

Applying empathy means that you can view the entire situation from the point of view of the other person. Empathy makes one realize that the other person is not selfish or evil. In fact, the person might not be wrong about the things he/she says. In most cases, the problem is more of a basic philosophical difference rather than the specific conflict occurring at the moment.

With empathy, one can understand the following aspects; what causes the other person to feel tenses thus making it hard to reason together? How does the person feel in the event of the disagreement? How does holding the argument exacerbate the fears and tension rather than calming them? What valid opinions does the person make for a particular situation? What are the intentions of the person and are they positive or negative? What is the idea behind the opinions and what motivates it? Is the conflict more important than the idea behind the differing opinions or is the situation worth of compromise?

Once one gathers the answers to these questions, the chances are that the level of anxiety and frustration in life will reduce. In fact, understanding the viewpoints of different people will help one to overcome some of the stressful interpersonal situations. This exercise might sound easy, but it takes practice to make it work.

Choose the Other Side

Empathy can empower a person to be able to see things from the perspective of a third person. Generally, it is hard for a person to take the same side as his/her enemy, and it requires a lot of discipline for one to understand another while thinking about personal emotions and stress. It is important to suspend personal judgment for a while.

Summarily, in order to use empathy effectively in real life, one should consider the following:

1. Put aside personal viewpoints and look at things from other people's perspective. When one does this, he/she realizes that other people are not just being stubborn, unkind, or evil. They just react to issues depending on the knowledge they have.

2. Validate the perspectives of other people. Once you understand why a person is supporting what he/she believes in, acknowledge it. Keep in mind that acknowledgment is not the same as agreeing with a different opinion. It is only accepting that different people have varying opinions for various reasons and they have a good course for holding their opinion.

3. Examine your attitude. Empathy should enable one to check their priorities. Is it more important for you to get

your way, win, or be right? Or do you prefer finding a solution, accepting others, and building relationships? Without an open attitude and mind, you will lack enough room for empathy.

4. Listen – As seen earlier in the topic, it is important to listen to the entire message before giving an opinion. The other person will be communicating both verbally and non-verbally; therefore, listen with your ears, eyes, instincts, and heart. The ears will detect the tone that is being used, the eyes will spot the body language, the instinct will sense when a person is not saying what they mean, and the heart will spot what the other person feels.

5. Ask the other person what he/she would do. When you are in doubt, it is okay to ask the other person about their position. Although most people avoid asking direct questions, it is probably the most effective way of understanding the stand of others. It is okay to ask and remember that figuring it out on your own does not give you extra points. The best part of asking is that you are more likely to get it right. For instance, it would be better if a boss asks the employees what an ideal holiday gift would be rather than giving them all turkey vouchers without checking if they enjoy cooking.

Why Is It Important to Apply Empathy in Real Life?

Without empathy, people would go about their lives without considering the feelings and thoughts of other people. Every person has differing perspectives on life; therefore, if we did not have something that made us accommodate each other, life would be very complicated. We all experience moods, joy, sadness, pain hurt et cetera, and if we focus only on the things happening in our lives, we will limit our capabilities. It is easy to jump into conclusions if we do not take a moment to truly understand what the other people stand for. Lack of empathy normally leads to bad feelings, misunderstandings, poor morale, conflict, and even divorce.

When one uses empathy in real life to understand why a person is angry, or a child is throwing a tantrum, he/she might learn about things in their lives that trigger the behavior. For example, one might find that something happened at home, thus pushing the angry person to act out or that the child did not have a meal in the morning thus they are not okay.

Empathy enables one to ask questions about the situation or behavior of another person before taking a defensive stance or reacting to some emotions. There may still be the need for disciplinary action, but one should use empathy first. Empathy makes a person feel valued and understood even if they are punished for the wrong deeds, and as such, they will accept responsibility for their action. Empathy is currently the missing link in schools, families, workplaces, and the world at large.

There are a few misunderstandings that arise when one is applying empathy in real life. Some people believe that being empathetic involves agreeing with the opinion of everybody else. That is wrong and will only lead to exhaustion. Understand the perceptions of the other person, acknowledge them but you do not have to sing along every tune.

Other people believe that being empathetic involves doing what everyone else wants or doing anything to make others happy. That is wrong. You are not obligated to please everyone; you do not have to cooperate in every other situation. Just because you fail to accommodate every other matter does not mean that you are evil. The world is complicated; therefore, use empathy but do not agree with everything.

Empathy does not mean being there for someone for a lifetime. After listening to a person and offering a solution, you do not have to always be there for them, you have other tasks to accomplish and if you feel that the person is just using you, walk away. Empathy does not mean you should have no ego or intention. Once you assist someone, allow your ego to help you walk away or change the discussion.

Applying empathy in real life can be challenging therefore, there are investments that one needs to make and they include time, patience and proactivity.

1. Time

   It takes some time for one to listen to others, pay attention and not jump into conclusions. Coming up with good solutions also takes time. In most cases, we want to arrive at an answer very first without taking the time to understand; this only leads to more problems. Empathy is like watching sand draining in an hourglass; it takes time, but not that much time, and it is very satisfying.

2. Patience

   Empathy does not only take time; it requires a lot of patience. Paying attention to someone, listening to everything they are saying, and selecting a comprehensive solution takes a lot more than just jumping into conclusions, listing arguments and repeating an opinion. Normally people fail to give the patience and attention required when making conversations; therefore, it becomes harder than it should be.

3. It takes proactivity

   Some people think that empathy should only be given when both parties have something to gain. In the real sense, we should show empathy even to people who show no sign of understanding our perspectives and opinions. This can be very frustrating, and one might find it very unfair, but empathy begins with you. It will not work if both of you wait on each other to start the conversation.

4. Be the role model, set the example, be a good listener and do not talk until the other person is done. Understand the opinions of other people but remember you do not have to agree with them. Being empathetic can be a tough challenge but still, there are many people that practice it. Apply empathy every day and enjoy the benefits.

Conclusion

Thank for making it through to the end of *Empath Survival Guide*, let us hope it was informative and able to provide you with all of the tools you need to achieve your goals whatever they may be.

The next steps will vary from one individual to the next. You may want to do further reading on the science of empathy, or the insights that the field of clinical psychology can offer. Working with a therapist or counselor can be enormously helpful, allowing you to more quickly process and release emotions that haven't originated within you. If you found the chapter on energy healing to be particularly compelling, you might instead choose to schedule a reiki initiation with a master, or look for a school of modern mysteries to provide further guidance on advanced spiritual practice. It is important for empaths with any degree of power to continually monitor their emotional balance, purge negativity, replenish energy, and seek higher clarity and truth. Embrace these practices as part of a lifelong journey and recognize that even if you ascend to the level of a spiritual teacher or guide for others, there will always be more to learn.

No matter how empowered one may become, and regardless of how well one has honed their empathic power, it is important to embrace humility, keep the mind open to unexpected possibilities. The self-righteous empath who develops a hermetic view of the world, unwilling to entertain ideas that do not strongly resonate with their interior knowledge, is likely to be deeply discontented or anxious, and struggle with communication and loving relationships, as others will perceive them to be arrogant and standoffish.

This type of attitude is also likely to weaken your empathic powers. Truth is multifaceted and always changing. In order to grasp even a sliver of it, the empath must maintain a balanced connection between their interior and exterior worlds. Shutting either out, or favoring one over the other, will eventually lead the empath to receive misleading messages, or lead them to misinterpret messages that would otherwise be clear and easy to decipher. Empaths are privy to knowledge that often goes unseen, unheard, unacknowledged, but from time to time, they can be flat out wrong--especially if the information they're receiving from the exterior world is limited, it can be skewed to support an incomplete hypothesis.

It can also be incredibly healing and inspiring to open your eyes to all the empathic power around you, much of which is still dormant, not yet fully realized or understood. Use the metrics outlined in the second and third chapter of this book and ask yourself if you might know other empaths who haven't awakened their sensitive powers. Or perhaps you know some self-aware empaths that you couldn't recognize as such before now. Whatever the case, you can benefit immensely from expanding your empathic support system. Since empaths are often able to see everything clearly except them; let your fellow empaths be a metaphysical mirror. Teach each other, trust each other; heal each other, replenish and amplify each other's energies. You may discover an echelon of both outward love and self-love that you never knew existed before.

Finally, if you found this book beneficial in any way, a review on Amazon is always welcome!

Empath Healing

How to Become a Healer and Avoid Narcissistic Abuse. The Guide to Develop your Powerful Gift for Highly Sensitive People. Emotion Healing Solutions

Introduction

Pain is a part of our lives now. It knows no boundaries. Our lives have been saturated with pain, stress, anxiety, and grief so much that we feel the emotions burdening our chests, making strain in our souls. There is hardly anyone nowadays who isn't burdened with problems. It causes us brevity of breath and makes us jump when we focus on it.

This is the thing that it feels like to live through the worldwide change of humankind in the mid-21st century. Be it climate change, family problems, workplace issues, they are deliberations, each one of them.

Yet, the sentiment of searching for peace and comfort has become increasingly futile with the passing time. No one seems to be happy. Don't our hearts bleed when we see our near and dear ones in pain? Don't we feel like extending our hand, pulling them into a hug and tell them that everything will be fine? These things are instinctive. They are physical and present. They are going on this moment and you can feel it in your bones, yet it is equally tough to find someone to lean upon when the world is slowly becoming desensitized to the emotions. Feeling sympathy is common, while empathetic gestures are increasingly becoming uncommon.

Social developments have led to the mechanization of everything, even emotions. Everything is guarded, a lie that we tell ourselves and others. For example, take social media-- we scroll and scroll, like and comment on cute videos and emotional stories of struggling human beings. However, how many of us would reach out to others to help those who are in distress? This is the moment when we have to realize that humanity needs to be awakened again. The emotions which we have been suppressing to fit into the crowd need to burn with passion again. It is a rallying call for us to decorate their defensive layer, get our weapons, and stand up to the foe at their entryway. Our enemy is none other than our insensitivity. It needs to be taken care of. The world needs healing; it needs the touch of love and genuine empathy. It needs healers.

Unfortunately misinformed in this methodology is the inability to perceive that what the world needs now, like never before, is healing. We have long overlooked our inner feelings and while doing this we take pride in the fact that we are moving away from what is significant. Not only us; everyone around us is going through the same painful situations. There is not a bleak of hope and our existence has been put for questioning. The present is so shaky that the future cannot find a ground to build itself. Giving way to emotions and helping others is seen as a weakness. It is a misinformed fact. Those who bare their souls are and would be the one to bring stability in the chaotic environment which we are living in.

These people are called healers.

The world needs healers and we continue encircling the procedure of social change as a progression of challenges. The polarization of emotions fused with material gains is creating driving a wedge among people who are supposed to love and care for each other.

Frantically required right currently is to look in reverse in time and truly comprehend the main drivers of our misfortunes. These issues emerged in the past when our predecessors were in unfortunate associations with our environment, other individuals, and ourselves. These problems are associated with each other. They are foundational. They occurred on our watch since we aggregately feel — someplace somewhere inside — this is actually what we merit. Our answers keep on being piecemeal on the grounds that every one of us, in manners we are too hesitant to even think about admitting, is broken and doesn't have the foggiest idea how to assemble the pieces back once more.

To fix things, we do not need fights and disputes. We need to look beyond our pigeonhole and look for solutions in the astral world. Believe it or not- this is the work for healers. While doctors, scientists, and humanitarians along with others are contributing to their part, sometimes it pays to widen our thoughts and beliefs and act upon them.

It might sound curious to state that affection is the appropriate response; however, it happens to be valid.

We need stalwart love, purifying and transformative love. We have to begin accepting that we are deserving of adoration with the goal that we can fabricate a world together that conveys it for us and who and what is to come.

The problem is that we see problems as a bystander. That needs to be changed. We cannot truly understand someone's issues without opening our emotional channels and absorbing what they are feeling. We can only mend our planet by perceiving that we are an integral part of it. We cure our wrecked lives and issues by a get-together in networks and building up solid social standards for initiative and portrayal. Our financial issues can only be solved by pulling back our help from the narcissists and putting rather in important connections among individuals who help us feel supported inside.

This is the thing that has been going on in a million little pockets of mankind all through the most recent fifty years.

We don't need to hang tight for it to start. It is completely in the procedure and developing day by day. All around the globe there are individuals framing agreeable organizations, putting resources into neighborhood networks, shaping ideological groups around life and mending (to supplant those of war, victory, and passing), making new advances that improve well-being and essentialness, making it simpler to associate with others in our very own networks and traversing the globe.

Individuals share these invigorating qualities at present. You are not the only one. There is power in numbers. The more insensitive we will be, the more the world around us will crumble as there is no one to take care of anyone. We are an army and our numbers develop every day. We have to tap into that power and do our best to make this world a better place.

However, there is much work to do and time is of the substance. Be a healer in your little pocket of this incredibly vast world. Hold firm to the sentiments of appreciation and to an option that is bigger than yourself and you will most likely think back on this progress with satisfaction and a warm heart. Give the individuals who a chance to react in dread and little mindedness live with their disgrace numerous decades from now, there will be some among us whom we won't most likely help. Discover comfort realizing that you opened your heart when the living things of this world called out in agony. What's more, you felt a similar hurt in yourself, constrained in this manner to sustain and recuperate.

However, it's not easy. Empaths are seen as weak. If you are an Empath, then you will probably be the worst sufferer as others will misuse your kindness and care. Since you understand the emotions of everyone around, you might encounter someone who will bully you, and you will almost always forgive them as it's not in your nature to hold grudges. Yes, you might end up facing abuse from a narcissist.

Here in this book, you will get to know more about Empath Healing, abilities, strengths, weaknesses, and much more. This information is essential for us to embrace our true, emotional selves as that would allow clearing our biases and becoming better human beings in the process. Feeling our inner love and those of others isn't a weakness. It will build up this world. In the time when empathy is buried deep inside somewhere and shallowness is riding with its head high, healers can be the saviors. If you feel you are the one, then do not hesitate to take charge. Do not be afraid to be charitable when it comes to servicing the humankind because this is precisely what we need now. And you need to protect yourself as well because without protecting yourself you cannot help others. It is essential to take a stand for yourself or else it will be too late-- for you and the world.

Chapter 1: <u>What is Empathy?</u>

To understand empathy, you need to go through the definition of empathy in detail, as described by different disciplines. This is the moment when you can seek a helping hand to protect yourself from the abuse you are encountering.

The word "empathy" appeared about a century prior in the form of a German term Einfühlung, it's meaning signifying "feeling-in." English-talking analysts proposed a bunch of different interpretations of the word, including "liveliness," play," compassion," and "similarity." Significantly, in 1908, two clinicians from Cornell and the University of Cambridge recommended "empathy" for the German word, drawing on the Greek "em" for "in" and "sentiment" for "feeling," and it took a flight since then.

At the time the term was new, and empathy was not fundamentally a way to feel someone else's feelings, yet the exceptionally opposite. The meaning was extremely different as compared to the way we use it today. Earlier, to have compassion meant to breathe life into an item, or to extend one's own envisioned sentiments onto the world. This is similar to the "white man's burden" when the west needed to enlighten other cultures. The absolute most punctual brain research investigates compassion concentrated on "kinaesthetic empathy," a substantial inclination or development that created a feeling of converging with an article. Expressions of the human experience pundits of the 1920s asserted that with compassion, a group of spectators individuals could feel as though they were completing the conceptual developments of the defined definition of empathy.

By mid-century, the definition of empathy started to change as certain therapists directed their concentration toward the study of social relations. In 1948, the test analyst Rosalind Dymond Cartwright, in a joint effort with her humanist guide, Leonard Cottrell, directed a portion of the principal tests estimating relational empathy. All the while, she purposely dismissed empathy's initial importance of inventive projection and rather underscored relational association as the center of the idea.

In the whirlwind of trial investigations of empathy that pursued, therapists started to separate "genuine" empathy, characterized as the exact examination of another's musings or sentiments, from what they called "projection" The term further experienced a change. Empathy was then described as the capacity to value the other individual's emotions without yourself ending up so sincerely included that your judgment is influenced. This definition has gained wide usage all around the world.

In a previous couple of decades, intrigue for empathy has spread to primatology and neuroscience as well. Important research also contributed to the study and understanding of empathy. During the 1990s, neuroscientists conducting research on monkeys found mirror neurons, cells in the creatures' cerebrums that fired when a monkey moved. The most important part was that they reacted when the monkey saw another make a similar action or gesture. The disclosure of mirror neurons prodded a rush of examination into empathy and brain action that immediately stretched out to people also. Other late investigations have additionally enlarged compassion's venture into fields like financial aspects and writing, finding that riches variations debilitate empathic reaction and that perusing fiction can improve it.

Understanding Empathy

The expression "empathy" is utilized to depict a wide scope of feelings. Psychologists and researchers, for the most part, characterize empathy as the capacity to detect other individuals' feelings, combined with the capacity to envision what another person may think or feel. It additionally is the capacity to feel and share someone else's feelings. Some accept that compassion includes the capacity to coordinate another's feelings, while others accept that sympathy includes being kind toward another person.

The most important part is to make a rational decision based on what the empath is feeling for others without being emotionally affected by it.

Contemporary analysts regularly separate between two kinds of empathy. One is

"full of feeling empathy" alludes to the sensations and sentiments we get because of others' feelings. This type of empathy can incorporate understanding what another individual is feeling, or simply feeling pushed when we recognize another's dread or nervousness. "Psychological empathy," once in a while called "point of view taking," alludes to our capacity to distinguish and comprehend other individuals' feelings. Studies propose that individuals with chemical imbalance range issue experience serious difficulties identifying. Martin Hoffman is an analyst who concentrated on the improvement of compassion. As per Hoffman, everybody is brought into the world with the ability of inclination empathy.

Empathy definitions envelop a wide scope of emotional states, including thinking about other individuals and wanting to support them; encountering feelings that match someone else's feelings; observing what someone else is thinking or feeling; and making less particular the contrasts between oneself and the other. It can likewise be comprehended as having the separateness of characterizing oneself and another a blur.

Empathy supposedly has profound roots in our mind and body. The same case goes with our evolutionary history. Basic types of empathy have been seen in our primate relatives and other animals such as dogs. Empathy has been associated with two zones in our cerebrum. Researchers have found that a few fragments of empathy can be safely linked to mirror neurons. Mirror neurons are the cells in the mind that start firing when we watch another person play out an activity in the same way as we do, that they would fire on the off chance that we played out that activity ourselves. Also, recent research has additionally linked heredity to empathy; however, studies recommend that individuals can improve or restrain their normal empathetic abilities.

Having empathy doesn't really mean we will need to help anyone anytime; however, it's frequently a crucial initial move toward spreading love and comfort to help ease those who are in distress, pain or misfortune.

Types of Empathy

As indicated by analyst and pioneer in the field of emotions, Paul Ekman, Ph.D., three particular sorts of empathy have been recognized:

Subjective Empathy: Also called "point of view taking," psychological empathy is the capacity to comprehend and foresee the emotions and contemplations of others by envisioning one's self in their circumstance.

Emotional Empathy: Closely identified with psychological empathy, emotional empathy is the capacity to really feel what someone else feels or if nothing else, feel feelings like theirs. In this case, there is in every case some degree of shared sentiments. This trait can be an attribute among people who are diagnosed with mental disorders, such as Asperger's Syndrome.

Compassionate or Humane Empathy: Driven by their profound comprehension of the other individual's emotions dependent on shared encounters, mercifully empathic individuals endeavor genuine endeavors to help.

Is Empathy Sympathy?

Sympathy and empathy are terms related to compassion. Definitions have changed over the course of years. Empathy is frequently characterized as a feeling we feel when others are out of luck, which persuades us to support them. Sympathy is a sentiment of consideration and concern for somebody out of luck. Some incorporate into empathy as empathic concern, a sentiment of worry for another, where a few researchers incorporate the desire to see them happier.

Compassion is often unintentionally equated with pity. Pity is an inclination that one feels towards others that may be in a tough situation or needing assistance as they can't fix their issues themselves, regularly portrayed as feeling bad for somebody.

Since compassion means understanding the emotional conditions of other individuals, the manner in which it is portrayed is gotten from the manner in which feelings themselves are described. In the event that, for instance, feelings are taken to be midway portrayed by real sentiments, at that point getting a handle on the real sentiments of another will be vital to empathy. Then again, if feelings are all the more midway portrayed by a blend of convictions and want, at that point getting a handle on these convictions and wants will be increasingly basic to empathy. The capacity to envision yourself as someone else is a refined creative procedure, which a lot of us confuse with the feelings of pity. Be that as it may, the fundamental ability to perceive feelings is presumably innate and might be accomplished unknowingly. However, it tends to be trained and accomplished with different degrees of force or precision.

Sympathy fundamentally has a "pretty much" quality. The worldview instance of an empathic connection, in any case, includes an individual conveying a precise acknowledgment of the criticality of someone else's progressing purposeful activities, related emotional states, and individual attributes in a way that the perceived individual can bear that. Acknowledgments that are both exact and middle of the road are focal highlights of empathy.

The human ability to perceive the substantial sentiments of another is identified with one's imitative limits and is by all accounts grounded in an intrinsic ability to relate the real developments and outward appearances one finds in another with the proprioceptive sentiments of creating those comparing developments or articulations oneself. Humans appear to make the equivalent quick association between the manner of speaking and other vocal articulations and internal inclination.

In Positive Psychology, sympathy has likewise been contrasted and charitableness and self-love. Selflessness is conduct that is planned for profiting someone else, while conceit is a conduct that is carried on for individual addition. Here and there, when somebody is feeling sympathetic towards someone else, demonstrations of selflessness happen. Notwithstanding, many inquiries whether these demonstrations of benevolence are roused by boastful increases. As per constructive analysts, individuals can be sufficiently moved by their emotions to be altruistic, and there are other people who think about inappropriate good points of view and having sympathy can prompt polarization, lead to viciousness and may cause 25066conduct seeing someone.

For example, you can feel pity for a beggar and even give them some money. But that's it. Going beyond "just giving money" and helping other people out of their miserable state is what empathy embodies. Teaching underprivileged children with a vision to make their future bright is empathy. Just giving attendance in the classroom and barely teaching is not. If someone is distraught or sick, staging an intervention is empathy, feeling pity is not. There are so many examples which can be given. Our world is full of them.

Here, what is important is to truly feel and do the needful action which not only gives you solace but benefits others as well. All of us watch videos where someone helped an animal out and rehabilitated them. Animal rescuers are the best example of empaths. Animals cannot pay anyone back in cash but in kind. Rescuing them is a shining indication of what empathy should look like. Those who go beyond wanting material benefits for themselves and help others genuinely are the pioneers of kindness which our world needs so critically now.

Chapter 2: Empathy Theories Straight from the Scientific Arena

A lot of research has been conducted on empathy. Mostly, the neuroscience and human's primitive social behaviors have been taken into consideration to understand the nuances of empathy. The theories mentioned below are results of several years of hard work scientists have invested in contemplating the sensitive side of human beings, and why some humans are more sensitive and receptive to others.

Hoffman's on empathy through the twentieth century is explained well in the developmental by therapist Martin L. Hoffman (2000), whose hypothesis of moral improvement has given the most exhaustive perspective on empathy. Hoffman mainly focuses on empathic trouble in his works. His hypothesis incorporates five ways to clarify how one becomes bothered when watching another person's trouble. The five methods are mimicry, classical conditioning, direct association, mediated affiliation, and role-taking. In Hoffman's (2000) initial three instruments, the eyewitness sees the subject's emotional experience legitimately. These instruments are viewed as crude, programmed, and automatic.

Mimicry. Empathizing through mimicry is a two-way process. To begin with, the onlooker naturally observes the objective's emotional facial, postural, or vocal articulations. Second, input from the imitated expressions causes the related emotional response in the eyewitness. For instance, if someone was bitten by a stray dog, you will unconsciously imitate their emotions. Your very own feeling of dread makes you feel frightened as well. This impersonation procedure of mimicry is the thing that Hatfield, Cacioppo, and Rapson (1994) called it primitive emotional contagion.

Classical conditioning. Classical conditioning of emotions starts with circumstances that make us feel emotional regardless of whether we have never experienced them. For instance, you may feel frightened when the dog bites you. After you experience the inherently emotion-inducing circumstance, we discover that specific signals are an indication that it is going to happen once more. Therefore, we begin to feel anxious when we see those dogs. You may discover that those dogs snarl before they run after you to bite; thus you start to feel terrified when you hear a dog snarl. In the language of classical conditioning, the dog bite is an unconditioned stimulus (UCS) that makes you feel frightened as an unconditioned reaction (UCR); the canine snarl is the neutral stimulus (NS) that is associated with the dog bite frequently enough to turn into a conditioned stimulus (CS) that makes you feel frightened as a conditioned reaction (CR).

Here, the thought is that others' emotional encounters can trigger a conditioned emotional reaction. In one variant of traditionally adapted empathy, during conditioning, we experience unconditioned stimulus (UCS's) with other people who are communicating feelings (NS's). This matching of the circumstance and others' emotional articulations makes the emotion-inducing articulations the prompts (CS's) that a comparative circumstance is going to happen. Therefore, others' emotional articulations cause us to feel emotions (CRs), which we experience as compassion. For instance, you may see a stray animal try to attack someone else who looks terrified (NS) directly before a similar canine assault you (UCS) and you feel apprehensive (UCR). Later on, when you see others' fear responses (CS), you will feel apprehensive once more (CR).

In the main form, the objective's emotional reaction causes empathic feelings, though in the second form highlights of the objective's emotional situation which causes empathic feelings.

Direct association. In this case, when the eyewitness sees the objective's emotional response or circumstance, it reminds the eyewitness of their own past emotional encounters. At that point, the eyewitness feels the feelings that they felt during the first encounters. For instance, on the off chance that you see a stray dog attacking someone, at that point you may recall when an animal assaulted you. You reexperience the first fear from the memory.

Mediated affiliation. In this case, onlookers find out about targets' emotional encounters through words. At that point, onlookers envision the objectives' emotional responses and copy them, recollect their own past encounters and feel the feelings from the recollections or both. This affiliation is like mimicry or direct affiliation however the eyewitness does not see the objective's experience in a direct manner.

Role taking. Role taking happens when eyewitnesses either envision themselves in the other person's circumstance or envision how they feel. Similarly, as with mediated affiliation, onlookers may copy envisioned emotional responses or might feel emotions by utilizing their emotional recollections to envision the objective's circumstance. By and by, role-taking is more tedious than mediated affiliation. It includes dynamic endeavors to comprehend an objective by bringing emotional recollections or imagined emotional articulations to mind, though intervened affiliation includes an increasingly programmed initiation of enthusiastic recollections or symbolism.

Hoffman talks about mimicry, direct affiliation, mediated affiliation, and role-taking as independent systems for empathy even in spite of the fact that they are put in the same category. For every one of them, the spectator's emotional experience originates from emulating emotional responses or reviewing emotional memories. The distinctions are whether the spectator must watch the objective's feeling or circumstance legitimately (mimicry and direct affiliation) or can construe them in a roundabout way (intervened affiliation and role-taking) and whether the eyewitness places in some push to empathize (taking) or not (the other four).

In his depiction of role-taking, Hoffman expresses that onlookers can envision the subject's emotional circumstance so clearly that they feel a similar feeling. This is the main case where Hoffman says that empathy probably won't depend on related knowledge or a context-free natural component (mimicry) and it starts to seem like an ordinary emotional experience. On the off chance that a spectator can feel the feeling by distinctively envisioning the objective's circumstances, at that point for what reason couldn't the spectator feel the feeling by straightforwardly seeing the objective's circumstance? Are the memory-based and mimicry components vital for sympathy?

Emotion theory

A baseline of emotion hypothesis is that feeling is a programmed system that is developed to manage flexible behavior. Emotion is additionally, be that as it may, a method for relational correspondence that brings out reactions from different people and situations. In this manner, feelings can be considered both to be intrapersonal and social states, and the development of empathy combines both such estimations and mirrors an intersubjective acknowledgment process which is helpful in sorting unfavorable emotions. Without rejecting it, a lot of research has been done on informative science, brain research, and emotion neuroscience. Collectively, they have blended together to define empathy as a characteristic competency that has developed in our brains to create and maintain social bonds, important for enduring, reproducing and keeping up prosperity.

These various segments include—

- Affective sharing is the primary component of empathy. This type of empathy reflects a person's capability to absorb the vibrations of others and feel energized by their valence and power of emotions.

- Empathic understanding revolves around the concept of in-depth attention to the emotional state of someone.

- Empathic concern, which alludes to the inspiration to think about somebody's well-being genuinely.

- Cognitive empathy is characterized by knowing, understanding, or appreciating on a scholarly level. As the majority of us know, to comprehend trouble isn't a similar thing as feeling miserable or sad.

Considering the multifaceted segments of compassion (or empathy, as we call it), there is no single locale in the cerebrum that underlies this limit. Or on the other hand, possibly, the neural system related with the dorsolateral prefrontal cortex, parietal cortex, and brainstem, operational hub, basal ganglia, and ventromedial prefrontal cortex- build up self-sufficient and firmly developed biological frameworks that help us in experiencing empathy. Additionally, the neural pathways included compassion and care are empowered and balanced by neuroendocrine frameworks. If we look at, in particular, the neuropeptide oxytocin initiates social relationships. It does so by diminishing stress and apprehension, and along these lines improves cognitive empathy.

Simulation Theory

Simulation Theory, says that empathy is conceivable on the grounds that when we see someone else encountering a feeling, we "recreate" or speak to that equivalent feeling in ourselves so we can know first-hand what it feels like. Actually, there is some fundamental proof of supposed mirror neurons in people that fire during both the perception and experience of activities and feelings. Also, there are even parts of the cerebrum in the prefrontal cortex (in charge of higher-level sorts of information) that show the cover of initiation for both self-engaged and other-centered thoughts and decisions. On an instinctive level, Simulation Theory bodes well, since it appears to be extremely clear that so as to comprehend what someone else is feeling. Notwithstanding its natural intrigue, Simulation Theory must be tried to perceive what proof exists for it in the mind.

The other proposed hypothesis that endeavors to understand empathy, which a few specialists think totally contradicts. Simulation Theory is known as the Theory of Mind-the capacity to comprehend what someone else is thinking and feeling dependent on principles for how one should think and feel. Research investigating Theory of Mind has turned out to be exceptionally famous in clinical work on neurotransmitter imbalance; the essential research demonstrating that medically introverted people can't viably speak to or clarify the psychological conditions of another. All the more as of late, errands those Tap Theory of Mind procedures have been executed in brain scans. The outcomes from these investigations demonstrate that there might be explicit cerebrum territories that underlie and bolster a Theory of Mind.

What's in all likelihood, possibly, is that empathy is a multi-faceted emotion, with certain parts of it being increasingly programmed and passionate (quickly getting agitated when we see a friend or family member who's disturbed) and different parts of it that are progressively intelligent and calculated (understanding why somebody may be angry or pissed-off depending on what we think about the individual, their character, and so on). Regardless of whether the more programmed or the more intelligent viewpoint "kicks in" will fundamentally rely upon the social setting wherein we get ourselves. This is an overwhelming, open inquiry, and we will need to sit tight for social neuroscience as a field to grow more and address it.

For the present, what we can say from compassion research is that we have started to see how the mind offers to ascend to the great limit we need to "feel into" another person. With the freshly discovered instruments of social neuroscience close by, therapists and neuroscientists are currently on the cusp of more disclosures about the empathic existence of the empathic cerebrum.

Social Baseline Theory

Social help is one of the most significant elements of social connections. Various researches have shown that it is basic for keeping up physical and psychological well-being, and an absence of help is related to not-so-good outcomes. An abundance of proof recommends that accessibility of a loved one or family or companions' support, by and large, eases stress and is related to well-being and prosperity. Then again, an absence of help and social detachment are significant indicators of depression and real risk factors for mental disease, just as mortality. In view of animal studies and human examinations, the proposed components for these "social buffering" impacts the guideline of stress-related action in the autonomic nervous system (ANS), and hypothalamic-pituitary-adrenal (HPA) gland. Social neuroscience looks into in. People have since a long time ago examined the neurocognitive components by which social help influences physiology and eventually well-being. For instance, in a bunch of studies, social help was found to decrease action in cerebrum locales that are regularly embroiled in the enthusiastic and homeostatic guideline. Specifically, neuro-hemodynamic changes were identified in the front cingulate cortex, dorsolateral and ventrolateral prefrontal cortex and midbrain regions.

The social standard hypothesis (SBT) suggests that life forms are adjusted to social biology—the nearness of different members of the same species.—more so than any physical nature. Thusly, the social nearness to different people (portrayed by nature, joint consideration, shared objectives, and reliance) ought to be considered as the default or standard supposition of the human mind. The base of SBT is the recently done observational investigations that have affirmed that neural pathways and hormonal stress responses identified with self-rule of inclination are less powerful when social assistance is given or even imagined. The neural response to peril sign is restricted when a social associate is accessible. Individuals whose associations are separate by commonality and responsiveness are depicted by reduced self-exertion, which results in a diminished reaction to peril signs.

The SBT is a valuable theory for analyzing singular contrasts in the social baselines of people, specifically with respect to their communication styles. Desire to communicate is an inborn natural framework advancing nearness looking for between a new-born child and a particular connection figure so as to improve the probability of survival, and compassion and connection are reliant. Connection hypothesis offers a convincing stage for understanding a person's ability to interface with others and create steady connections including adapting assets. Studies have exhibited an explicit association between correspondence style and empathy. These detailed researches have demonstrated that individuals with the secure association are progressively open to and understanding others. has been connected with diminished pain constrains. It is said to be a prognostic factor for perpetual pain. It has been additionally demonstrated that unreliable communication may prompt better view of tentatively actuated pain especially within the sight of empathic spectators. All the more, for the most part, communication style directs the advantages of social help, with the end goal that unreliably communicating people report less apparent social help and securely attached people report lower tension levels. Apparently, people that are progressively uncertain in their communications view steady people as less trustworthy, rendering them unfit to involve wholeheartedly in their contacts, and less inclined to profit by social help and empathy.

Trial work has begun to uncover a part of the key neuroanatomical and neurochemical foundations of communication-related techniques and their relationship with other social practices. Such research has clarified different neuropeptides that are unquestionably drawn in with an assortment of association-related social works on including vasopressin, opiates, and oxytocin. It is found that traces of oxytocin can adjust various communication-related practices including trust, empathic concern, and empathic precision. Intranasal oxytocin organization has as of late been appeared to influence cerebral blood perfusion in basic regions in the mind hardware engaged with social discernment and enthusiastic handling, independent of any attending psychological, emotional, or social controls. Critically, oxytocin organization specifically decreases full of feeling responses to compromising social boosts and differentially adjusts visual consideration toward the social sign of positive methodology. In addition, it gives the idea that people lacking amazing social associations show essentially diminished reactions to oxytocin.

In general, there is a developing variety of research demonstrating that emotions give quick, typified data about ebb and flow assets and logical requests, controlling basic leadership by altering the abstract impression of the world. Through the foundation and support of social connections, the assets of social accomplices (guardians, companions, life partners), just as doctors, come to be seen as assets accessible to the person.

Chapter 3: Empath Characteristics, Types and Test

The accompanying rundown of qualities will tell you more about how empaths are.

- **Profoundly sensitive**

Individuals who are normally empathic are exceptionally sensitive to their condition and rapidly since even the smallest changes in others. Their affectability isn't simply restricted to physical sensations – it particularly incorporates relational perspectives. They can "feel into" other individuals and can profoundly comprehend their feelings, inspirations, and emotions.

Exceptionally instinctive

In numerous cases, empaths are profoundly in contact with their own sentiments and feelings. They have a greatly improved understanding of their own emotions than numerous others. Thus, empathic individuals have figured out how to observe their gut impulses and are extremely instinctive. They can detect things sometimes before others observe. Simultaneously, their instinct causes them to evade individuals that are exceptionally dangerous and manipulative.

- **Extremely withdrawn**

You may likewise detest swarmed places, for example, malls, crowded markets, train stations or just such a large number of individuals in the same room. Regularly it's where there is turbulent energy, and the individuals around you are pushed and simply need to get what they are there to do over and finished with.

Because somebody is withdrawn does not really infer they are an empath and the other way around. Not every single empathic individual are essentially self observers. In any case, numerous empaths want to restrain their social cooperations to great lively, kind, and understood companions or relatives. They rapidly feel overpowered when associating with vast gatherings of individuals. Subsequently, they frequently want to invest energy alone, as social cooperations will, in general, enhance their intuitive capacities. An empathic individual explicitly looks for time alone in light of the fact that it encourages them to revive their batteries. One purpose behind this is they can't completely unwind within the sight of other individuals. They can't completely release themselves in these circumstances, which make it unfathomably hard to feel completely calm and agreeable when others are near.

- **Selfless**

Empaths frequently will in general totally overlook their own needs. By and large, they are so worried about the prosperity of others that they thoroughly neglect to deal with themselves. Now and then, empaths may even turn out to be so drenched in a helpful undertaking that they totally dismiss whatever else, regardless of whether it causes them incredible challenges.

- **Associates with others rather quickly**

An empathic individual is capable of connecting with others. Therefore, they can completely comprehend others on a passionate level. Considerably more along these lines, empathic individuals are uncommonly sensitive to how other individuals feel. Because of this extraordinary association with other individuals, empaths are all around prone to assimilate the state of mind and feelings of those they connect with. This intrinsic capacity can make them unknowingly take on a lot of cynicism from others.

Simultaneously, it can happen that they associate way too rapidly with others without taking a note. It could be said, they associate with other individuals on such a private and profound level in such a brief span, that others will most likely be unable to pursue their pace. Thus, these individuals may feel as though the empath is excessively rapidly holding with them, which basically feels unnatural to them.

- **Excessively receptive**

Empaths regularly observe themselves in others. Therefore, they profoundly comprehend the issues and difficulties other individuals are gone up against. Much more in this way, they are very mindful how the psychological weight that a few people carry on their shoulders impacts their conduct. Hence, they are now and then excessively empathetic of other individuals' unsatisfactory and discourteous conduct. Rather than not enabling others to treat them insolently, empaths are in all respects liable to rationalize other individuals' conduct. They are, in a way, magnets to people's emotions.

- **The inclination to put others before themselves**

Individuals that are empathic are not just caring; be that as it may, they likewise tend to put others before themselves. They are normally disposed to accept that the requirements of others are definitely more significant than their own special needs. Empathic individuals are exceptionally caring for others. They are tolerant of other individuals' frailties, shortcomings, and mix-ups. They are regularly ready to see themselves in others, which is the reason they treat others all around benevolent – regardless of whether they don't generally merit it.

- **Finds untruths and duplicities incredibly speedy**

From various perspectives, empaths seem to have one of a kind capacity to rapidly observe through other individuals' untruths and controls. They might be exceptionally suspicious of untruthful individuals, while a large number of their companions haven't seen a thing. Another character characteristic of an empath is that they basically can't stand it to be around dangerous and pompous individuals. They don't just disdain the conduct of these individuals but at the same time are repulsed by the manner in which they treat others.

- **Intrinsic want to better the world**

A considerable lot of the activities of exceptionally empathic individuals are driven by their desire to improve the world. They invest significantly more energy with exercises of a compassionate or magnanimous nature than on progressively conceited undertakings.

- **Curious in nature**

Another character attribute of empaths is their curiosity. They only here and there are happy with the proof that will be found superficially. Consequently, they persistently attempt to perceive what is taken cover behind the window ornament. Also, they over and over again ask about the idea of the real world. Not exclusively are they continually looking for answers yet they likewise love to suggest themselves provocative conversation starters that cause them to philosophize.

- **Inattentiveness**

Empaths are frequently seen to be preoccupied, distracted, or oblivious. In practically all examples, empathic individuals are so overpowered by the ocean of feelings they are swimming in, that they thoroughly lose their ground. They are influenced by the confused feelings they are encompassed with, which regularly drives them to turn out to be completely submerged in this contemplation and feelings.

- **Ability to acknowledge full duty**

Various individuals are stood up to with the issue that they constantly reprimand others for their own deficiencies. An empathic individual is a remarkable inverse. Rather than routinely looking for the deficiency in their condition or outer conditions, empaths assume full responsibility for their very own activities. In numerous occurrences, this enormously causes them to impact helpful changes in their lives. In any case, it can likewise happen that they acknowledge duty regarding things they are not in any manner in charge of.

- **Profoundly imaginative**

An empathic individual is imaginative. They want to invest their energy with exercises that enable them to utilize their creative mind and inventiveness. Empaths are bound to be craftsmen, scholars, performers, painters, and planners than bookkeepers, legal advisors, and specialists.

- **Effectively diverted, the propensity to wander off in fantasy land**

Empaths battle to stay in reality, particularly when connecting with numerous individuals or when performing undertakings they despise. These two circumstances frequently lead them to turn out to be completely inundated in their own thoughts.

- **The propensity to invest much energy alone**

To an empathic individual, communicating with individuals can be – both rationally and physically – depleting. This is particularly evident when they are gone up against insensible, little disapproved, and narrow-minded individuals. Consequently, empaths are all around liable to plan some "alone time" so as to revive their drained batteries. In any case, if empathic individuals can't invest energy with themselves, they rapidly experience passionate over-burden.

- **Regularly fixated on keeping things spick and span**

On the off chance that there's one thing empathic individuals completely don't care for it is disarray and mess. Consequently, they incline toward moderate and mess-free conditions. In numerous examples, they themselves are minimalists.

- **Trouble to distinguish the wellspring of feelings**

At the point when an empathic individual is interacting with others, they may regularly struggle to separate between other individuals' feelings and their own. Subsequently, they are not constantly ready to distinguish if certain feelings they experience to begin from inside themselves or not.

- **Frequently abused as a dumping ground for psychological weight**

Empaths frequently comprehend the enthusiastic scene of another person much superior to anything the individual themselves does. Subsequently, a large number of their companions will look for an interview and help during times of incredible challenges. Lamentably, a few people abuse empaths just to dispose of their psychological weight without really thinking about the empathic individual.

- **Experiences exhaustion**

Numerous empaths continually feel depleted without truly knowing why. This can form into an extremely serious issue, particularly when the individual being referred to doesn't know about their high reasonableness towards other individuals' feelings. Fortunately, numerous empathic individuals gradually start to comprehend that investing energy alone encourages them to energize their batteries after social connections. This, thusly, encourages them to diminish the weakness they experience.

- **Aversion of savagery and dramatization**

It's nothing unexpected that one never goes over an empath that appreciates observing any type of savagery on TV. They are, by and large, truly hopeful individuals, which is the reason they are not especially enamored with watching or perusing dread based news reports. Additionally, they don't prefer to take part in merciless or vicious extra time exercises.

- **Unequivocally associated with animals**

Another extremely fascinating quality of empathic individuals is that they can associate more profoundly with animals than general others. They connect with animals without any effort. In a way, they communicate naturally. Most of them are animal lovers and enjoy connecting with animals' emotions.

- **They can't say "no"**

Empathic individuals staggeringly struggle in circumstances where they need to dismiss others. By and large, they don't generally prefer to say "no." actually, they will regularly give their absolute best to keep away from such circumstances. The explanation behind this is very straightforward: they profoundly see how harmful it is to be rejected. They likewise know instinctively how terrible a "no" can be, particularly when one actually needs assistance. Subsequently, empathic individuals regularly acknowledge duties without thinking about their very own restrictions.

- **Issues with digestion**

Try not to ask for what valid reason this is the situation, however, strangely enough, numerous empaths have stomach related issue. One explanation behind this could be that empaths, for the most part, have fiery issues in the territory where the sun oriented plexus is found.

- **Overpowered when connections get excessively private**

As was at that point referenced in the above mentioned, numerous empaths need much time for themselves. Be that as it may, when they are in a cozy relationship, time alone can be very rare. Subsequently, numerous empathic individuals feel extraordinarily overpowered with connections that get excessively personal. To

374

them, such a relationship imperils their capacity to revive drained batteries. Simultaneously, they might fear to lose themselves and their character in the relationship.

- **Facelower back issues**

It was at that point tended to that numerous empathic individuals experience the ill effects of stomach related issues. Another result of vivacious issues in the sunlight based plexus zone can show as lower back issues. Different sources describe these issues to the way that an individual that does not realize that they are an empath, so they are less inclined to take part in exercises that ground them.

- **Completely abhor unfair treatment in all aspects**

Empathic individuals just can't stand it to be gone up against with treacheries. To them, it doesn't make a difference whether they are influenced by it or not. They are frequently totally overpowered by the foul play they themselves and other individuals are encountering. Such shameful acts to give them a hugely extreme time as well as motivation empaths to look for potential arrangements, regardless of whether this hunt takes weeks or months.

- **Like to help unfortunate people**

An empath feels attracted to dark horses and will regularly give their absolute best to help them in any capacity they can.

- **Free-lively**

Elevated amounts of control, rules, and tight guidelines are soul-pulverizing according to an empath. Also, complying with such principles and being compelled to adjust to fixed schedules feels profoundly detaining to an empath. While numerous others have a sense of safety in such stable conditions, empathic individuals incline toward opportunity, independence, and experience. They just love to be independent.

- **Especially focused on genuinely feeble individuals**

Empaths are always targeted by individuals who – either intentionally or unknowingly – try to deplete their energy. The impact of these vampires frequently leaves empathic individuals feeling drained, depleted, and mysteriously discouraged. These sincerely frail individuals are, for example, narcissists, dramatization rulers, self-saw exploited people, and numerous other damaging individuals.

- **Headed to invest energy in nature**

Nature encourages empathic individuals to revive. They may some way or another vibe calmer and revived when being in nature. Investing energy outside causes them to ground themselves and to discharge the weight of a chaotic and occupied condition.

- **Regularly went up against with synchronicities**

It regularly appears as though empathic individuals are more tuned in to themselves as well as other people. Therefore, they frequently experience unexplainable synchronicities. They might consider a specific individual just minutes before this for an individual calls them on the telephone. Or on the other hand, they may feel that a darling individual is by one way or another in a tough situation, regardless of whether that individual is far away.

- **Effectively controlled by others**

In the abovementioned, we've officially secured that empaths have attempted to state "no." Consequently, they are regularly gone up against individuals that have figured out how to control them by utilizing remorseful fits. These controllers have found that the empathic individual battles to meet choices that make others feel baffled or irate, which is the reason they can without much of a stretch adventure them.

- **As a rule excessively liberal in viewpoints and lifestyle**

On the off chance that one of your companions is a profoundly empathic individual, you will realize that their generosity and enormous heartedness (nearly) knows no restrictions. Empathic individuals care, as it were, for the prosperity of others. In many cases, they attempt to tackle other individuals' issues and to assuage their misery. In numerous occasions, nonetheless, empaths give so liberally that they are either misused or essentially don't have the foggiest idea when they have arrived at their restrictions.

- **Finely-tuned faculties**

Another significant normal for practically all empaths is the way that their faculties are profoundly tuned. For some others, such an individual may show up as excessively sensitive.

- **Secret confidante to huge numbers of their companions**

Without truly knowing why, numerous empaths are the picked associates of their companions, relatives, and those they connect with. They regularly hear sentences, for example, "I've never told this anybody" or "I don't realize for what reason am disclosing to you this." by and large, numerous individuals feel truly good around empaths and are hence bound to share personal privileged insights that they wouldn't impart to any other individual.

Other than the characteristics mentioned above, you can always check out if you are an empath.

- You might be sensitive to loud noises. They may not be disturbing, however, they have an inclination that they affect you directly. You are sensitive to harsh lights, strong scents. The energy of these things can really initiate a state where you are encountering negative sentiments activated by them.

- You may encounter times of nervousness for no obvious reason. Regardless of what you do, you can't release it or get over it, and you have no clue why.

- You are clinically discouraged or feel discouraged for no evident reason. By and by, regardless of what you attempt, you can't 'get over it'.

- You take a great deal of blame, regardless of whether it's for another's activity or for something you have done that has been gotten in a manner you didn't expect or want.

- You feel overly sensitive to individuals whether there is a need to associate with you or not. In reality, in the event that you sense that you are not invited at someplace or by somebody willingly but the other person is not conveying it, you will quickly take the nearest exit which you can find.

- You feel ungrounded. That is, you are all in your psyche, as opposed to your body. When you are someplace where you don't feel great or are exhausted, or simply don't wish to be there, you will frequently withdraw into your creative mind, and travel to far away and inaccessible spots. This kind of not-being-rooted feeling is highly disturbing to an empath as they derive their energy from natural elements. Being among people may drain them of their empath abilities.

- You can generally tell how another person feels, regardless of whether they reveal to you something different. This is frequently taken actually, however, by and large, it's simply the other individual having issues, which have nothing to do with you. The closer you are to somebody, the more you will fear it has to do with you.

- You will, in general, assume the best about individuals. You ensure that somebody has been given every opportunity, and that's only the tip of the iceberg before you act to prevent them from accomplishing something that might damage or putting you under strain. Regardless of whether this individual is acting like a total jerk, despite everything you will attempt to give them understanding and empathy. Tragically, in this present world, doing such things is regularly mishandled, or worse, you end up being the terrible individual.

- You feel an extraordinary association with creatures and things of nature, including plants and trees. In fact, you may detect the vitality of a zone in all respects empathically, be it positive or negative.

- If you see somebody in trouble, pain or who are suffering, you will naturally feel inclined to them, so as to make them feel that they are not the only one. You may even feel their physical pain and unquestionably feel their emotional distress. You may really feel regretful in the event that you don't understand such an individual and will regularly set aside your own needs, regardless of whether you happen to feel better. You can't stand another's anguish.

- You may want to help, recuperate and spare others from themselves. It is significant for the empath to not bounce directly in an attempt to 'fix' somebody who they see to experience an unpleasant time. This is a snare numerous empaths can fall into, however frequently their assistance isn't constantly welcomed, or is mishandled, and the empath winds up being utilized and depleted of crucial energy and assets. An empath has a method for recognizing on the off chance that they ought to support somebody or not.

- You have an inbuilt untruth finder. Somebody can be revealing to you a flagrant deception; however, you will know whether it's not valid. The intriguing thing about this is you may not know immediately, however you will know, and soon. Individuals will frequently attempt to trick you; however once you have had the opportunity to strengthen each one of those sentiments, you will consistently know whether somebody is attempting to deceive you or control you.

- Many empaths are common healers and can recuperate others either with the laying of hands or from a separation.

Empaths are commonly attracted to healing others or a calling that guides others somehow or another.

- If somebody discovers something entertaining or dismal or has a solid assessment about a specific subject, you may end up connecting with them, so as to coordinate their energies. At that point, you may end up doing it with the following individual who tags along. You generally wind up in concurrence with who you are with and you possibly feel your actual emotions when you are along. This doesn't mean you are indecisive or powerless, it implies that you are checking out who the individual is and what they are feeling, and enabling their energies to overpower yours. Numerous empaths do this since they feel it will help construct an affinity with the other, yet all it truly does is discredit what your identity is, and nobody expresses gratitude toward you for it either. Remaining in your very own space and power can be very tiring for an empath.

- You do not feel like you have a place with this world. Surely, the empath will regularly feel like a fish out of water, and genuinely accept that they do not have a place here. That is on the grounds that the conduct of others is so odd and an outsider to them, they can't relate.

- You may feel overpowered by such a large number of individuals, energies or feelings happening at the same time. Being an empath resembles being a clairvoyant sponge. On the off chance that you do not have command over your capacities, and ability to cleanse, you will, in the long run, go into harmful over-burden, particularly when there is so much clairvoyant contamination out there. In some cases having a purging, shower can do some amazing things.

- You and others see yourself as an exceptionally touchy individual. Indeed, even the littlest change in dispositions can be grabbed by you. It very well may be extremely perplexing.

- While somebody might be an empath, it doesn't restrict them to simply being an empath. They may likewise have or create other mystic capacities, for example, clairvoyance, directing, special insight, and so forth. Sympathy is one part of our mystic capacities.

- There is no disgrace in being an empath. You ought not to need to conceal this from others, or even yourself. What your identity is a gift, and you can possibly improve other individuals' lives so much that they will rush to associate with you. The empath can get feelings, yet they can likewise send, and where they feel torment in others, they can, rather than taking on the agony, send happiness and recuperating. You can truly bring somebody out from their most profound sadness just by doing this, and being you.

- If you feel that you fit a portion of the qualities, or even every one of them, at that point truly, you are an empath.

- When you show profound compassion toward others, their protective energy goes down, and positive vitality replaces it. That is the point at which you can get progressively inventive in taking care of issues.

EMPATH TEST

After going through the empath characteristics, you might have a lot of questions. There must be so many questions in your mind about you being an empath. On the off chance that you identified the majority of above-mentioned characteristics, here is your chance to quickly take an empath test which will affirm your beliefs. This empath test is a short version. If you say "yes" to these inquiries you might be an empath.

Everyone has empathy in lesser or greater degree but only a few are empaths at heart. Of course, if you are curious about your empathic nature, this

This test scores you on a few classifications, including regardless of whether you are an out of control healer, how well you utilize your own empathic protection tools, the amount of empathy you unconsciously mirror to other individuals, and how logical versus intuitive you are.

To decide how empathic you are, take the accompanying self-evaluation test.

1. Do people think that I am overly touchy or humble?

2. Do I oftentimes get overwhelmed by different sensations and feel on-edge?

3. Do I hate loud noises and they make me feel sick?

4. Do I feel different from others?

5. Do I constantly become overwhelmed when in-crowd and find a way out when I feel trapped?

6. Does commotion, scents, or constant talkers make me feel uneasy and repulsed?

7. Do I feel overly sensitive to strong scents or too tight clothes which constantly rub on my skin?

8. Do I always need my vehicle around myself so I can escape when I want to?

9. Do I indulge to adapt to pressure?

10. Am I terrified of getting to be choked by personal connections?

11. Is it easy to make me scared?

12. Do caffeine or drugs affect me a lot?

13. Do I have a low threshold for pain?

14. Do I avoid people in general?

15. Do I retain other individuals' feelings or stress?

16. Do I feel crumble under pressure by multiple tasks?

17. Do I feel relieved in natural surroundings?

18. Do I need quite a while to recover in the wake of being with troublesome individuals or vitality vampires?

19. Improve in little urban areas or the nation than huge urban areas?

20. Do I lean toward coordinated collaborations or little bunches instead of

On the off chance that you addressed yes to one to five inquiries, you're at any rate somewhat an empath.

If you said yes to 6 to 10 of the questions implies, there are good chances that you are a moderate empath.

If you answered yes to 11 to 15 questions, it means you have dense empathic inclinations.

If you answered yes to more than 15 questions, you are undoubtedly an empath.

Empath Types

Like other things, even empaths have types. Have a look at them to know more about your empathic abilities.

Emotional empath

This is the class regularly partner with empaths. Emotional empaths are known for detecting and feeling the feelings of others. They will see through any façade or front that someone else might set up to shroud how they are truly feeling. Not at all like other empathic or exceptionally delicate individuals, have enthusiastic Empaths really experienced the feelings that other individuals are feeling.

Restorative empath

Restorative empaths will feel or realize other individuals' hurts, agonies, and ailments. This might be instinctive mindfulness or a feeling of what indications another person has. They may feel the equivalent physical manifestations or torment in their own body. The pressure, agony, sensation, and feelings of others' ailments can be washed over them and effectively showed through the empath's body. They additionally frequently sense what the other individual may require regarding mending and this leads them to be gifted healers.

Animal empath

An animal empath can tune into the sentiments and thoughts of other creature life around them to a degree that they can collaborate and empathically impact the creature's behavior. These empaths know what a creature is feeling, facing and needs. They feel a more profound shared connection with almost all animal species.

Nature empath

Nature empaths are people who can communicate with nature and needs of plants and trees. They are plant specialists and cultivators who love being in nature. They can hear the thoughts of the plants, which enables them to be exceptionally talented plant specialists, as they can tune into what the plants they work with require to flourish. These empaths likewise feel a deep connection with the earth. During natural disasters, nature empaths regularly experience negative energy.

Scholarly empath

Scholarly Empaths see how the mind functions and can undoubtedly get a handle on another person's point of view. They want to learn and keep on examining an assortment of subjects for the duration of their lives. These Empaths can change their correspondence style in a split second to coordinate any discussion they are having.

Precognitive empath

Precognitive empaths experience dreams about future occasions. They may encounter these as a hunch, feeling, or as a clear dream.

Psychometric empath

Psychometric empaths perceive the energy in lifeless things including apparel, photos, souvenirs, and adornments.

Precious stone empath

Precious stone empaths feel a ground-breaking association with gems and utilize these for information, motivation, and profound investigation.

Clairvoyant empath

Clairvoyant empaths are regularly considered "personality perusers" since they can encounter someone else's unexpressed thoughts.

Mechanical empath

A mechanical Empath intrinsically gets machines. They can detect what is important to fix a machine, even without specialized learning.

Astral empath

Astral empaths can straightforwardly connect with astral creatures, including angels, pixies, heavenly attendants, or ETs.

Law enforcement empath

Law Enforcement empaths share the uncommon capacity to fathom wrongdoings and find missing people.

Atomic empath

Atomic empaths experience others at the sub-atomic level, which gives them a profound comprehension of an individual's quintessence. This capacity is useful for healing and instructing.

Geomantic empath

Geomantic Empaths feel the vitality left in a particular spot. They can stroll into a room and realize that a noteworthy contention occurred there only hours sooner. These Empaths are regularly attracted to investigate cemeteries, places of worship or old houses for reasons unknown. Certain spots can trigger forceful feelings and the Geomantic Empath might be attracted to an area or feel a solid direness to leave.

Spiritual empath

Such empaths have astuteness about someone else's association with the divine powers. They see profoundly the relationship other individuals have to a higher power.

Claircognizant empath

Claircognizant empaths can see past non-verbal communication, outward appearances and words to comprehend someone else's profound mysteries. They can detect an individual's genuine emotions, paying little heed to what that individual is stating.

Medium empath

Medium empaths have a setup association with the heavenly world. They can interface with the spirits of the deceased. These empaths can encounter the emotions, thoughts, and mental impressions of divine creatures.

How Empathy Works for Empaths

While there is much we don't yet comprehend how empathy functions, we do have some information. Everything has an energetic vibration or recurrence and an empath can detect these vibrations and perceive even the subtlest changes imperceptible to the unaided eye.

Expressions of articulation hold a lively design that starts with the speaker. They have particular importance specific to the speaker. Behind that articulation is a power or power field, otherwise called energy. For instance, the feeling of hate frequently achieves an extraordinary inclination that promptly goes with the word. The word hate gets escalated with the speaker's feelings. It is that individual's sentiments (vitality) that are gotten by empaths, regardless of whether the words are verbally expressed, thought or just felt without verbal or real articulation.

Psychic empathic qualities include the capacity to receive energy, yet in addition, incorporate the capacity to heal much of the time. Therefore, an empath's life way is most appropriate to the healing expressions, regardless of whether it is in the field of human services or guiding, or working with children, plants, animals, or notwithstanding healing spots through structure and redesign. There is a wide range of ways for how to turn into an empathic energy healer - you simply need to figure out which attributes and levels of an empath impact you most. When you have a constructive option for the mystic capacities of being empathic, you can encounter harmony and satisfaction. This enables you to conquer the staggering sentiments of why an empath feels the tension.

Meditation can be useful for anybody to accomplish a condition of harmony, yet what is significantly increasingly significant for those with mystic empathic

qualities are to keep up steady grounding and assurance. You should envision yourself encompassed by an air pocket or cover of white light that shields and shields you from outside energies. On the off chance that you are a highly sensitive one, you might need to build these limits of security by envisioning a rainbow of layers around yourself, beginning with an air pocket of encompassing your body, trailed by a layer of orange light, at that point yellow around that, at that point green, at that point blue, at that point indigo, at that point a layer of violet light, lastly a layer of white light around them all. It is likewise imperative to imagine yourself grounded and associated with the Earth so you can stay adjusted, steady and secure.

It is useful to utilize the phrase "I will get all that is for the most astounding and best for me to know, and I am shielded and protected from all else consistently." For empaths, it is essential to protect themselves from the negative energies of others (narcissists).

Keep in mind that those with mystic empathic characteristics are not just ready to receive and absorb the energy of others; they can likewise emit healing vibrations as well. The reason that empaths receive energy and information, in any case, is on the grounds that they have the ability to take care of others.

What an Empath Feels

Perhaps the most effortless strategy for how to turn into an empathic vitality healer is just by utilizing your aim. When you get emotions from others, or even from the entire world, you can invert the extremity and convey healing energy. Close your eyes, envision that there is a huge sun above you that is sending down a light emission into your heart and down into your hands. With the majority of your will and aim, send that light out from your heart and your hands, and direct it to any place it needs to go for the most elevated and best great of all.

This is the thing that will give you harmony. What's to come isn't unchangeable and we are not unfortunate casualties. We have an endowment of freedom and the ability to change, so we should not be apprehensive, notwithstanding when it appears to be overpowering.

Empaths have unstructured energy zones. They move their energy fields in and around the energy fields of other individuals so as to look at how they are feeling. They do this naturally so as to realize how to get what they need, so as to be sheltered, or so as to comprehend what is around them. As they develop more established a few people learn different strategies for protection, seeing verbally, or techniques for getting data. A few people don't learn different techniques and keep on being empathic, sponge-like in absorbing energy, information, and feelings from other individuals. These individuals think that it's extremely hard to comprehend where they stop and someone else starts. They tend to enable their limits to be attacked by other individuals. They don't comprehend the idea of individual limits. At the point when an individual is empathic, it is hard for them to have a decent mental self-view that isn't constrained by the musings of other individuals about them. They don't have an unmistakable impression of selfhood and "others." This endowment of having the option to peruse other individuals empathically turns out to be to a greater extent a curse rather than a blessing. Thus, it is important that empaths learn to protect themselves from the negative influences of people.

It is an opportunity to quit any pretense of being empathic and to rather get information for and about other individuals by conversing straightforwardly with their soul. In being empathic they are getting information from others and conveying it for them or acting it out for them, unknowingly. It is hard to separate between what are our sentiments and feelings and the feelings of others. Being empathic makes numerous individuals be stressed and to be exorbitantly emotional. They can stop to work on being unwittingly empathic by introducing purposeful inflatables of protective energy around ourselves, and by having an expectation to convey clairvoyantly (as opposed to an empathically) with the souls of those we experience. Trust just your very own instinct. Trust just what resounds with your very own reality.

Chapter 4: Empathy in Different Life Zones

Empathy is the capacity to experience and identify with the musings, feelings or experiences of others. It is the capacity to venture into another person's shoes, know about their sentiments and comprehend their needs. But how is it relevant to our lives? It is. We need empathy in our life experiences, and this is essential to maintain the collective conscience of humanity. Be it workplace, relationships, sex, friendships, and/or strangers; empathy is lacking in all of these life segments. Having a look at empathy's role is crucial. The main problem is that stress has been so normalized that tensions, feuds, and everything negative are considered normal. What's worse? If you are an empath who is in stressful and pressured situations, you might end up being exploited. But it can be a good thing too. Let's have a look at empathy's role in different scenarios to understand better.

It is generally agreed upon that empathy is something worth being thankful for, and that it should be the premise of frames of mind towards patient care, or ought to, at any rate, assume a significant job in the patient-doctor relationship which includes physical assessments, and treatment. Increasingly more frequently, therapeutic instruction highlights the importance of empathy in the medicinal field, and a developing number of medical schools have started instructing their understudies about the importance of being empathic with the patients. Quite recently, an abundance of studies and research has inspected the empathy from various viewpoints. Be that as it may, the vast majority of this scholarly research has concentrated on the empathizer.

Empathy certainly has found a way to intrigue the researchers. This will lead the way to more research in this field.

Importance of Empathy at Medical Establishments

Regardless of the variety that portrays the idea of empathy, this idea is generally utilized in patient-centric practices and progressively unmistakable in contemporary healing techniques. A few theorists contend that empathy is neither fundamental nor adequate to ensure great medication. While empathy has consistently been viewed as a fundamental segment of empathy-based patient care, there has been a significant research on the significance of empathy in medical field, how it can be utilized properly, and how it can be enhanced in medical practitioners' daily behavior when they are at work tending to people they don't know.

Such studies and researches have led to the flood of intrigue and excitement in the idea which is about contemplating empathic patient-doctor relations. In psychiatry and clinical psychology, an empathic mental state enables the practitioner to communicate and garner essential data about the patient. It also adds to building a dependable, reliable relationship between the patient and caretaker. Empathy is likewise a significant component of value human services in the medical field. Doctors who endeavor to comprehend what their patients are feeling, regardless of empathic precision or just truly imparting their empathic concern, accomplish various important results for their patients. On the other hand, it could just be truly imparting empathic concern which can result in churning out various important results. For instance, a specialist's mindful contact instead of an analytic touch is seen as passing on clinical empathy and advances healing.

All the more important in the healing fields, tolerant impression of doctor's empathy is related to improved well-being results. Patients give more full narratives to those medical practitioners sensitive to them without telling it. Empathic care is shown to improve patient satisfaction, better adherence to treatment, and fewer cases of medical negligence. It goes the same way for better wellbeing, prosperity, and expert fulfillment of doctors.

Critically, intellectual empathy can improve understanding of fulfillment. One of the most important aspects of empathy goes a long way than anyone can imagine.

Empathic concern is essential to patient adherence to treatment schedules, with a beneficial connection between patient-doctor empathy and expanded fulfillment and consistency to treatment. Patients tend to respond better to those doctors who do not treat them merely as subjects but as humans. Rude doctors tend to have stressed outpatients which may affect the recovery rate. Even if witnessed in real settings by a layman, this thing is shown to be true and impactful.

In medicine, empathy has significant ramifications for the patient's well-being results, and also in addition to doctor achievement. Specialists who show empathy commit less negligence and a better understanding of fulfillment and consistency. One research revealed that while there is much irregularity in regards with the impact of psychological consideration, doctors who receive a warm, benevolent, and consoling way are considered more trustworthy than the individuals who keep meetings formal and don't offer consolation. Care based intercessions that upgrade consideration, mindfulness, and relational abilities, increase compassion and improve the doctor's prosperity and mental health as well.

What Problems Healthcare Providers Can Face?

Empathy has limits for medical practitioners as well. We need the specialist to see how we feel, yet we don't really need them to cry when we cry, and we surely need them to stay cool in crises. What's more, such are the circumstances human services experts need to go up against once a day – pain, stress, and death– that not many could get by without a level of expert detachment. These mental weights of care can be a central point in staff 'burnout', which can make it harder to be compassionate. Yes, a line has to be drawn.

It is critical to take note of that being too empathic can be stressful for medical professionals. In any case, a tiny level of individual stress (or emotional sharing/attunement), is essential for the doctors' proficient personal satisfaction. Since doctors are presented to large amounts of negative feelings in unpleasant situations, they can develop empathy weakness and serious emotional depletion, which may desensitize them and increase the danger of medical blunders. Studies and neuroscience research shows that people who can direct their very own full of feeling reactions to keep up an ideal degree of emotional excitement have more prominent articulations of empathic worry for other people

By and large, there is a strong and collective proof that all features of empathy assume a significant job in therapeutic practice and affect both the patient and doctor. Empathy at medical settings can improve the patient's mental as well as physical well-being especially after recovering from an illness, add to recuperating, and can influence the general prosperity of the beneficiary; a reality that requires an unthinking clarification.

Empathy at the workplace

Social collaboration in our work environments is progressively significant as robotization replaces basic assignments, pushing our employees and employers into more learning-based and the board jobs. The functional economy depends on social communication and societies that advance and encourage these connections. At present, we are seeing a reduction in empathy and increment in narcissism, especially in our young people. Empathy, the capacity to comprehend and share the sentiments of another, encourages correspondence, assembles trust, and debilitates hostility and tormenting. It is a basic fixing in positive authoritative societies that are social capital.

Such huge numbers of our representatives are presently immune to empathy. Those who have less empathy are celebrated as dedicated workers. Sociopath tendencies are increasing as a result. Since sociopathy is a continuum of seriousness we essentially mean somebody who has some trouble understanding or sharing someone else's emotions. For instance, we all have experienced bosses who refuse to listen to employees and expect them to work like machines. One single day of problem and the chances of getting fired increase. This pattern of lessening in compassion and increment in narcissism has been credited to the ascent of technology-dependent workplaces. It's most likely settled in parts of current culture, for example, intensity and fundamental dread of not succeeding, the rat race to earn riches, massive pay disparity, voyeurism, and fear.

Indeed, technology-based life empowers self-advancement and the chase to be successful that outcomes in narcissism. Having little regard for others is so normal that an emotional person is not seen as a perfect fit to be an employee. Even if an empath ends up in a company, the consistent presentation to issues and stressful occasions can prompt empathy exhaustion and affirmation predisposition that adds to a relative passionate separate from others. At the same time, individuals collaborating through innovation miss the meaningful gestures related to close and personal communication, lessening their capability to peruse and decipher these signs. These signals are crucial to sympathy so it's sensible that an absence of capacity to comprehend expressive gestures will bring about diminished compassion. Remember, an empath's only weakness is to not being able to draw a line. Most of the empathic employees end up being exploited as they understand and the pressure their boss is facing from superiors.

This is especially critical for young adults who are as yet learning and discovering their place in the public arena. Youngsters and grown-ups who invest energy in the technology-infiltrated life are passing up close and personal cooperations that would enable them to learn meaningful gestures and create sympathy. It is anything but an act of futility. We need to battle the tide of the more extensive cultural culture; however, we can make our way of life inside our association or gathering. Furthermore, that is a battle worth battling.

What can be done?

To changing degrees relying upon the person, when individuals enter another circumstance they glance around for prompts to how they should act. They look for data about how things work in our association or gathering, how they should act and even think. Whether you are a boss or not, you can still initiate change. To encourage a more profound comprehension of the significance of sympathy in the work environment, we need to understand how empathy contributes to the workplace.

Empathy is a learned trait. A great many people who score high on appraisals for compassion have no clue why; maybe they are raised that way or they have seen things spiraling out of control, and they lend an ear or shoulder for another person to lean upon. They don't comprehend what it is they do that makes others consider them to be empathic. They can just express that they like individuals, appreciate working with and helping other people, and consider individuals as people worthy of compassion. Empaths might never notice their inner compassion, but they are useful elements who make things better for everyone. Some draw a line, some don't. Yet one can never dismiss the importance of empathy.

For instance, show others how empathy can be a useful tool. Show compassion towards everybody in your association or group. Urge others to demonstrate compassion and discover approaches to recognize the individuals who do. An act of kindness and understanding never goes waste. Lending an ear to listen to another person at the workplace will only be beneficial. This is especially true for new joiners, who are finding out about the new, very different way of life than their previous company. Making them feel comfortable is the first step to gain trust. At first, their faculties will strain for any proof of "how it is," however as they settle in they will develop trust in the company's way of life.

You have to guarantee clear messages are sent from the earliest starting point and nothing repudiates the way of life you need to make. We might utilize compassion tested individuals yet we can't think little of the job of working environment culture in making increasingly sympathetic activities in our association. In the working environment, compassion can demonstrate profound regard for associates and demonstrate that you give it a second thought, rather than simply passing by standards and guidelines. An empathic initiative style can make everybody feel like a group and increment profitability, resolve and faithfulness. Compassion is an integral asset in the initiative belt of a well-enjoyed and regarded official.

We could all take an exercise from medical attendants about being sympathetic. On numerous occasions, medical attendants rate as the most reliable in calling. Since they utilize legitimate compassion to make patients feel thought about and safe. Stress is there too, but their main job is to make the patient comfortable. And most of them do know the right things to say to put other people at ease.

Most of the people do it without making much effort.

By understanding others we grow nearer connections. The radar of each great official just went off when they read "connections." This is not an awful thing since a great many people comprehend the issues that happen when inappropriate connections are created in the working environment. All together for a group of employees and their pioneers to work intensely together, legitimate connections must be manufactured and extended. A fist is stronger than individual fingers and empathy is the glue which binds all together with mutual understanding, care and respect. At the point when this occurs through empathy, trust is ingrained in the group. At the point when trust is assembled, beneficial things start to occur.

Empathy requires three things: tuning in, receptiveness and comprehension.

Compassionate individuals listen mindfully to what you're letting them know, placing their total spotlight on the individual before them and not getting effectively diverted. They invest more energy tuning in than talking since they need to comprehend the challenges others face, all of which gives everyone around them the sentiment of being heard and perceived.

Compassionate officials and administrators understand that the reality of any business is just come through and with individuals. Accordingly, they have a frame of mind of receptiveness towards and comprehension of the sentiments and feelings of their colleagues.

Let us put it this way; when we understand our group, we have a superior thought of the difficulties in front of us. Empathy enables us to have a sense of security with our disappointments since we won't just be accused of them. If we talk about getting late to work, it is considered as one of the main things an employee dreads. As explained earlier, having the position of "boss" should not stop one from being an empath. Even if an employee is late, empathy urges the authority figure to comprehend the main driver behind terrible showing without compromising with the office work. Being compassionate enables pioneers to help battling representatives improve and exceed expectations. Having a narcissist boss or colleague is a nightmare for a lot of us. So, why an act of compassion isn't being taken when the benefits are immense?

Empathy assumes a noteworthy job in the working environment for each association that will manage disappointments, terrible performance, and representatives who need to succeed. The job of a boss (and even an employee) is straightforward—manage the group, be empathic and watches them create a solid and prosperous association.

However, the main problem is that despite knowing about the benefits of empathy, we aren't being progressively compassionate at work. Why? Because one needs to take a step forward to move ahead. If the boss is super strict and considers that empathy is a weakness, they need to realize the benefits it would do to others, and them. As an empathic employee, you can be supportive, understanding and encouraging while taking a step back to recharge yourself. Sympathy takes work. Exhibiting empathy requires some investment and exertion to indicate mindfulness and comprehension. It's not in every case straightforward why a worker thinks or feels how they do about a circumstance. It also means putting others in front of yourself, which can be a test in the present focused working environment. Numerous associations are centered on accomplishing objectives regardless of the expense to representatives.

While the pressure is immense a yelling boss or an uncooperative colleague will never be appreciated. What recognizes normal to average pioneers from the individuals who exceed expectations?

The differentiation gets through the capacity of the pioneer who effectively neutralizes all the supposed "reasons" and consolidates a frame of mind of sympathy all through their association. That sort of pioneer will exceed expectations.

By investing more energy finding out about the requirements of their workers, bosses, leaders, and employees can establish the pace and approach taken by their representatives to accomplish their company's objectives.

This is a reality that has long stood the trial of time. It is valid for our connections all through the working environment.

EMPATHY IN ROMANTIC RELATIONSHIPS

Empathy is the core of the relationship and there is no doubt in that. Without it, the relationship will find it hard to survive long-term. That's since sympathy requires empathy. Also, without sympathy, couples can't build up a bond. This is a bond which needs a strong glue of love to survive.

The significance of empathy for a romantic relationship is that it bridges the partition between being independent people with various foundations, sentiments, and viewpoints.

Empathy combined with love is a strong mix of transparency and warmth, which enables us to reach, to take get a kick out of and acknowledge, to be at one with ourselves, others, and life itself. Without empathy, we can't reach the couple goals.
To have a sound, solid relationship, it's significant for you and your accomplice to feel profoundly associated with one another.

While it might be simpler to keep up this during the special first-night stage, being powerless in your relationship and observing approaches to be progressively sympathetic to your accomplice can help with fortifying that passionate bond.

Being empathic you are mindful of your better half's feelings and can see from their point of view; you feel what they feel, you get hurt when they get hurt. In spite of the fact that it's essential to be empathic in each domestic relationship you have, it's fundamental to keep up strong love and empathy for each other. Regardless of to what extent you've been with your partner, feeling comprehended and heard is an extraordinary method to feel like you and your accomplice are tied together strongly with the strings of love. Be that as it may, to totally comprehend being empathic, it's great to know the distinction from simply being thoughtful. Empathy drives association and can strengthen a marriage.

For what reason is an absence of compassion an issue for a marriage or a close relationship?

An absence of empathy is one of the characterizing attributes of low emotional quotient.

You should be happy to step outside of your own needs and sentiments so as to be available and drawn in with another person.

Empathy calls for persistence, undivided attention, closeness, and magnanimity. It requires a liberal and giving soul and a genuine want to sit with somebody in their most troublesome minutes or offer in their most blissful achievements.

A few people are normally compassionate, yet individuals who need empathy can learn and strengthen their abilities by making an effort.

To do that, we should perceive its worth in our connections, yet additionally in our very own development. Rehearsing compassion extends our comprehension of ourselves as well as other people.

It interfaces us to the human condition. The anguish, the delights, the distresses, and the longings both partners share as a whole. It attracts us closer to the individuals around us and liberates us to be powerless and genuine with them.

We have to rehearse empathy in the majority of our own and expert connections, yet the one relationship wherein compassion is fundamental are your marriage or love relationship.

Empathy causes you to settle struggle and mistaken assumptions, as you are additionally ready to see your accomplice's point of view and comprehend their emotions. It gives you knowledge into the most profound openings of your accomplice's passionate world, permitting you a fuller encounter of the individual you are hitched to. Not only that, empathy demonstrates your partner that you cherish them enough to be completely drawn in love with each other.

An absence of empathy makes you have less sensitive and be increasingly judgmental with other individuals throughout your life. You start focusing more on yourself while completely neglecting your partner.

Self-ingestion in the entirety of its structures kills sympathy, not to mention empathy. When we center on ourselves, our reality contracts as our issues and distractions pose a potential threat. In any case, when we center on others, our reality grows. Our own issues float to the fringe of the brain thus appear to be trivial, and we attempt to increase our ability for association or care.

For a relationship or union with a flourish, the two accomplices must grasp the estimation of empathy and practice it energetically. The two accomplices ought to be inspired to learn and defeat any absence of sympathy.

Signs that you aren't getting empathy from your partner

On the off chance that you are an empathic and merciful individual, you may wind up working twofold time to be there for your loved one at whatever point the person needs you.

- You drop everything when your mate needs you. You tune in with empathy and love. You save your decisions and suppositions and enable your accomplice to completely express their sentiments.

- Your accomplice's agony causes you incredible torment. You endure when the individual in question endures.
- No matter what you do, your accomplice seldom responds. Actually, the person in question may see your feelings as minor, exaggerated, or disturbing.
- Your accomplice doesn't get on your outward appearances or temperaments since they are excessively caught up in personal worries. Your significant other doesn't set aside the effort to ask you examining inquiries or endeavor to comprehend the agony behind your terrible mind-set.
- Maybe your companion or accomplice sees your issues or stresses as less significant or difficult than their own. Instead of looking to all the more likely get you, your accomplice utilizes the chance to vent and think about their very own issues.

Some of the time a generally adoring and good-natured partner has an absence of empathy out of obliviousness or lack of mindfulness. Your accomplice may not be normally compassionate, and may not comprehend what empathy is and what it means for your relationship.

Maybe your accomplice never saw an empathic connection between their folks and never took in the aptitudes of sympathy.

Notwithstanding, it's conceivable that you are involved with somebody who has an absence of empathy. A narcissist needs empathy since they are too self-ingested, controlling, manipulative, and uncertain to offer you what you need in the relationship.

Dealing with narcissism in marriage

Recognize that narcissists aren't persuaded to change their conduct. For what reason would it be a good idea for them to be the length of they are getting their needs met?

This individual couldn't care less about improving the relationship or better understanding you by venturing into your perspective. He needs you to occupy his shoes consistently. She needs you to address every last bit of her issues and be accessible for her without using any passionate vitality consequently.

A genuine narcissist utilizes you to support their confidence and will once in a while see you as an equivalent. It's not healthy for your relationship in any way.

In the event that this is your circumstance, attempting to get your accomplice to indicate more compassion is a pointless activity.

You're the most logical option is to acknowledge that you won't get your passionate needs met by your accomplice or experience the delicacy and sympathy you want. You'll have to discover compassionate surrogates who can fill the excruciating hole and figure out how to deal with your very own passionate longings.

How to manage the lack of empathy from your partner?

When you need emotional assistance with empathy, don't keep attempting to cause them to get you or offer you the empathy you require. Your accomplices proceeded with childishness will just exacerbate you feel and undermine your confidence.

1. Quit making every effort to be available and accessible for your accomplice with the expectation that the person in question will respond. Your accomplice will keep on being an enthusiastic vampire, depleting you of the vitality you require to watch out for your own passionate needs.

2. Create or fortify your fellowships and associations with other grown-up relatives. Locate a couple of individuals with whom you have a sense of security to share your inward emotions — the individuals who have demonstrated compassion previously. Make certain to respond when they need you and your comprehension and backing.

3. Locate a minding, strong counselor who can be there for you during extremely troublesome or agonizing occasions. Your loved ones can't give the majority of your enthusiastic help, and since your life partner or accomplice is

relationally repressed, you will require somebody who can fill in when you feel overpowered.

4. Practice self-empathy by focusing on your own misery and agony and offering yourself love and consideration. Rationally step outside of yourself, as if you were your own closest companion or cherishing life partner, and give yourself the compassion you would offer others.

5. Tragically, as long as you are in a marriage with somebody who can't or reluctant to demonstrate your sympathy, the thoughts above won't enable you to make an all the more adoring, close, and empathic association with your accomplice.

6. You will either need to acknowledge an uneven association with a narrow-minded accomplice and adapt as well as can be expected, or settle on the troublesome choice to proceed onward and look for an association with somebody who doesn't need empathy.

In the event that your accomplice shows an ability to be progressively sympathetic and minding, at that point you have more to work with and a genuine chance to reinforce your marriage.

If you are one of the partners who are deprived of empathy, attempt these means in managing their absence of compassion:

1. Request that your accomplice read this post about compassion so the individual in question can more readily comprehend what it is and why it's such significant expertise for your marriage.

2. Tell your accomplice precisely how you need the person in question to be progressively sympathetic. Here and there you should be immediate instead of trusting your accomplice will intuit what you need.

3. Give your accomplice more understanding into your inward world and why you feel and react in the manner in which you do. Your accomplice may not understand why something causes you so much stress or torment or what may trigger these emotions except if you verbalize the more profound reasons.

4. Converse with your accomplice about your very own non-verbal communication and what it implies. Consider how you respond physically when you are baffled, harmed, or pitiful. What are your demeanors? How would you hold your body? Help your accomplice figure out how to peruse the physical indications of your feelings so the person can react with empathy.

5. Request that your accomplice maintains a strategic distance from decisions, spontaneous counsel, or genuine beliefs when you are communicating your sentiments or stresses. A sympathetic accomplice ought to tune in with open sympathy and delicacy and approve your emotions,

regardless of whether the person in question doesn't concur with them.

6. Show more empathy toward your accomplice or companion. Perhaps the most ideal approaches to encourage compassion is to be a decent model of it. Demonstrate your accomplice the sort of compassionate practices you need that person to demonstrate to you.

7. Recognize and recognition of your life partner when the individual shows compassion. Tell your accomplice how much their endeavors intend to you and how they bring you two closer. Everybody reacts well to encouraging feedback.

It might require some investment and persistence before they will defeat their absence of empathy and improve the relationship.

Here are some different ways you can turn out to be progressively empathic with your accomplice. If you want to show empathy to your partner, practice the following points.

1. Put yourself in your partner's shoes

Demonstrating empathy in a relationship can cement your accomplice's bond. That is the reason perhaps the most ideal approaches to be progressively compassionate is by basically envisioning yourself in their position and understanding what they feel like. A great beginning stage is to remind your partner to think about how they feel as they bear life's diverse emotions-- good, terrible and unbiased encounters. This activity will put down neural pathways that take into consideration an individual to understand – first their own, at that point that of another person.

2. Acknowledge their emotions

Upbeat couples frequently demonstrate their empathy by conveying verbally that they are setting aside the effort to envision what their accomplices are encountering. Notwithstanding tuning in, communicating to your partner that you comprehend what they're experiencing can demonstrate to them that you're in effect increasingly compassionate to their feelings rather than simply rejecting them.

3. Ask active questions

Being more adjusted with your accomplice's feelings can enable you to see when they're down before they even notice anything. When you begin to pose inquiries about their passionate state, it can demonstrate that you're put resources into their joy and in the relationship. They can pre-emptively ask their accomplices inquiries about how things are going, without holding back to be told.

4. Don't judge

A genuine association involves developing and adapting together. That implies helping each other out when they need it most, without making a decision about the other individual and making them feel little. They can retain judgment of their accomplice's decisions and accept that those decisions were made after cautious thought, paying little mind to whether they at last prompted achievement. Accepting that their accomplices are kind and clever people makes way for every single beneficial thing.

5. Share responsibilities

For long haul a connection, an incredible method to be increasingly sympathetic in a relationship is by just engrossing a portion of your accomplice's errands and everyday obligations. It can enable you to comprehend what they experience on every day and can enable you to quit judging. A fun method to demonstrate empathy in a long-haul relationship is to take on a portion of your accomplice's obligations regarding a timeframe.

6. Consider your better half's needs

Having empathy, or the capacity to look past your very own point of view, to that of an accomplice, advances basic leadership since it takes into account important thought of an accomplice's needs and needs before acting. Regardless of whether you purchase vegetables before they ask or you offer them an outing when they're feeling down, being on the ball with regards to your accomplice can enable them to feel nearer to you, which consequently, can make you more joyful.

7. Never stop being empathic

Regardless of whether you're in school or not, it's constantly a smart thought to adapt new things, particularly if it will profit your relationship. A few couples struggle while showing empathy toward each other on the grounds that having empathy is high-request relationship expertise that not every person has been educated or has set aside the effort to learn and ace. A lot of it can be attributed to the couples' individual exposure to empathic acts within their family when they were children.

8. Make sure to be with your loved one in hard times

Increasing comprehension of the critical estimation of exhibiting empathy towards an accomplice can urge couples to organize this relationship ability. Despite the fact that one accomplice is experiencing a hard time, which may slant their objectivity, they should attempt to turn out to be totally sensitive to their accomplices' sentiments in light of the conditions. This will end up being a nonstop two-way road, especially in light of the fact that one accomplice's difficult occasions regularly significantly affect different. While it's never simple to see your partner struggle with problems, which can in some cases cause conflict in a relationship, it's critical to be there for them notwithstanding during the hardest occasions. Envision yourself in their situation as opposed to guiding them to get over it.

9. Attempt to make progress

The thing about being empathic all the time is that it can turn out to be rationally debilitating. Your accomplice's feelings may turn into your feelings, as well. In a similar domain, attempt to indicate more empathy in your relationship to help lighten that. When you show empathy, you feel warm emotions and worry for your accomplice without overpowering yourself with taking their feelings. This is an incredible method to even now demonstrate sympathy without losing your own individual feeling of how you feel in some random circumstance.

While there are a lot of approaches to be there for your accomplice, having empathy for your better half's feelings and considerations can truly drive an association between both of you.

EMPATHY IN LOVE AND SEX

People reach out far and wide for the way to a sound, fulfilling sexual coexistence. Some people take part routinely in—and even commit their lives to—the everlasting discourse encompassing sexual fulfillment and delight.

We humans as a whole are mind-boggling, entrancing sexual creatures and the best way to comprehend and appreciate each other explicitly is to have empathy and the capacity to comprehend and share the sentiments of another—close to the individuals we share our bodies with. It bodes well, considering sex should be commonly pleasurable and fulfilling; in any case, it appears to be dreadfully uncommon that we put ourselves in the enthusiastic, physical and mental prosperity of the individuals with whom we take part in such an exceptionally personal act.

Who is a sexual empath?

Compassion is one of the most significant capacities that help individuals see one another. So for what reason is it significantly increasingly significant in your relationship? And who is a sexual empath?

An empath is portrayed as somebody who can get on and is delicate to the enthusiastic or mental condition of someone else. A sexual empath can be described as somebody whose empathic capacities heighten during a sensual experience so the individual in question detects more pressure or delight. A sexual empath is more tuned in to these emotions than even an ordinary empath. Sexual empaths are profoundly sensitive during lovemaking. In short, a sexual empath is somebody whose empathic capacities strengthen during a sexual experience. They are exceptionally delicate during sex and even snapshots of a tease, regularly encountering elevated pressure or ecstasy. They are more mindful of their accomplice's feelings than expected, and to feel their best, they should figure out how to impart physical closeness to somebody who can respond to their adoration and regard.

The truth is that there is no single method to have a decent sexual coexistence. A few people need sex toys, others prefer BDSM, a few people need to begin laying down with an alternate sexual orientation, a few people need to move out and explore intimacy with different people and others simply need to begin jerking off. While sex itself is a pleasurable experience, why sexual empathy is important? Why some people have great sexual experiences over time, while others don't?

It appears that in numerous occasions, individuals go into sexual relationships bearing in mind the end goal of the sex being great immediately. Sadly, sex can't turn out to be great without correspondence and understanding, the two of which require some degree of enthusiastic closeness with our sexual accomplices. Regardless of whether correspondence happens the absolute first time, the straightforward certainty that exchange happened implies you have turned out to be closer with that individual than you have with a great many people throughout your life.

We're all human. To expect that a specific degree of enthusiastic powerlessness doesn't go before great sex is a supposition that will set you up for disillusionment and disappointment.

To get proper feedback from our sexual partners, we should learn to be empathic. We need to think about our weaknesses and insecurities about sex and pleasure our partners. We need to ask each other what we need, what feels better and what doesn't, because, without compassion, communication is almost difficult to accomplish.

However, we can't simply ask. We need to think about the feedback we get. We need to mind that sex feels great for our accomplices, as opposed to painful and dissatisfying. We need to think about our accomplices having orgasms. Not only that, we need to comprehend if our partners aren't in the mindset, then we need to analyze our situation and theirs as well. We need to quit being insensible to the point that we'd want to have intercourse with individuals.

Notwithstanding during a passing sexual experience with an outsider, having empathy toward your partner grants you the chance to turn out to be increasingly experienced and see progressively about how an individual's body functions. You get the chance to leave liking what you took part because you gave joy, delight and opened your psyche up to finding out about the inclinations of an individual other than yourself.

Empathy is the motivation behind why we long to engage in sexual relations with genuine, live individuals. Compassion is the motivation behind why pornography, vibrating dildos, telephone sex, strip clubs, and different substitutes simply don't work for the vast majority. The more sympathy that is associated with sexual experience, the better the sex will be for the two gatherings. Having compassion toward your accomplice implies you get to encounter your pleasure, however the joy of another genuine individual.

Effect of Sexual Empathy and Empaths

While heightened sentiments of pleasure seem like a distant dream, this isn't generally the situation. Sexual empaths can frequently get excessively cleared up by the rush of another sexual relationship since it feels so exceptional. On the off chance that somebody tags along who starts their sexuality, they are so anxious to enter a relationship, they overlook natural cautioning signs. So they take part in a sexual relationship at an early stage with an individual who's a poor decision.'

Rather than agreeing to simply anybody, one can step away for a while from searching for the right sexual partner and rather dedicating your energy during the act. This is how, when somebody who is truly well-coordinated to you goes along, you can believe that you're not blinded by sensation and rather settling on a positive choice. Empaths lead to blooming of much-needed sexual pleasure. Whenever sex, soul, and heart are consolidated in lovemaking, it is a brilliant experience together.

Keeping up a Solid Relationship Through Setting Limits

When you're seeing someone, recommends being observant of your accomplice's mental and emotional state. If your partner has had a troublesome day and is irate, it probably won't be the best time to be sexual since empaths can ingest this annoyance. You have to talk honestly to your partner about this. Your cherished needs to comprehend for what reason you're deciding not to be personal when the individual in question is furious or under outrageous pressure.

Regardless of whether you're single, dating, or in a long haul relationship, sex is a significant point to talk about—particularly in case you're an empath or profoundly sensitive individual.

Since empaths are delicate to vitality, there is nothing of the sort as "easy-going sex." During lovemaking, energies join; we can get both uneasiness and happiness from our sexual accomplice, and regularly sense their considerations and sentiments. That is the reason we should pick our accomplices astutely—something else, sex can be loaded up with lethal vitality, stress, or dread—especially on the off chance that we are a sexual empath.

433

Sexual empaths dread that since it has taken such a long time to discover somebody even remotely intriguing, they have to stay with this individual regardless of the warnings. In any case, we open ourselves to superfluous hurt when we become appended to inaccessible individuals who simply don't want to cherish us back.

Rather than simply trusting that the correct individual will appear, find out about the intensity of our sexual vitality.

When we've discovered the correct accomplice, the reason for closeness is to join our heart vitality with our sexual vitality. Empaths blossom with heart vitality; when sex, soul, and heart are consolidated during lovemaking, it is wonderfully nurturing.

EMPATHY IN PARENTING

Empathy has never been progressively essential, yet the capacity to see how others feel can be supported. It's up to the grown-ups not to allow let our future generation be insensitive, or worse, turn into narcissists. There is no absence of the bounty of advice when it comes to child-rearing. Be that as it may, it appears to be evident that if needed the world to be a superior place, we do need to sustain sensitivity and empathy in our children. As talked about before, kids who experience empathic surroundings are the ones who will have sympathy towards others when they grow up.

Some pieces of advice center around expanding enthusiastic education as a rule, by helping children to all the more likely comprehend their feelings and the feelings of others. Others include helping children to cultivate a feeling of themselves as minding individuals, by connecting with them in exercises where they can be liberal and by demonstrating liberality toward others ourselves. Still, others include helping children to end up good legends, in school and out of it.

For instance, you can help children build up an ethical character. It is your duty as an empath. Children who are lauded for helping other people are more averse to act more liberally later on than children who were commended for being having empathy towards others. We have to help children build up an ethical personality, not simply commend them for good deeds. To react empathically, kids must consider themselves to be individuals who care and worth others' worries and feelings. Missing that vital piece leaves an immense void in a child's empathic character.

Also, giving them second chances is yet another benefit which you will be providing to your children. It's not in every case simple to get children to take another's point of view. When they talk or act uncaringly, it very well may be useful to enable children to have second chances as opposed to just rebuffing them. You can highlight uncaring behavior and assess how unfeeling influences others, thus helping your children to comprehend another's point of view. Then comes the action part where the child must be taught to repair the hurt and present appropriate reparations. One can teach them to express frustration for cutthroat conduct while focusing on desires for minding conduct later on. Try to search for those control minutes when we can enable our youngsters to get a handle on how their activities influence others so it extends their compassion, and one day they can act directly without our direction. Learning empathy is essential for children's character to develop and help them live a satisfying life ahead without being exploited.

Empathy Lessons Begins at Home First

Parents are children's first school. Adults must help children learn empathy through play-acting, and books and other activities that let them get inside the characters' brains.

Exercises that permit cautious reflection on how others are feeling in a given circumstance help manufacture the abilities required for good activity. For instance, reading books is found to be effective in inculcating empathy in children. The correct book can blend a kid's sympathy superior to anything any exercise or talk ever could. What's more, the correct book coordinated with the correct kid can be the passage to opening their heart to humankind. Of course, you can throw in some wisdom of yours to avoid toxic empathy which will ruin them.

All things considered, over and over again these are disengaged endeavors by individual instructors or schools. Some portion of the issue comes from our excessively aggressive culture, and the way that numerous children are pushed to succeed scholastically as opposed to pushed to be kinder, better individuals. Regardless of whether parents state they value thoughtfulness and empathy, if they just acclaim accomplishment, they give an inappropriate impression to their children. If we are serious about raising a sympathetic, empathic child, at that point our desires must be a great deal more clear to our children. Also, seeing how graciousness benefits youngsters and gives them a preferred position for progress and bliss may be simply the help to alter our own particular way of living.

To build up the ability to feel empathy for other people, a youngster must feel seen, felt, heard, and comprehended by in any event one essential parental figure. Relatives who know, acknowledge, and regard a youngster paying little mind to outside achievements help that child feel genuinely appreciated by their adult family members. These sorts of connections increase a child's capacity to think about others.

There are some important steps which must be taken to ensure that your child grows up to be a compassionate individual

-Ingrain empathy at home

Families impart empathy at home by providing chances to rehearse sympathy, helping kids experience kindness and teaching youngsters to self-control their feelings. Peruse progressively about sympathy.

-Sustain positive citizenship

Bringing up children to observe kindness does not happen by coincidence. It happens when they connect with others out of luck, confront moral difficulties, reflect on their qualities, notice how social issues are associated, and create positive and energetic inspirational figures.

-Undivided attention

Undivided attention is a training that enables guardians and youngsters to develop in their comprehension of one another. Three aptitudes regularly connected with great listening are--- respect the other individual, listening more than talking, and looking towards understanding others. Whenever you and your kid experience issues tuning in, attempt a straightforward listening activity created by the family advisor,

-Show kids why giving back pays

Families who show mindfulness, collaboration, empathy, benevolence, cooperation, and the significance of coexisting with others are ground-breaking compassion manufacturers. As children are growing up, they ought to advance through three formative stages as they take on jobs in the public arena: being mindful residents; improving their networks; and contributing to taking care of cultural issues. Being social pays as the child learns a lot. If they see empathy in others, chances are that they will adopt the same state of mind.

-Show a progressive outlook

Tell your kid that compassion is anything but a fixed characteristic—that it creates after some time. Empathy can be expanded with training simply. The more you practice, the better you will be at understanding another's considerations and emotions.

-Open them to various perspectives

At the point when families develop an interest in how people and gatherings of individuals see the world in an unexpected way, they grow youngsters' erudite person, relational, and passionate limits. They help kids perceive and comprehend contrasting points of view. At the point when tested to investigate partialities, discover shared characteristics, and gather importance from what they envision life might be want to stroll in someone else's shoes, youngsters fabricate a more noteworthy limit with regards to sympathy.

-Reconsider how children learn benevolence

It is nothing unexpected that grown-ups like themselves when they show consideration to their kids and grandkids. Not exclusively do great deeds make us feel much improved, \yet individuals who are thoughtful and empathic are frequently the best. All things considered, we don't satisfy youngsters when we just empower them to be collectors of thoughtfulness. We increase their sentiments of joy, improve their prosperity, decrease painful emotions, enhance their friendships, and construct harmony by instructing them to be providers of benevolence.

-Communication during family gatherings

Blessing giving during special events such as festivals and birthdays can shape your child's long-lasting personalities. The qualities your family holds about blessing giving can be transformed into ground-breaking exercises that show sympathy, compassion, and consideration. Be proactive about your qualities as you create occasions which are saturated with positive feelings. Incorporate kids in discussions about how to provide for other people. Peruse increasingly about blessing giving.

-Help children gain from volunteering

Children increase formative advantages by taking an interest in building and nurturing connections. Tweens and teenagers are particularly prepared to embrace kindness when they are taken out by parent figures and watch them helping others. In any case, to do as such, they need grown-up help and support. It is important to realize why taking out your child for volunteering can enable them to take full advantage of their experiences.

-Lead with compassion

Parents need to step up as the inspirational figures for their children. At the point when guardians lead with empathy, appreciation, and benevolence, children figure out how to do likewise. It is essential to figure out how to be well-spoken and express your family esteems with the goal that kids comprehend and gain from them.

-Talk about cash and generosity

Each discussion about money is additionally about qualities. Giving is about liberality. Work is about determination." The more children learn about money management since the beginning, the more they can add to family discussions that tap into the benefits of giving. These discourses can enable youngsters to place themselves in others' shoes and help them experience the joy of giving without damaging their finances.

The seed of empathy has to be planted at the earlier stage, and then it will bear the fruits of empathy. Your child and you can be agents of change in this increasingly insensitive world.

Empathy in Friendships

In the beginning periods of friendships, it very well may be anything but difficult to put together your association concerning straightforward unity and fun. For a more profound, progressively significant enthusiastic bond, in any case, you need a firm handle on empathy. Empathy in a kinship will assist you with getting each other through troublesome occasions just as hold each other under tight restraints. Simultaneously, figuring out how to develop your compassionate comprehension of a companion can enable you to extend your comprehension of one another.

There is a way you can be empathic to your friend. Figure out how to abstain from offering guidance or attempting to fix their issues when they come to you simply needing understanding. Offer empathy as your regular behavior and shun offering guidance and arrangements except if your friend asks you legitimately. For instance, in some situations, your friend may ask for advice or pose questions like, "What can I do now?" Otherwise, expect that they are searching for a shoulder to lean on and you are their choice.

Keep in mind that empathy helps individuals through disturbing and troublesome circumstances by helping them feel they don't need to confront their torment alone. Help them realize that their sentiments are typical and reasonable to other people. This will engage them to deal with their feelings maturely and settle on their own choices about what to do.

How to Use Empathy to Help your Friend?

-Echo their emotions

Figure out how to express your empathy by resounding your companion's sentiments back to him in your very own words. This activity not just offers a voice to the compassion you feel, it will assist you with growing more grounded sympathy for them. Reword their emotions, yet besides, help them to end up mindful of sentiments they might battle with. In unstable circumstances, help them to evade rash activities by keeping them concentrated on comprehension and handling their emotions instead of concentrating outward on individuals who they feel have wronged them.

-Creative mind

Utilize your creative mind to enable you to empathize completely and effectively. Put yourself in your friend's shoes and envision how they would feel and think in the circumstances they are facing. Full empathy requires envisioning the occasions existing apart from everything else, except attempting to envision how it would feel to be them as far as how their background has affected them. This requires seeing how your background has impacted you and how your emotional pattern is not the same as theirs. You will always be unable to completely comprehend someone else's understanding, yet the more subtleties and contrasts you can consider, the more grounded your sympathy will be.

-Confinements

Regard the confinements of your sympathy. Realize that you may not generally comprehend what a companion feels and may need to tune in with a receptive outlook in circumstances where their sentiments are confounding to you. Pose inquiries, particularly on occasion when your efforts to understand them might end up disappointing them rather than making a difference. Perceive that they likewise must help cross over any barrier when you two don't see one another.

-Body language

Utilize nonverbal communication that communicates to your companion that you are focusing on them. Keep up eye to eye connection, don't fold your arms or tap your foot and lean internal when your companion is talking. These sign will demonstrate your companion that you are centered on them and care about what is being said. Seeming occupied - regardless of whether you are not - may appear to be egotistical or cold-hearted.

-Rewording sentences

Reword what your friend has quite recently let you know however make a point to utilize diverse wording. This demonstrates you were tuning in and comprehend the message that your friend is attempting to confer. It will likewise help clear things up if you didn't completely get a handle on what your friend was attempting to state, and avert future miscommunication.

-Verbalize

Verbalize how you accept your friend is feeling. An expression pursued by an exact feeling demonstrates your partner that you get it. This central idea of empathy is significant because imparting emotions to a friend fortifies the obligation of kinship.

Your companion may quit communicating emotions to you if they figure you don't appreciate what is being talked about.

-Clarify if not understanding

Clarify that you comprehend why your friend would feel that way. Relate your friend's present inclination to a circumstance in your very own life that caused a comparative feeling in you and discussion about how you took care of it. Demonstrating your companion that you have experienced comparative circumstances and felt a similar way will further underline what you share practically speaking and help reinforce the obligation of your kinship.

Compassion is an enthusiastic response to the situation of others. Sympathy can prompt unselfish conduct, for example helping somebody with the sole goal of improving that individual's prosperity. On the off chance that we see individuals in trouble, for instance, we feel similar feelings, and this may provoke us to support them. However, the connection between compassion and charitableness is still a long way from clear. When we help companions out of luck, we are provoked by sentiments of empathy, and that when we help relatives we do as such because we have desires for correspondence.

Why do some people help friends more than families?

We as a whole contrast ourselves and the individuals around us, yet few people do this more than others. At the point when the individuals in this gathering contrast themselves and somebody in a more awful position, they regularly experience negative feelings, for example, strain, disturbance, nervousness, and aggravation.' These negative feelings are a statement of empathy. These individuals feel engaged with the individual out of luck and relate to them. The negative feelings are a method for communicating this. But haven't we observed that some people help friends more than families, especially when we are not obliged to help them.

There is an explanation for this. Friends are family we choose not out of an obligation arising out of blood relation. We help companions for unexpected reasons in comparison to relatives. Individuals help companions out of sentiments of empathy, yet they help relatives since they have assumptions regarding responses. It was constantly expected that empathy was principally normal for family connections. Be that as it may, it makes sense when you consider it. You can, as a rule, depend on family. We don't pick our families, yet we do pick our friends. We feel a more prominent feeling of association with companions, so sentiments of empathy are progressively significant.

Empathy patterns differ from people to people. That makes it increasingly hard to examine charitableness. There is a model for this called 'unselfish decision model'. The model fills in as pursues. You see the pain of others and this prompts a sentiment of empathy, over which you have no control. This can be trailed by different emotional reactions: identifying/relating to the individual being referred to, concern or 'considerate nature' (delicate sentiments). These are reactions that we can impact. These reactions can prompt empathy and selflessness, for example understanding the other individual's anguish and the ability to mitigate it. Charitableness is a choice and something that we can effectively develop when we watch others in the problem.

Sadly, unselfishness is underestimated in our general public. We are pack creatures. We can't exist without social contact, so it is no outrage if we are eager to help one another. You are not obliged to help others, but still, you do. Selflessness makes the world an increasingly lovely place. It is remunerating to support somebody. 'A few people say, in this manner, that helping other people depends on narrow-minded thought processes. On the off chance that you help somebody and it has positive ramifications for you, that does not intend to state that your basic thought processes are not charitable.

Chapter 5: The Plight of Empaths

While empathy can offer importance to our lives, it is warned that it can likewise turn out badly if a line isn't drawn. While demonstrating an empathetic reaction to the disaster and misfortune of others can be useful, it can likewise, whenever misled, transform us into emotional parasites.

When empaths lose track of reasonable empathetic response, it can lead to several negative impacts on their lives. It is good to be good, but too good never did well to anyone.

Sympathy can aggravate individuals, so on the off chance that they erroneously see that someone else is compromising an individual they care for. Hostility may arise as one may misinterpret the intentions of others. For instance, if someone is trying to hug your child, an empath (being too sensitive) may wrongly read another person as a threat. Although you are trying to protect your child, your paranoia might turn out into an inconvenience for the person whose intentions were not malicious. Thus, sympathy and hostility are also described as "existential twins."

Not only that, empaths tend to lose money more than usual; sometimes, to the point where they end up penniless. For a considerable length of time, instances of excessively compassionate people imperiling the prosperity of themselves and their families by giving ceaselessly their life investment funds to destitute people have served as the prime example. Such excessively compassionate individuals who feel they are by one way or another in charge of the misery of others have built up empathy-based blame.

The blame goes on to the point of self-ridicule as well. The state of "survivor blame" is a type of sympathy based blame in which an empathic individual erroneously feels that their very own satisfaction has come at the expense or may have even caused someone else's wretchedness. People who normally carry on of compassion-based blame, or neurotic philanthropy, will, in general, create gentle discouragement in later-life.

Since money is involved, it must be remembered that a lot of us have families who need our care, empathy, and love. The neurotic philanthropy can damage relationships if an intervention is not sought. The main thing which must be remembered is that empathy ought to never be mistaken for affection. Love isn't enough to cement the bonds; stable and better finances play a massive role as well. While love can make any relationship better, empathy can't. Love can fix, compassion can't. One who is getting involved in empathetic spending must carefully weigh their priorities. For instance of how even good-natured empathy can harm a relationship, we must look around ourselves.

Not only do people end up being bankrupt while trying to help others, but the vines of empathy can also wrap onto their physical, mental and emotional states. Empathy fatigue or weariness" alludes to a condition of physical fatigue coming about because of rehashed or delayed individual inclusion in the constant sickness, incapacity, injury, distress, and loss of others. An empath can become so involved in the welfare of others that they may forget their well-being. Any excessively sympathetic individual can encounter compassion exhaustion.

On top of it, if an empath encounters a narcissist, it's done for. So, we need to understand the opposite side as well.

Narcissism

As a matter of first importance, we have to comprehend what are narcissism, abuse, and narcissistic abuse to understand how they can damage empaths.

Narcissistic Personality Disorder alludes to self-important conduct, an absence of compassion for other individuals, and a requirement for the reverence which must all be reliably clear at work and seeing someone. Narcissistic individuals are much of the time depicted as arrogant, conceited, manipulative, and needy. Narcissists may focus on impossible individual results and might be persuaded that they merit exceptional treatment. Narcissism is a variant of Narcissistic Personality Disorder. It includes presumptuousness, manipulative nature, childishness, linear thought processes, and vanity-adoration for mirrors.

Narcissists will, in general, have high confidence. Be that as it may, narcissism isn't simply something very similar regard; individuals who have high confidence are frequently unassuming, though narcissists once in a while are. It was once imagined that narcissists have high confidence superficially, yet where it counts they are uncertain. Nonetheless, the narcissists are secure or self-important at the two levels. Spectators may construe that instability is there because narcissists will, in general, be cautious when their confidence is undermined or they are being criticized; narcissists can be hostile when they feel that they are being attacked. They tend to read between the lines a lot more than necessary. The occasionally hazardous way of life may all the more by and large reflect sensation-chasing or impulsivity such as reckless spending. Narcissists don't need empathy in the manner we commonly accept – they need empathy, regret, and lament-- all of which they lack.

In the previous chapter, we learned that a lot of us equate feelings like sympathy with empathy; however as referenced over, an individual can comprehend what someone else feels, thinks, and encounters without inclination the human feelings that accompany it. Narcissists lack it. So, it will, in general, let them free for harmful conduct. The narcissist's absence of compassion thought infers that their oppressive conduct is unexpected. It's amazingly manipulative and very purposeful when they are dealing with people who are highly receptive of them, especially the empaths.

Empaths Facing Narcissist Abuse

Individuals who are shafts separated may be drawn together for all inappropriate reasons. The pairing of an empath and a narcissist is a 'poisonous' fascination bound for disaster.

Most of the times, empaths embrace people's emotions and needs as they have been in a condition, in childhood or somewhere when they were growing up. There are a good number of chances that empaths are the way they are as they have been in a condition of vulnerability or tragedy, and as a result, they have experienced such a great amount of pain that they basically surrender their self-sufficiency, go beyond their financial and emotional means to help others, and do not take a stand for themselves even at the cost of emotional harm. Also called "learned helplessness," it can prompt gloom and other psychological maladjustments. And it is the most lucrative playground for narcissists. Narcissists, for instance, are pulled in to individuals they will get the best use from. Frequently, this implies they seek after and target empaths.

If a narcissist needs to constrain their subject into learned helplessness, the initial step is to set up an association. And empaths, being compassionate, almost always are willing to lend an ear for the distressed person, who could or could not be narcissistic. Intellectual sympathy is a narcissist's weapon for setting up the association.

As should be obvious, the narcissist's absence of empathy is a fantasy since they have to utilize psychological compassion to get what they need from everyone around them. They utilize Emotional Empathy to get what they want, and they do not care about the effect on other people. When someone is desperate for support or assistance or in serious circumstances, they utilize psychological sympathy to get into the subject's head. They have to comprehend the subject's sentiments and thoughts which they would then be able to control into creating a result that is most useful to them. Convenient, isn't it?

That is the reason you've likely wound up bobbing forward and backward commonly pondering about what they feel for you. Narcissists keep empaths on edge. It is much simpler to accept this isn't deliberate. However, these activities are determined. Narcissists decipher feelings like love, receptiveness, thoughtfulness, and liberality as shortcomings. Also, on the off chance that you offer a bit of leeway, they'll take a mile, back up, and travel a similar mile again and again until you're hauling your hair out.

What narcissists see in empaths is a giving, cherishing individual who is going to be dedicated, adoring and most genuine shoulder to lean upon. The very fact that an empathetic person is willing to hear them out makes them alert and interested. Be that as it may, sadly empaths are pulled in to narcissists because from the outset this is about a bogus self. Narcissists present a bogus self, where they can appear to be enchanting and shrewd, and notwithstanding giving until you don't do things their way, and after that they get cold, retaining and rebuffing."

Empaths are something contrary to narcissists. While individuals with narcissistic character issue have no compassion and flourish with the requirement for profound respect, empaths are exceptionally touchy and tuned in to other individuals' feelings. In a way, empaths are like sponges that absorb sentiments from other individuals in all respects effectively. This makes them appealing to narcissists since they see somebody who will satisfy their every need in a benevolent manner.

At the point when a narcissist is attempting to snare somebody in, they will love and mindful, yet their veil soon begins to slip. Toward the starting, they just observe the great characteristics and accept the friendship that will make them look great. This doesn't last since narcissists tend to be loaded with hatred, and they consider most to be as beneath them. When they begin to see their accomplice's faults, they never again deal nicely with them, and soon begin to reprimand them for not being impeccable.

It can at times take some time for the real nature to appear. In any case, this conflicts with an empath's responses, as they believe they can fix individuals and mend anything with empathy. They truly have faith that they can listen more and give more. That is not the

458

situation with a narcissist. And the empaths have a hard time facing that other person is devoid of compassion. It's unbelievable for some empaths that someone simply doesn't have compassion, and that they can't mend the other individual with their affection. Empaths buckle down for concordance, though narcissists are hoping to do the inverse. They appreciate disorder and like to realize they can pull an individual's strings. This is a strategy narcissists use to reel their accomplice back in. With empaths, it is exceptionally powerful; because they need to help their accomplice and help them develop. Eventually, they are simply being abused further.

Narcissists' strategies on empaths

Narcissists control empaths by leading them on with irregular expectations. They will incorporate compliments and thoughtfulness into their conduct, causing the empathetic individual to accept that if they carry on in the right way, they will recover the happiness of others. And that is what empaths believe in doing. Sad, but a dangerous combination.

The push and pull nature of the narcissistic relationship can create a damaging partnership between the person in question and the abuser, where it can feel practically difficult to leave the relationship, regardless of how much harm it is doing.

With compassion comes the capacity and readiness to take a gander at ourselves and take a gander at our deficiencies and that gets exploited while the toxic bond is going on. It turns into a cycle for an empath who has been immune to self-damage because they begin taking a gander at themselves, and what do they have to do to change, and what do they have to do must be beneficial to others. It's the ideal set up, lamentably.

Evading the cycle of abuse

Besides, the cycle continues until the Empath lose the sense of who they are any more, and feels incredibly exhausted, self-ridiculing and disheartened from endeavoring and missing the mark with the Narcissist over and over. They feel exhausted and disheartened while continuing to evade and redirect their feelings towards themselves to keep up the bond and benefit others. The precise inverse thing they have to do is hurt their tricky Narcissist, who will quickly use the empath's outward renunciation of anger to demonstrate how hurt they have been by them, and as evidence for them being the veritable Narcissist.

The key to an Empath truly vanquishing this cycle and being adequately ready to leave, and retouch, is to truly re-perceive themselves with and feel their annoyance, and recognize that they in conviction cause hurt, and are in like manner allowed to feel rage, and lose their patience and care. That, without a doubt, it is okay to use unskilful or inadequate strategies in characterizing a resentment awakened point of confinement. It is acceptable to anger the narcissist if the latter is to make certain authoritatively going to have their feelings hurt anyway. That every so often it is critical to use ill will and capacity to get someone to finally back off, in case they have felt equipped for your essentialness, time, and resources, and this doesn't make someone Narcissistic, problematic, or entitled, yet rather is verification of confidence and regard.

Chapter 6: Personal emotional healing solutions

Empaths find it hard to protect themselves. Hence, they must understand when to stop others from exploiting their genuine emotions. Since they usually absorb others' energies, it can be hard for them to distinguish between their feelings and those of others.

An indication that you are holding someone's feelings is when you experience a sudden distinction mental or physical state when you are around a particular individual Almost certainly, if you didn't feel tense, disheartened, drained, or cleared out already, the trouble is at any rate generally beginning from the individual being referred to.

In case you move away and the trouble hits you, it is not yours. The identification of problems is one aspect; one true question is how an empath gets rid of them?

How empaths heal themselves?

1. **Go into Your Pain Rather Than Trying to Escape from It**

    It sounds irrational, doesn't it--going into your emptiness. Nevertheless, it's a huge development for releasing the built-up emotions inside you. When we are diverted with sidestepping, checking and avoiding our desolation, we continue the cycle of our pain. Instead of respecting the impulse to run – stop – stay there. Plunk down and let yourself feel the shortcoming, the confusion, the disappointment, the hurt. Just once you face the truth of the pain you feel you can then head to the period of discharging the suffering.

2. **Breathe in and reiterate your realization to counter negative emotions**

As you breathe in, the force of your voice can channel the uneasiness out of your body. Your breath is the vehicle that transports it back to the universe.

Say, "I release you." Also, while saying this, you can expressly breathe in deadly emotions out of your lumbar spine in your lower back. The spaces between your vertebrae are useful to be utilized as channels for getting rid of disastrous feelings. Imagine the burden of leaving through these spaces in your spine.

3. **Securing Is Not a Useful Technique**

As a fleeting method, ensuring can be helpful; anyway, it's not a whole deal course of action. Securing to "secure" yourself beforehand and how it uses the language of victimhood which is counterproductive to transforming into a repaired empath. Securing is essentially about restricting either people's imperativeness and resistance just serves to continue with the cycles of fear and pain inside. Instead of fighting with what you are feeling, open yourself. Empower yourself to experience the emotions, yet furthermore, let them pass by not holding onto them as yours. This requires huge speculation and practice. In any case, non-association is an incredibly improved whole deal course of action.

4. **Step away from the source of disturbance**

Move away several feet from the suspected source of negative energy. Check whether you feel light. Make an effort not to worry over at fault outcasts. Wherever you are, don't hesitate to change your place. Move to an undeniably quiet place as soon as possible. Don't worry about what others will think of you. It's fine to stand up for yourself and give yourself the approval to move. It's called self-care and there is no harm in that. Empaths much of the time end up in overwhelming social conditions. If that unfolds, make a point to take out time to recharge yourself. Once you feel fine, you can return to the gathering.

5. **Purgation and Body-Mindfulness**

As an empath, it is basic to the point that you intertwine some reliable decontamination into your common regular practice to free yourself of the suffocating emotions you may harbor. Favored sorts of cleansing methods among empaths are journaling, walking and running. Various kinds of purgation consist of singing, walking, yelling (furtively), laughing and crying. It is in like manner unfathomably significant as an empath to tell yourself the best way to connect with your body. This is called body-care or physical consideration. Making sense of how to be in contact with your body is an incredible technique for protecting and building up yourself right rather than getting to be stirred up in the flood of emotions and vibes that come to your course. Body-care is also a not too bad technique for making sense of how to check out your needs, similarly as continuing and managing yourself.

6. **Avoid most extreme physical contact**
   Emotions travel through the eyes and contact. If you're absorbing negative energy from someone, limit eye to eye contact, including grasps and hand-holding. In spite of the way that grasping a companion or relative in a tough situation routinely helps you feel good. However, do not go near if you are affected by it. You can continue sending positive vibrations from a distance.

7. **Detoxification in water**

Detoxification in water is one of the most effective ways empaths can recharge themselves. Water is a life-giving element. Using some essential oil drops and healing salts can help you calm especially when you have faced a tiring and exhausting day.

If this is not working for you, there is always another way. You can go for water-based spa treatments. The perfect empath release works best in normal mineral springs that flush out all of that causes trouble to you.

8. **Set limits and cut-off points**

There's no way to get around it. To suffer and thrive, you have quite far with people. Don't be someone's venting bucket. Always make sure that you spend less time taking staying concerned about another person. It's perfectly fine to say no. Simply telling them that you don't want to talk or communicate at the moment is perfectly fine. Remember, your purpose is to protect yourself, not fall into the trap of so-called emotional vampires. It's possible that they don't realize it, but you can. Changing the pattern of communicating with your friends or acquaintances would certainly be helpful to you. You can be empathic without staying too much in contact. That way you would not only help yourself but them too.

9. **Set aside a few minutes to regroup**

The main strength of empaths comes from their ability to connect with others even though they are the ones to bear the brunt in the end. Spending alone time without any interference helps an empath reconnect with their ability and recharge themselves. It's important to be alone without anyone around to interrupt your flow of unidirectional thoughts. Keep everyone aside and think of yourself. You are your best friend and caretaker first. You won't face any harm in spending some alone time. Respond only when some critical issue comes up and needs your instant attention. Once again, you are the one to define what is critical to you.

10. **Take a break from social media**

You need a standard break from social media that saturates you with an unreasonable measure of information. Online media triggers your emotions, for instance, Twitter social affairs, Instagram, unpleasant news channels—can cripple your ability to fall asleep. It's not hard to get emotional in the virtual world, so put aside a couple of minutes for yourself.

11. **Spend time and energy in nature and work on 'earthing' yourself**

From soil we came; to the soil, we will go back. There is hardly an empath who doesn't love connecting with the earthly elements. Empaths love nature and feel calm there. The Earth transmits healing. Go to grassland and lay down with your hands and legs stretched. Try to absorb the natural emotions in your entire body and connect them with the vibrations of soil. Go shoeless. Walk barefoot. Channel others' negative energies, feel the grass between your exposed toes, walk around the sand or the soil.

Realizing the gift of empathy

With training, enabled empaths can mend, venture, work with, and intensify emotional energy. Indeed, even without preparing, those skilled with empathy are profoundly sensitive to the feelings of others. At the point when individuals are feeling happy, cherishing, energized, or tranquil, empaths can feel it. Then again, when individuals are feeling pitiful, irate, alarmed, or lethargic, empaths feel that as well.

More than monitoring feelings, empaths absorb feelings intuitively, especially negative feelings. Individuals experiencing melancholy frequently feel better in the wake of being around empaths in light of how they naturally siphon away negative feelings. This is extraordinary for anybody with gloom, yet to some degree risky for an untrained empath.

Numerous empaths are helpless before their blessing and live subject to the enthusiastic climate made by everyone around them. The endowment of empathy consequently brings mindfulness and absorption of feeling yet no learning of how to manage it a short time later. Be that as it may, similar to some other blessing, compassion can be an amazing resource when it is appropriately prepared. With training, empaths can change the feeling they retain, recuperate the feelings in others, use feelings to power show, and even effectively venture more joyful passionate atmospheres.

At the point when individuals talk about being an empath, it is regularly with a feeling of pain. At the point when empathy is untrained, it very well may overpower to feel and assimilate to such an extent. It can be overwhelming for many untrained empaths who don't know how to properly utilize their gift. If you are one of them, do not be afraid. Your answers are out there. Keep in mind that you are the core of humankind, and you are a healer who will heal the world.

Chapter 7: Empath Strategies

There are three important strategies which empaths can use to help those in distress. These techniques help empaths normalizing and maintain their gift without putting themselves in problems.

- **Liquid Empathy**

Before working with empathy, utilize this procedure to help deal with your inexperience. At whatever point you feel mysteriously pitiful, apprehensive, or angry out of the blue, you can utilize the liquid sympathy procedure to free yourself of these feelings and help you become accustomed to working with enthusiastic vitality.

Empaths are intended to fill in as the core of mankind. They can feel the feelings of others since we are intended to heal and work with them. Looking at the situation objectively, this implies they can work with and control emotional energy. They can take in emotional energy, yet that does not imply that they need to get a hold of it.

So, take a full breath and look inside yourself. Know about any negative feelings keeping you down. Negative emotional energy will, in general, be substantial, cloying, and dim. The weight is the sign. To state that a feeling is substantial infers that it reacts to gravity. It does.

So now grab hold of all the substantial, negative energy within yourself, and send it where it needs to go. Send it to the focal point of the Earth. The Earth's center is hot and liquid. It can separate and dissolve any component into its most perfect structure. On the off chance that the core can soften overwhelming metals, it can positively liquefy down negative vitality.

So push, channel, and siphon any negative energy inside you down into the Earth. See it move through the ground past the roots and earth, past layers of fossil and coal, lastly arrive at fluid hot magma. The negative energy is disintegrated with extreme heat and light, and the antagonism blurs away to discover just harmony. You in the interim, feel lighter than you would have suspected conceivable.

Practice this strategy regularly. The more you do, the better control you will pick up the emotional condition you live in. When you deal with it, you can attempt effectively depleting negative feelings surrounding you before they even touch you.

- **Projective empathy**

This procedure is valuable when somebody is experiencing negative feelings and you need to enable them to feel good. If somebody feels disappointed, angry or furious, you could dissolve or flush the negative feelings and help them quiet down. If somebody is disturbed, you could enable them to feel tranquil. On the off chance that somebody feels despair, you could extend trust straight into their heart. You could share and enhance your most joyful sentiments to make an emotional atmosphere of unadulterated satisfaction.

This procedure depends on the hypothesis that an entryway once opened might be ventured through in either bearing. On the off chance that you feel another's feelings, at that point, you have a connection legitimately to their heart. So for what reason should you feel the feeling? Some portion of the reason you get they are communicating that they wear not have any desire to feel that way. So help them feel something better by turning around the feed and anticipating a feeling through the connection rather than just accepting it.

To do this, it is fundamental to develop ammunition stockpile of happiness, tranquillity, peace, confidence and cherishing memories in your brain. To extend a feeling, you need to feel it. To find or gain a couple of experiences, empathy needs to be kept in the cutting edge of your psyche. When have you felt joyful, successfully cheerful? When have you felt so quiet and loosened up that you could have remained as such until the end of time? Construct an information stockpile of these recollections in your psyche. Record them if it causes you to show them. Work on inclination them regularly. This will do some incredible things in a larger number of ways than one.

So on the off chance that you go over somebody whose feelings are shouting for assistance, do the following. Take a full breath and settle on what feeling you wish to extend. In the wellbeing of your psyche, review the memory that inspires your picked feeling. Make the memory as solid as conceivable in the present. Give the feeling of that memory a chance to fill your heart. At the point when your heart is overflowing with your picked feeling, send the abundance enthusiastic vitality you've created towards your objective. Give the vitality a chance to saturate the connection between your souls. Your passionate projection will gradually overpower and change their negative enthusiastic state until it mirrors your inspiration.

- **Showing with Empathy**

Energy streams where feeling goes. Empathy gives a genuine lift with regards to showing the empaths' deepest longings in all actuality. To show, you can utilize your creative mind, you can make a dream board with pictures of what you need, and you can record what you need in the request structure. The majority of that is fine, yet what truly makes it work is the feeling.

The feeling is a widespread language that the universe comprehends at a base level. Sentiments have so much vitality and power in our lives that it just bodes well that they assume such a significant job in showing.

One minimal known favorable position of being an empath is that since we are associated with the core of the universe so personally when we feel something, we feel it into reality. So when you compose your petitions or make your vision sheets, utilize the full intensity of your feelings. Whatever you are drawing into you, feel what it resembles to have it now. Task how astonishing it feels to have what you need most, regardless of whether you don't have it. With regards to showing, empathy is an exceptional blessing!

Being an engaged empath

As a sensitive and empathic individual, there is a lot to be thankful for: you are equipped for encountering lovely enthusiasm and happiness. You can see the comprehensive view on a more profound level. You are sensitive to the magnificence, verse, and energy of life. Your empathy enables you to help other people. You are not hard or closed off or wanton. Your sensitivities enable you to mind, helpless, and mindful. You have a unique relationship to nature. You feel a family relationship with creatures, blossoms, trees, and mists. You might be attracted to the tranquillity of the wild, the calm of the desert, the red shake gorge, the woods, or the boundlessness of the sea. You may move under the full moon and feel her exquisiteness in your body. You realize how to wind up one with the quietness of nature. You need to secure the earth, our mom, and save her valuable assets. Empaths can empathically change themselves, their families, and the remainder of the world.

Empaths speak to another model for authority by being defenseless and solid. They can hugely affect humankind by advancing common comprehension—the way to harmony in our own lives and comprehensively. In any case, such upsets will stick just when the inward enthusiastic and otherworldly work is finished by the progressives. At that point, external positive changes—political, social, and ecological—are conceivable.

Chapter 8: Empathy Revolution: Need of the hour

We live during a time of hyper-independence, a period where an overdose oversimplified self-improvement, have persuaded that the most ideal approach to lead the great life and accomplish human joy, is to seek after our limited personal circumstances, to pursue our wants. Sadly, we have become so selfish that the world is facing a looming crisis. Someone has to take any action; a cure is needed. That cure is empathy.

For a large number of years, humankind's history has been commanded by developing advances that focuses on making tasks easier and provides convenience. Up until now, we have kept away from across the calamity; however, that point is not far away. Be that as it may, as our reality turns out to be increasingly interconnected and our advances progressively coordinated and incredible, we are in peril of losing the capacity to deal with the difficulties that self-serving innovation development makes.

Presently, we as a whole realize that empathy has any kind of effect in our everyday connections. Be it with humans or animals, we see empathy around us. However, the main concern is the rising cases of apathy, cruelty and capitalistic mindset. No doubt, empaths are so overwhelmed all the time. Their ability to communicate is being overloaded with each passing day.

In any case, empathy can accomplish more than assistance in our connections. Compassion can make radical social change. It can give rise to a revolution of which our world is in dire need. What's more, we desperately need this social change because of a developing worldwide empathy deficiency.

Why empathy revolution is needed?

Empathy levels have declined by almost half in the course of the most recent decades. We have overall developed social partitions. In a majority of western nations, the bridge between rich and poor is more prominent today than it was earlier. Simultaneously, over a billion people on the planet are living in poor conditions. Wherever we turn, we see the contentions brought about by religious fundamentalism, ethnic strains, and xenophobia. We desperately need empathy to make the social glue to hold our social orders together and to disintegrate the harmful egoistical attitudes, that is the reason for so much social unrest.

Biologically, our cerebrums are wired for empathy. We are Homo Empathicus. In any case, not very many of us have truly arrived at our full empathic potential. Furthermore, as a general public, we haven't yet truly figured out how to saddle the intensity of empathy, to make social and political change. Initiating a worldwide empathy revolution would do nothing but good to this world.

How can we do it?

Empaths have to prepare our future generations. Since empathy can be educated and learned, it very well may be adapted simply like riding a bicycle or figuring out how to drive a vehicle. It's ideal to learn it when you're youthful. The world's most noteworthy program for training sympathy is the one you can see on the screen here which is known as the Roots of Empathy. It started in Canada, in 1995. An interesting thing about it is that the educator is a child. An infant comes into the study hall, at regular intervals, a similar child for an entire year. What's more, the kid's lounge around the infant and they begin talking to the infant. What's the child thinking, what's the infant feeling, for what reason is the infant crying, for what reason is the infant snickering? They're attempting to relate, into the shoes of the infant. What's more, they at that point utilize that action to begin thinking about empathy on a more extensive scale.

Be that as it may, we can hardly wait for a long time. For these change-producers to develop, we have to turn out to be progressively empathic ourselves and lead the empathic unrest as people, as grown-ups. That is the reason we have to build up an eager creative mind. The most recent brain science research lets us know that on the off chance that you carefully center around another person's sentiments and necessities, that is, feel for them, that expands your ethical worry with them and can spur you to make a move on their sakes.

One of the best empathic travelers in humankind's history, Mahatma Gandhi, indicated that we need to be somewhat yearning about whose shoes we choose to step into. He broadly stated, in a statement called Gandhi's Talisman, he said "At whatever point you are in uncertainty, or when oneself is a lot with you, apply the accompanying test. Review the substance of the least fortunate man who you may have seen and inquire as to whether the progression you think about will be of any utilization to him. At that point, you will discover your questions and yourself dissolving ceaselessly."

Simply envision if that empathic message was on the work area of each financial titan or media noble, or even without anyone else. In any case, Gandhi likewise indicated that we need to propel ourselves considerably further, that we have to identify just with poor people and the feeble, yet additionally venture into the shoes of our adversaries. We, as a whole, need to figure out how to feel for our foes, to build our degrees of resistance, to make us more astute individuals, and furthermore to create more brilliant methodologies of social change.

How would you individuals here today get the chance to meet individuals who are not quite the same as you, and venture into their shoes? Well, that is the reason we have to accomplish something different in the empathy revolution, which is to start our interest. Presently, the vast majority of have lost the interest that we once had in our childhood. We stroll past outsiders consistently, without realizing what's happening in their psyches. We scarcely know our neighbors. We have to develop an interest in outsiders to challenge our partialities and stereotypes. The considerations in other individuals' heads, is the extraordinary apathy that encompasses us. Furthermore, the empaths along with others have to utilize developing discussions with outsiders to enter that obscurity.

We have to start somewhere. To bridge the gap, we could talk to a new person each week. Regardless of whether the individual vacuums the floor in the workplace, or somebody who, you know, you purchase a paper from each day. The significant thing is to get past shallow talk and simply discussing the climate, and discussion about the stuff that truly matters throughout everyday life: love and passing, legislative issues and humanity.

Yet, we additionally need to develop an interest in outsiders on a social level and advance undertakings like the Human Library Movement which you can see up here on the screen. It started around 10 years back in Denmark and the Human Library

Movement is presently spread to more than 20 nations. On the off chance that you go to a Human Library Event, similar to this one in London, what you do, you come and, rather than acquiring a book, as you would do from an ordinary library, you get an individual, for discussion. It may be a Nigerian soul vocalist, or it could be a single parent living off welfare. The fact of the matter is to have discussions with individuals who are concerning you, challenge your generalizations. Simply envision, on the off chance that you sorted out a Human Library Event in your locale, who might you welcome along for individuals from the general population to converse with, to start their interest?

Presently, how would we realize that these discussions and experiences between outsiders, can truly have any kind of effect? History lets us know so. We have to gain from history. We typically consider empathy as something that occurs between people. In any case, empathy can likewise exist on a mass scale, on an aggregate level.

Presently, if you glance through history, there have been snapshots of mass empathic breakdown. Think about the Holocaust, for instance. Be that as it may, there have similarly been snapshots of mass empathic blooming.

We have to make experiences this way, today. Fortunately, they are as of now occurring. In the Middle East, for instance, there is an association called the Parents' Circle. What's more, it does phenomenal grass-roots harmony building ventures. My preferred one, that they did was known as the 'Welcome Peace' phone line. Presently, on the off chance that you are an Israeli, you could telephone this phone free telephone number, and you are put through to an irregular Palestinian outsider. You could converse with them for up to 30 minutes. Palestinians could telephone the number and they were put through to Israelis. In the initial five years of activity, more than one million calls were made on this line.

Simply suppose you could set up one of those telephone lines today among rich and poor or environmental change cynics and environmental change activists. One thing I haven't spoken about, however, is making experiential experiences. Simply suppose we didn't simply have discussions with individuals however we could encounter something of their lives. I think a model of this is an association called 'Exchange in the Dark', which is a one of a kind type of historical center experience where you go into a space for an hour in complete haziness, and a visually impaired guide takes you through to find what it resembles to be denied of your sight for 60 minutes. You do exercises like attempting to purchase foods grown from the ground and you mishandle with your cash. You go into a bistro, attempt and plunk down and drink espresso and, you know, discover how troublesome it is. This exhibition hall experience is uncommonly ground-breaking for individuals, and this association has spread the world over. 'Discourse in the Dark' has shown up in more than 130 urban communities, in 30 nations. Indeed, it's as of late simply opened in Athens, and more than 6 million individuals have experienced its entryways. So we have to make experiential experiences to grow our circles of good concern.

We likewise need to figure out how to tackle innovation. Innovation's consistently been significant in empathic developments. In the battle against subjugation in the late eighteenth century, the innovation that was utilized was the printing press to print blurbs, a huge number of them of what number of African slaves could be fitted on a British slave ship heading off to the Caribbean. This notice prompted mass open objection, petitions and it prompted, in the long run, the cancellation of servitude and the slave exchange itself.

To make it workable for the Sustainability Revolution to win, we need to discover another way going past the extraordinary shafts of the perfect world and oppressed world. If we need to reclassify connections between states, business, and society, we must be available to helpful discourse and molding open worth – a procedure which depends on straightforwardness, responsibility, and respectability, just as incorporating all on-screen characters in the planetary scene.
On the off chance that we don't comprehend that taking a stab at the normal social great is the most ideal approach to spare our

living space and ourselves, we will convey the fault for the hardships of the ages to come. Each unrest first occurs in quite a while and hearts. Sympathy, empathy, and solidarity can give the urgent force for the significant and durable difference in the all-inclusive mentality. An Empathy Revolution ought to be viewed as essential for the Sustainability Revolution.

In the previous two decades, the appearance of MRI in neuroscience has created fantastic accomplishments in the investigation of the human mind. Researchers have unfortunately affirmed that individuals naturally will, in general, be egocentric. In any case, fortunately, there is a particular piece of our cerebrum, called the privilege supramarginal gyrus, which is in charge of sympathy and empathy. This region of the mind makes it feasible for us to disengage the view of ourselves from that of others. Additionally, the privilege supramarginal gyrus is brilliant to the point that it can perceive an absence of empathy and autocorrect it. The demonstrated neuroplasticity of our cerebrum guarantees that our ability for sympathy is never fixed. By intentionally placing ourselves in another person's shoes, we can fortify the pliability of our neural systems and impressively improve our potential for sympathy and empathy.

Empathy is our responsibility

Being empathic isn't useful for our kindred individuals yet similarly serves our circumstance. Neuroscientists have demonstrated that exceptionally empathic individuals feel increasingly satisfied, are progressively positive, alert and idealistic, and furthermore, for the most part, will, in general, live more joyful and longer lives than their egocentric partners!

With regards to the corporate world, it would imply that those organizations that see aggregate enthusiasm as their own, and are guided by the standards of open worth and social great, would thus, by implication, be working for their bit of leeway and could just make win-win circumstances.

In our worldwide world with all its worldwide entertainers, areas, networks, systems and developments, is there any valid reason why we wouldn't try to accomplish and spread worldwide compassion also? The Empathy Revolution could unquestionably carry us a lot nearer to the worldwide execution of the Sustainability Revolution. In this way, let us enact the privilege supramarginal gyrus of our minds and show signs of improvement world for all!

Today, the innovation we have to consider is long-range informal communication advances, computerized advances. Presently, we realize that they can be incredible. We realize that during the Arab Spring and in the Occupy development, long-range interpersonal communication stages helped spread amazing feelings, similar to outrage and empathy. Someone could snap a picture of a young lady called Nedā, shot in the city of Tehran, and inside hours a large number of individuals around the globe knew her name, about her family, what her identity was, and went on to the lanes to challenge at state fierceness.

In any case, you likewise need to perceive that cutting edge advancements, computerized innovations, have a risk to them. Since, most interpersonal interaction stages have been intended for the proficient trade of data, not for the trading of closeness and sympathy. They will in general advance, once in a while, shallow connections. There's a peril that they advance the amount of the associations we make instead of the quality. They will in general associate us with individuals who are especially similar to us, who offer our preferences in music or movies. So we have to make another age of person to person communication advances, which spotlight on extending profound empathic association and interfacing us with outsiders.

Be that as it may, just as this, we have to figure out how to be empathic pioneers. Since we are for the most part pioneers, we as a whole have authoritative reaches, regardless of whether it's in schools or the work environment, in places of worship or network associations. We can take a lead from renowned pioneers, for example, Nelson Mandela who understood, that in the progress from Apartheid, it was indispensable to attempt to make sympathy and common comprehension among highly contrasting South Africans. He is one of the most famous and respected empathic personalities so far. These personalities did what others hesitated to do- being empathic.

So those are the fixings to begin an empathy insurgency. Socrates broadly said that to carry on with an astute and great life, we have to 'know thyself'. What's more, we have generally imagined that this implies peering inside yourself, looking at your very own soul. We have to adjust thoughtfulness, with what we call-- introspection. Outrospection is finding what your identity is, and how to live by venturing outside yourself, and glancing through the eyes of other individuals and finding other individuals' universes. Empathy is a definitive fine art for the time of outrospection.

Presently empathy, as an idea, is better known today than at any crossroads in mankind's history. It's on the lips of legislators and neuroscientists, business pioneers and spiritual gurus. We need to accomplish something other than discussion about empathy or searching for it on the internet. We need to transform empathy into a type of social activity. We have to outfit its capacity for social and political change. That is how we will make an upheaval of human connections in the 21st century.

Empathy revolution is the need of the hour. It's something which our world would be thankful for eternity. Selflessness is the tool which humans must learn to make use of. No, empathy is not a weakness; it's the biggest strength one can ever possess.

Be an empath and see the happiness unfolding around yourself.

Conclusion

Being sensitive or empathic is something with which quite a few people are blessed. Sadly, the world is not understanding the importance of empathy.

Nowadays, no one seems to be happy. Don't our hearts bleed when we see our near and dear ones in pain? Don't we feel like extending our hand, pulling them into a hug and tell them that everything will be fine? These things are instinctive. They are physical and present. They are going on this moment and you can feel it in your bones. Yet it equally tough to find someone to lean upon when the world is slowly becoming desensitized to the emotions. Feeling sympathy is common, while empathetic gestures are increasingly becoming uncommon.

A change has to come.

Empaths have to start from somewhere. To bridge the gap, they could talk to a new person each week. Regardless of whether the individual vacuums the floor in the workplace, or somebody who, you know, you purchase a paper from each day. The significant thing is to get past shallow talk and simply discussing the climate, and discussion about the stuff that truly matters throughout everyday life: love and passing, legislative issues and humanity.

Social developments have led to the mechanization of everything, even emotions. Everything is guarded, a lie that we tell ourselves and others. For example, take social media-- we scroll and scroll, like and comment on cute videos and emotional stories of struggling human beings. However, how many of us would reach out to others to help those who are in distress? This is the moment when we have to realize that humanity needs to be awakened again. The emotions which we have been suppressing to fit into the crowd needs to burn with passion again. It is a rallying call for us to decorate their defensive layer, get our weapons, and stand up to the foe at their entryway. Our enemy is none other than our insensitivity. It needs to be taken care of. The world needs healing; it needs the touch of love and genuine empathy. It needs healers.

Here in this book, you will get to know more about Empath Healing, abilities, strengths, weaknesses, and much more. This information is essential for us to embrace our true, emotional selves as that would allow to clear our biases and become better human beings in the process. Feeling our inner love and those of others isn't a weakness. It will build up this world. In the time when empathy is buried deep inside somewhere and shallowness is riding with its head high, healers can be the saviors. If you feel you are the one, then do not hesitate to take charge. Do not be afraid to be charitable when it comes to servicing the humankind because this is precisely what we need now. And you need to protect yourself as well because without protecting yourself you cannot help others. It is essential to take a stand for yourself or else it will be too late-- for you and the world

Lightning Source UK Ltd.
Milton Keynes UK
UKHW020808130121
376933UK00003B/237